The Mood/Interest Theory
of American Foreign Policy

The
Mood/Interest Theory of American Foreign Policy

JACK E. HOLMES

With a Foreword by Frank L. Klingberg

THE UNIVERSITY PRESS OF KENTUCKY

Publication of this book has been
aided by a grant from Hope College.

Copyright © 1985 by The University Press of Kentucky

Scholarly publisher for the Commonwealth,
serving Bellarmine College, Berea College, Centre
College of Kentucky, Eastern Kentucky University,
The Filson Club, Georgetown College, Kentucky
Historical Society, Kentucky State University,
Morehead State University, Murray State University,
Northern Kentucky University, Transylvania University,
University of Kentucky, University of Louisville,
and Western Kentucky University.

Editorial Offices: Lexington, Kentucky 40506-0024

Library of Congress Cataloging in Publication Data

Holmes, Jack E.
    The mood/interest theory of American foreign policy.

    Bibliography: p.
    Includes index.
    1. United States—Foreign relations.   2. United States
—Foreign relations—Public opinion—History.
3. Public opinion—United States—History.   4.United
States—History—Philosophy.   I. Title.
E183.7.H65   1985   327.73   84-25679
ISBN 0-8131-1533-7

To Professors Frank L. Klingberg and Robert E. Elder, Jr., and my students at Hope College who provided the encouragement and suggestions to express my thoughts in written form.

Contents

Figures

Foreword

In this book, Jack E. Holmes has made a major contribution to the understanding of American foreign policy, by developing his mood/interest theory and relating it to other major approaches. His analysis helps Americans to understand themselves and other nations to understand America.

American foreign policy has often seemed to be unpredictable and undependable, especially to observers overseas. The American system has sometimes been regarded as fickle, with sudden changes of policy. Often given is the example of President Woodrow Wilson's role as the chief architect of the League of Nations, followed quickly by the league's repudiation in the Senate in 1919.

A common theory in the inter–World War period was that the United States was traditionally and powerfully isolationist, so that World War I appeared to be an aberration. After World War II, it could be argued either that this second war could prove to be only another aberration, or that the American people had been forced by the war to drop political-military introversion (or isolationism) forever.

My 1947 study of American diplomatic history showed that not only had the United States become deeply involved in world affairs from about 1893 to 1919 and then "isolationist" from 1919 to 1940, but that such an alternation had occurred ever since 1776. When this theory was published in 1952, it was applied to the future to suggest that the American people would support a strong extrovert policy at least until the late 1960s, when they would be likely to revert again to a relative introversion (a leveling-off of political-military involvement).

The theory was little noticed until 1967–1969, when it looked as if the predicted introversion was coming to pass. The State Department, some columnists, and some scholars discussed the idea in relation to the growing reaction against "Vietnam." Holmes began work on the theory in 1969 and continued to develop and apply it in many ways, while presenting many professional papers on it. The present book is a most fruitful result of his research, as he took the mood theory and developed it into his "liberal mood/interest" theory.

Holmes helps explain the fairly regular alternation of long-time foreign policy moods by positing America's basic *liberal* stance (whether "reform" liberal or "business" liberal) as the steady motivating force in inducing mood shifts. Since liberals tend to dislike the exercise of concentrated power, especially military, except when a crusading spirit takes hold, there is a fundamental conflict between the liberal *moods* and America's political-military *interests* (which require the use of some degree of power).

A new mood may originate with political leadership, Holmes writes, but once it is grasped by the people, it is they who dictate its continuation. In an introvert mood, one generation of Americans will underestimate the political-military factor until the security of the country appears to be endangered, inducing a shift to extroversion. In an extrovert mood, the next generation may stress the political-military factor so much as to finally violate America's liberal norms.

Thus, Dr. Holmes supports basic democratic pluralist theory, believing that the mass public has commendable intelligence, even though it may be lacking knowledge, and that it sets the parameters within which political leaders must act. He avers that the impact of public moods on foreign policy has been insufficiently identified and analyzed, since perhaps most scholars have supported an "elitist" view of the determination of policy. At the very least, the public chooses which of the competing elites it desires to place in power.

In Chapter 2, Professors Holmes and Robert E. Elder, Jr., evaluate and compare a number of behavioral or statistical studies to show that they lend general support to the theory. Then, in addition to analyzing the "elitist" approach, Dr. Holmes demonstrates how the "liberal mood/interest" theory of alternation tends to dominate or explain the application of other common theories, including pragmatism, moralism, conservatism, fortunate circumstances and modern technology, and the recurrence of certain types of "events."

After applying the theory to America's whole historical development since 1776 in Chapter 3, the author similarly clarifies United States policy in the six major regions of the world, enabling him to discuss America's current problems in all of them, including the role of nuclear weapons.

In Chapter 4, there is a full analysis of the impact of the theory on the formulation of foreign policy by the United States government, as affected by pressure groups, business, the press, and the general public. Evidence is presented to show that the presidency has been strong during extrovert phases, while the influence of Congress and pressure groups has increased in introvert phases. The president indicates direction and is informed by the federal bureaucracy, but is normally guided by the public mood, particularly as delineated in the press. There is a good discussion of the "military-industrial complex," showing that its influence depends largely on the public mood. The author notes that the general American liberal spirit rather consistently supports economic and humanitarian activity on the world scene, so that only political-military actions are normally subject to the alternations of moods.

With a full analysis of the current dominant mood of introversion, characterized in part by a lack of basic consensus, the book is up-to-date and projects the theory onto the future, noting the possibility that America could again allow introversion to endanger its political-military interests in the world, and lead toward a major crisis. For example, other powers could try to take advantage of this introvert mood just when a new spirit of American extroversion would be ready to respond. The next mood of extroversion can be expected by the late 1980s, if the historical pattern continues.

Dr. Holmes sees a particular danger in the tendency of each of the alternating foreign policy moods to move to extremes and suggests ways in which these extremes might be prevented or minimized. Modern weapons of destruction, he writes, cannot be combined with the past degree of mood extremes. Educators have a special opportunity and responsibility, he believes, to help explain America's historical foreign policy in terms of these alternating moods, to prepare students and the public for coming shifts, and to try to develop a broader understanding of America's *interests* which could reduce these extremes and perhaps even help "break the pattern." The author also points out areas where further research would be helpful, such as in studying elite/mass interaction, the role of competing elites, legislative-executive competition in the light of the mood/interest theory, and the like.

The book is well-written and convincing, with a balanced and fair point of view. A large number of American foreign policy studies are used and logically analyzed. This fresh and broad perspective and the coverage of all the basic topics affecting American foreign policy make the book suitable indeed for use as fascinating text or for general reading by students, policy makers, and the interested public. It is especially valuable for those who try to educate or mold public opinion.

FRANK L. KLINGBERG
Professor Emeritus of Political Science
Southern Illinois University-Carbondale

Preface

The mood/interest theory is a macroanalysis of United States foreign policy covering more than two hundred years of American independence. It advances a broad, regular pattern which can aid in the analysis of past, present, and future American foreign policy.

This book presents and explores the mood/interest theory, in the process summarizing material researched and developed in a variety of settings over the course of a decade. Refinement could easily continue into future decades. The theory is presented at this time to encourage thinking about larger issues of American foreign policy.

The author would like to thank students at Hope College who have aided his continuing efforts to develop and refine the mood/interest theory. Charles W. Gossett, Daniel Blauw, and Scott Dwyer were most resourceful as summer research assistants. James Van Heest made valuable suggestions for improvement of the introductory chapter and diagrams and Robert Pocock made helpful contributions to some of the case studies, both as part of their senior seminar project. Paul Bolt, Brian Crisp, Peter Maassen, Stephen Muyskens, Ben Vonk, and Dirk Weeldreyer each spent a highly productive summer on editorial matters. William S. Graham made several significant contributions to Chapter 2, did research, and offered editorial suggestions for the better part of three summers. Lee Bechtel, Kim Japinga, Gary Koops, Nancy Piersma, and Beth Van Hoeven helped in research for Chapter 2; useful background papers were prepared by Kim Duffy, Kirk Hoopingarner, Kathy Stratton, and George Wiszynski; and Professor James Zoetewey made a number of useful suggestions for improving this application.

Billy Beaver, Patricia Cecil, and Dan Stid were very helpful in preparing the final copy of this manuscript. Sally Budd, Brian Gardner, and Lon McCollum worked diligently and efficiently on tables. Paul Bolt helped compile and edit the index. Sandy Tasma patiently and expertly typed many drafts of the text. Anne Buckleitner, Steve Cochrun, Jeff Fraser, and Dave Rhem kept the author's office in order so that he could have the time needed for this project. The Mellon Foundation and Hope College provided valuable assistance for conducting research and preparing the manuscript. Many excellent suggestions were made by reviewers. Responsibility for all matters of interpretation and fact is, of course, solely the author's.

Introduction

The mood/interest theory argues that alternating introvert and extrovert public moods, first identified by Frank L. Klingberg and manifested in American liberalism, regularly pass in and out of an interest zone established by the realities of international politics. Public mood, which can conflict with foreign policy interests, limits the feasible foreign policy actions of the United States government. The above concepts can be utilized to construct a two-hundred-year framework which aids in the analysis of American foreign policy.

The mood/interest analysis emphasizes the need for greater attention to long-range macroanalysis by making a strong case for one such framework. Often concepts are advanced on the basis of detailed study of a few current instances and can be disputed when applied to other instances. An interpretation valid in the context of the next few years might be invalid in the context of the next few decades. Optimum understanding requires attention to a number of concepts developed within various frames of reference.

Differences between long- and short-term views of the same situation are important enough to indicate that long-range analysis deserves attention. A common explanation for the reassertion of congressional foreign policy prerogatives after 1968 is that the Congress could not abdicate its foreign policy responsibilities to the executive. From the long-term viewpoint, this reassertion might lead to excessive congressional power. The actions of presidents Wilson and Johnson in 1918–20 and 1966–1968, respectively, can be explained from the short-range viewpoint as efforts by presidents to sustain American involvement in two quite different situations. The long-range mood/interest perspective identifies the end of two extrovert eras, with actions taken by the two presidents seen as setting the stage for reactions. From a short-range perspective, immediately following World War II the United States entered a new era of international leadership largely divorced from its past history. The mood/interest theory, evaluating the new situation from a long-range historical perspective, could imply that public enthusiasm for the new United States role would eventually wane.

KLINGBERG'S FOUNDATION

The mood/interest theory starts with Frank L. Klingberg's 1952 article on American foreign policy moods. In that article Klingberg defined four "introvert" periods averaging twenty-one years and three "extrovert" periods averaging twenty-seven years. Klingberg based his dates on analysis of State of the Union and inaugural addresses, major party platforms, election results, naval expenditures, treaties, diplomatic warnings, annexations, and wars. He speculated that a new introvert mood could begin in the late 1960s, since the fourth extrovert phase had started in 1940.[1]

When, in fact, this took place in 1968, much attention was paid to Klingberg's article. This attention subsided gradually until a movement toward extroversion, which appeared to exist around 1980, became a questionable proposition a few years later. Accordingly, interest in Klingberg's 1952 article has again increased. In general, analyses of Klingberg have noted his contribution and added a few speculations. Thus, analysts have generalized rather than explained the forces behind Klingberg's 1952 cycle.[2]

This author was first exposed to Klingberg's work in 1969 and has found it a remarkable tool for looking at events in context. The mood/interest theory was formulated in order to promote knowledge about exactly how Klingberg's cycle might work in a more specific sense. This work uses Klingberg's dates until 1940, identifies 1968 as the start of the current introvert phase, and formulates propositions to present a macrotheory of American foreign policy.

In recent years, Klingberg has developed his introvert/extrovert cycles as an international cycle in conjunction with a political cycle and a cultural cycle.[3] The mood/interest theory applies the international cycle alone based on the 1952 article and dates. In view of the significance of this endeavor, additional research on the other Klingberg cycles would be valuable. However, a study of how the international cycle alone might work proved to be a sufficient challenge for a single volume.

MOOD/INTEREST PROPOSITIONS

The mood/interest theory is built upon six sequential propositions, each of which can be argued independently; in fact, support for each can be documented in the literature. What is different in the mood/interest theory is the manner to which the several propositions are fit together into a macrotheory.

Public Rule Proposition

Public mood is a dominant force in American foreign policy and limits governmental actions. The mood/interest theory contends that, in the American system of government, the people set the parameters within which the political leadership must act. The theory does not contend that the American public determines the specific of individual issues, but rather that it guides the decision-making process by determining an allowable "channel" for policy makers, which can be illustrated graphically by two heavy parallel lines (Figure 1). This channel of proper action may have originated with the political lead-

Figure 1. American Public Opinion and Foreign Policy Parameters

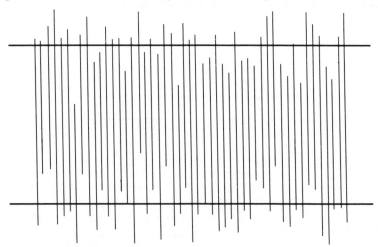

ership, but once grasped by the people, it is they who dictate a continuation along this path, regardless of new leadership decisions of what is best.

Short-term public opinion on specific issues is shown as vertical lines varying in position and length and assumes adjustment for the intensity of opinion and the context within which the opinion is formed. Foreign policy movements within the parameters are acceptable to the public, although short-term public opinion fluctuates on various issues. Thus, the foreign policy mood parameters are more important to a macroanalysis than is public opinion on specific issues.

Decisions made by foreign policy leaders are expected to be concentrated within the parameters set by the public. The foreign policy maker is not required to act within the parameters in every instance, but should aim toward results within the parameters, particularly on important issues. When foreign policy decisions regularly violate the general will of the public, the policy-making officials involved are removed through the electoral process, and important policies are altered to conform to public mood. Such removal and alteration could result from an unrecognized change in the public mood, as depicted in the Liberal Moods Proposition.

Liberal Moods Proposition

American foreign policy moods are expressed and channeled by American liberalism and fluctuate between extreme introversion and extreme extroversion with intervening periods of moderation. American foreign policy moods are subject to extreme fluctuations best expressed by liberalism and its dislike of concentrated power.[4] When analyzing problems, Americans are primarily

Figure 2.   The American Liberal Mood Curve

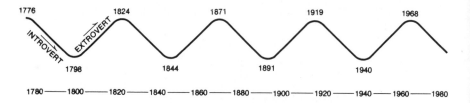

reform liberals (often referred to simply as liberals), business liberals (often referred to in America as conservatives), or some combination thereof.

Although often regarding domestic policy differently, both camps of American liberals are constantly dissatisfied with the harsh realities of international politics and continually try to change them in one of two ways. One alternative is to minimize active United States participation while setting an example that the liberal would have other nations follow; this is a basic tendency toward introversion. The other alternative is to engage in active participation in an effort to change international politics; this is a basic tendency toward extroversion. Since 1776, American foreign policy has regularly alternated between introvert and extrovert phases, reaching an unrealistic extreme in one orientation before abandoning it for the other.

Figure 2 provides a rough representation of the regular alternation of underlying moods. As noted previously, Klingberg's dates are used until 1940, and 1968 is used as the start of the current introvert phase. This alternation is reflected by a change in the public mood parameters. On this and subsequent diagrams, the two parallel lines representing the public parameters in figure 1 will be merged into one heavy line.

In terms of figure 2, the preferred dichotomy for moods in this book is introvert/extrovert. The isolationist/internationalist dichotomy is worded to favor the internationalist, just as the globalist/limitationist is worded to favor the limitationist. All three dichotomies are included in the diagram to relate to pertinent literature.

Interests Proposition

The United States has generally definable foreign policy interests. The interests pursued by the United States in the international system must be defined before they can be analyzed. The discussion of how such interests relate to the mood/interest theory centers on matters of a political and military nature. The theory acknowledges the secondary importance of economic and humanitarian concerns, but maintains that they are not directly subject to the shifting moods manifested in American liberalism.

Figure 3.   United States Politico-Military Interests

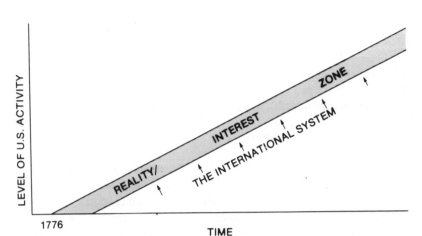

The most basic United States interest is, of course, the preservation of its territorial integrity and well-being. On a global basis this interest has been reflected in two ways: attempting to maintain freedom of the seas and, since 1945, preventing a nuclear, chemical, or biological exchange.

The mood/interest theory rejects the argument that American interests are so global that regional variations are of minimal significance. On the contrary, it asserts that an early point in the identification of interests is the recognition of regional variations. American foreign policy necessarily treats certain geographical areas as constituting a higher level of interest than others. These areas include Europe and East Asia, where the United States seeks to prevent one-nation dominance, and the Western Hemisphere, where the United States endeavors to preserve its dominance among major powers.[5] The United States also seeks to keep other areas of the world, especially the Middle East, open to necessary United States activity.

Figure 3 provides a representation of the United States politico-military interests as dictated by the realities of the international system. The reality/interest zone represents the approximate level of United States activity necessary to guarantee the satisfaction of its fundamental politico-military interests. The time dimension reflects the development of the international system and its relation to United States politico-military interests. As the international community continually increases its ability to challenge United States interests, the level of United States activity necessary to guarantee national interests must rise accordingly. This is not to say that United States activity will always necessarily increase. The rising level depicted could start downward if there were a decline in United States interests abroad. However, the current ever-rising line gives a general picture of the United States' increasing role and commitments in the international arena thus far in its history.

Mood/Interest Conflict Proposition

There is a fundamental conflict between the moods manifested in the liberal American ideology and the dictates of United States politico-military interests. Achieving the interests determined by the harsh realities of the international system usually implies the use of some degree of power.

However, the liberal American orientation to politics includes an aversion to power and, therefore, an aversion to the notion of pursuing politico-military interests. Yet, the extant international situation demands that America pursue its interests to some degree.

Occasionally the United States does too much or too little in pursuit of its interests. Historically, each mood phase has concluded in unchecked excesses above or below the interest zone, resulting in a shift to the opposite phase. After the time required to correct previous excesses, each new phase passes through a middle range reality/interest zone in which the liberal mood corresponds to politico-military interests. Eventually, however, the fluctuating mood results once more in excesses beyond realistic foreign policy interests, setting the stage for the next phase.

This periodic tendency of public mood to deviate from national interest is roughly depicted in figure 4. This diagram takes the American liberal mood curve from figure 2 and adjusts it for the steadily rising reality/interest zone depicted in figure 3. When mood lies within the shaded zone, mood and interest are in relative harmony. The mood/interest conflict is most apparent when mood is above or below the dictates of realistic national interest, represented by the vertical lines above and below the reality/interest zone. An introvert or extrovert mood begins at a time when overall mood leans strongly in the opposite direction.

Executive/Legislative Proposition

Application of the consistent fluctuation in the mood/interest theory can improve understanding of the executive and legislative roles in the determination of American foreign policy. During extrovert phases the executive plays his strongest role in formulating foreign policy, while during introvert phases the legislature gains power. During extrovert phases, people are not only willing, but also anxious for the United States to assume an active role in international affairs, whether it be "Manifest Destiny" or "Guarding the Free World." In such times, the sense of urgency implied by stirring slogans allows little patience with the ponderous workings of the legislature. Thus, foreign policy tends to be delegated to "the man in the best position to know," the chief executive. The Congress, the historical source of isolationist sentiment and

Figure 4. The Mood/Interest Conflict (abbreviated)

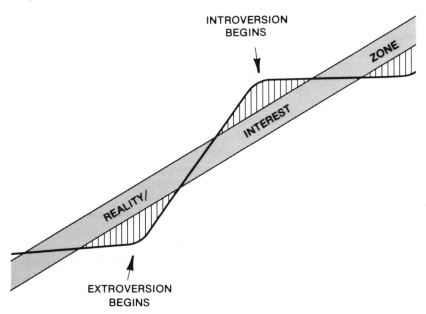

INTROVERSION
BEGINS

ZONE

INTEREST

REALITY/

EXTROVERSION
BEGINS

necessarily looking to be reelected, is often content during extrovert phases to let its power slide over to the White House, particularly since the public approves of decisive presidential action.

Introvert phases feature a greater foreign policy role by the Congress. The congressional response to an introvert public mood is to place greater restrictions on foreign policy activity. The Congress can best exercise its foreign policy muscle through its ability to say "no." The president can urge action, but he sometimes needs to accept a more introvert policy than he believes desirable in order to get along with the Congress. Indeed, given the divided structure of American government, a stalemate can lead to an introvert policy given the rising foreign policy interest zone.

Extreme Introversion Proposition

The possibility of a return to an extreme form of introversion is more likely than is commonly recognized. Most of the literature that accords some validity to the concept of mood change is optimistic that previous forms of excessive introversion will be avoided in the future. The mood/interest theory indicates, however, that avoidance of extreme introversion will be difficult at best, considering the other propositions. The result could be that the United States may again fail to do enough to maintain its interests.

Much of the American understanding of the dangers of extreme introversion is based upon experience of forty to fifty years ago. Protection of American interests is now more complex simply because more American action is required, a situation resulting in part from strong American action during the 1940–1968 extrovert phase. Since extreme introversion occurs late in a mood phase, it is a very relevant matter now, while time might remain to avoid or mitigate the end-of-phase extremes of past mood fluctuations.

Late 1983 featured a United States determination to keep Marine peacekeeping forces in Lebanon and place new missiles in Europe, as well as an active U.S. role in an invasion to restore order in the Caribbean island of Grenada. By early 1984, the pace of American activity slowed down. From a long-term perspective, these moves do not appear to represent a change of the type experienced at the beginning of past extrovert phases. The moves could be typical late introvert adjustments for previous weakness that has gradually promoted increased challenges to U.S. interests by other countries. It also is possible that they could herald a breakdown of past patterns or an earlier than expected return to extroversion.[6] The passage of time will, in any event, tell which interpretation has the most validity. However, it is a misuse of long-range analysis to make a definitive judgment from events in the recent past until a long-term pattern is established; sets of events can be unique. For purposes of this theory the author will assume that the country is still in an introvert phase as is indicated by history. However, it must be emphasized that the purpose of this theory is to present one interpretation of American foreign policy to date and not to make definitive judgments on the long-term meaning of recent events or to predict the future.

For the policy maker or scholar seeking relevancy in foreign policy literature, this proposition may have the greatest value.

METHODOLOGY AND VALUE

American foreign policy can be analyzed in many ways, but traditional approaches predominate. Gene Rainey has identified four American foreign policy "images": the liberal image, the realist image, right-wing revisionism, and left-wing revisionism.[7] Although it does not entirely reject any of these four ideological images, the mood/interest theory fails to conform to any one of them.

In agreement with the liberal image that foreign policy should be determined by the people, the mood/interest theory emphasizes a strong element of pluralism. The mood/interest theory further argues that elite influence on American foreign policy exists, yet maintains that the elites regularly change according to the will of the public. Unlike the liberal image, however, this study views the forging of interests common to all nations as unrealistic and, hence, unachievable at present.

Similar to right-wing revisionism in that it views a considerable portion of American foreign policy problems as internal, this theory advances an argument that emphasizes internal causation. The public mood, an internal cause, pushes American action to the extreme of introversion or extroversion until the external realities of international affairs force the mood in the other direction. Contrary to right-wing revisionist views that the defeat and reformation of communism constitutes an underlying goal of American foreign policy, this study places the anticommunist objective within the perspective of realistic politico-military interests.

This study concurs with the left-wing revisionist advocacy of the need for a changed perspective of American foreign policy. Although in agreement that change is necessary, the mood/interest theory proposes a differing solution. Contrary to the left-wing revisionist image, this study does not emphasize economic causation, plots by American elites, or the need for an enlightened view of adversaries.

In its emphasis upon national survival through the use of a balance-of-power philosophy, the mood/interest theory is perhaps most similar to the realist image. However, unlike most realist analyses, this study asserts that the public ultimately decides American foreign policy questions and holds the key to the solution of foreign policy problems. Only in the long-term sense, after experiencing extremes, does the United States adjust to power realities.

The relation of the nontraditional, behaviorist approach to the mood/interest analysis also should be considered. Some adherents to behaviorism are overly attentive to detail, yet their stress on data collection greatly benefits further studies which wish to build on a strong data base. All too often, however, scholars advance new material on specialized topics rather than categorizing or relating existing material. Herein lies the value of the mood/interest analysis of American foreign policy. The author's macrointerpretation seeks to relate a number of existing theories within the framework of an historical analysis.

Unfortunately, American social scientists are so wary of cyclical theories of history that Klingberg's study, however perceptive, has not achieved its deserved recognition. Analysts still concentrate on detailed studies of events, which indicate that each historical situation is unique and, therefore, of limited value to understanding the present. The price paid for this overly sensitive attention to detail is immense. The mood/interest theory seeks to redress past academic neglect by emphasizing, within the bounds of intellectual integrity, the role of moods in the foreign policy process.[8]

The historical perspective of the mood/interest theory improves understanding of America's international stance more than do many conventional foreign policy studies which downplay the significance of history, long-range trends, and internal causation. Through the integration of six individual propositions into a plausible, coherent interpretation of foreign policy behavior, the theory advances a new framework for analysis. The theory asserts that, if changing public mood is acknowledged, America's interactions with other nations will be viewed less as random responses to world events and more as a pattern of responses conforming to mood.

In order to incorporate two hundred years of American history into a manageable theory, the author must make generalizations. If the theory is applicable to actual situations, if it contains realistic suggestions for an improved view of its subject matter, and if it has been constructed with belief in its validity, then those generalizations are justifiable. An attempt at relating what is often seen as an entangled morass of details and circumstances will be made through the incorporation of some statistical data, further supporting and justifying those generalizations. This gives a better idea of what is known and what is unknown. A statement of one way in which moods operate may work to stimulate others to look for further approaches. The next step, of course, would be an extensive quantitative study. Such a study would be difficult to conduct without a greater consensus by the academic community, because academics often build on one another's work. This work is designed to stimulate moves in such a direction.

The mood/interest theory as presented here thus argues that long-range cycles in American foreign policy can be placed in a framework that is meaningful to both scholar and policy maker. This framework, which relates Klingberg's mood analysis to American liberalism and foreign policy interests, cannot provide automatic answers to American foreign policy problems. It is only one prospect for a macroanalysis of American foreign policy and does not claim to be the sole and authoritative long-range study. The mood/interest theory can, however, demonstrate the necessity of learning from history and considering long-range moods, and it is the hope of the author that this study will inspire other macroanalyses. Indeed, the author would be pleased to see refinements and modifications of the mood/interest theory, or even an improved replacement.

1. Liberalism, Moods, and American Foreign Policy

The writings of John Locke articulate well the basic liberal ideological stance of almost all Americans. Locke, one of the early theorizers of liberalism, describes some characteristics of political and social human beings particularly relevant to American beliefs. Peace, not war, is the natural state. People are basically good, born free with natural rights to property and human equality. People enter society on their own accord to better secure their natural rights. Government must be limited to prevent it from reducing individualism more than is necessary to maintain the benefits offered the individual by society. Governmental authority should be divided. The powers of the government are subordinated to the people, who act as the ultimate judge. Problem-solving is left to the faith in human ability to rationally meet the needs of each new situation.[1] These liberal ideological values are embraced by most Americans.[2]

That the vast majority of Americans are liberal is not a new assertion. Louis Hartz argued forcefully in this direction almost three decades ago, placing American history in the context of an all-embracing liberalism. His book, *The Liberal Tradition in America,* argues that the American business community, often thought of as conservative, is unquestionably liberal in the Lockean tradition. Other ideologies, Hartz maintains, have been ineffective in America simply because they were not formulated to address the dominant liberal situation in America. Hartz summarizes that "the outstanding thing about the American community in Western history ought to be . . . that the American community is a liberal community."[3]

The continuity of American liberalism has been a significant motivational force for action, particularly in the field of foreign policy. Even business liberals, those Americans currently called "conservative" in conventional American terminology, are, in reality, conveyors of American liberalism. Thus, "conservative" is not an entirely accurate term for business liberals in the American context. If Americans in general can be considered conservative in any way, it is in their tenacious protection of the liberal ideology as advanced by John Locke, not in their protection of traditional technology and methods in business dealings. For this reason, it is profitable to replace conventional liberal/

conservative terminology and instead designate different kinds of liberals. The predominantly liberal American public is best divided into two major strands: business liberals and reform liberals. Business liberals want to change things by allowing individuals to pursue their own self-interests unencumbered by institutions. Reform liberals, on the other hand, generally want to change things by reforming institutions throughout America.[4]

In principle, reform liberals emphasize humanitarian improvement and business liberals emphasize economic improvement. The differing emphasis is often overshadowed when American liberals assume a unified stance, particularly on American foreign policy issues. Both types of liberals believe that progress is necessary and leads to an ideal, that peace is the natural condition, and that individual rights, as described by Locke, are the most important rights. While both are distrustful of the politico-military power relationships that lie at the heart of international politics, both sometimes justify the use of power to achieve liberal objectives.

Liberal beliefs are articulated in the 1801 inaugural address of reform liberal Thomas Jefferson, the 1969 inaugural address of business liberal Richard Nixon, the 1977 inaugural address of reform liberal Jimmy Carter, and the 1981 inaugural address of business liberal Ronald Reagan. The similarities among the varieties of liberalism are striking. Jefferson expressed the following ideas:

All . . . will bear in mind this sacred principle, that though the will of the majority is in all cases to prevail, that will to be rightful must be reasonable; that the minority possesses their equal rights, which equal law must protect, and to violate would be oppression. . . . Error of opinion may be tolerated where reason is left free to combat it . . . entertaining a due sense of our equal right to the use of our own faculties, to the acquisitions of our own industry . . . a wise and frugal Government, which shall restrain men from injuring one another, shall leave them otherwise free to regulate their own pursuits of industry and improvement, and shall not take from the mouth of labor the bread it has earned. . . . Equal and exact justice to all men, of whatever state or persuasion, religious or political; peace, commerce, and honest friendship with all nations . . . a jealous care of the right of election by the people . . . freedom of person under the protection of the habeas corpus, and trial by juries impartially selected.[5]

Nixon's address includes these phrases:

The greatest honor history can bestow is the title of peacemaker. . . . The American people are ready to answer this call. . . . We have given freedom new reach, and we have begun to make its promise real for black as well as for white. . . . But we are approaching the limits of what government alone can do. . . . What has to be done, has to be done by government and people together or it will not be done at all. The lesson of past agony is that without the people we can do nothing; with the people we can do everything. . . . Each of us shares in the shaping of his own destiny. . . . No man can be fully free while his neighbor is not. . . . As all are born equal in dignity before God, all are born equal in dignity before man. As we learn to go forward together at home, let us also seek to go forward together with all mankind. . . . We seek an open world—open to ideas, open to the exchange of goods and people. . . . I know the heart of America is good.[6]

Carter also emphasized basic tenets of American liberalism:

We reject the prospect of failure or mediocrity or an inferior quality of life for any person. . . . We have already found a high degree of personal liberty, and we are now struggling to enhance equality of opportunity. Our commitment to human rights must be absolute, our laws fair . . . the powerful must not persecute the weak, and human dignity must be enhanced. . . . The passion for freedom is on the rise. Tapping this new spirit, there can be no nobler nor more ambitious task for America to undertake on this day of a new beginning than to help shape a just and peaceful world that is truly humane. . . . Because we are free we can never be indifferent to the fate of freedom elsewhere. . . . We do not seek to intimidate, but it is clear that a world which others can dominate with impunity would be inhospitable to decency and a threat to the well-being of all people. . . . I join in the hope that . . . people might say this about our Nation: . . . That we had torn down the barriers that separated those of different race and region and religion, and where there had been mistrust, built unity, with a respect for diversity; . . . That we had insured respect for the law, and equal treatment under the law, for the weak and the powerful, for the rich and the poor.[7]

Strong support for the similarity of reform and business liberalism as twin offspring of dominant American liberalism can be seen by comparing reform liberal Carter's inaugural with the similar ideas found in business liberal Reagan's address:

We are a united people pledged to maintaining a political system which guarantees individual liberty . . . . We as Americans have the capacity . . . to do whatever needs to be done to preserve this . . . bastion of freedom. . . . From time to time we've been tempted to believe that . . . government by an elite group is superior to government for, by, and of the people. But, if no one among us is capable of governing himself, then who among us has the capacity to govern someone else. . . . This administration's objective must be a healthy, vigorous, growing economy that provides equal opportunities for all Americans with no barriers born of bigotry or discrimination. . . . We are a nation that has a government—not the other way around. . . . Our government has no special power except that granted it by the people. It is time to check and reverse the growth of government which shows signs of having grown beyond the consent of the governed. . . . we unleashed the energy and individual genius of man. . . . Freedom and the dignity of the individual have been more available and assured here than in any other place on earth. . . . We, the Americans of today are ready . . . to do what must be done to ensure happiness and liberty for ourselves, our children, and our children's children. . . . No arsenal or no weapon in the arsenals of the world is so formidable as the will and moral courage of free men and women. . . . The crisis we are facing today does . . . require . . . our willingness to believe in ourselves and to believe in our capacity to perform great deeds; to believe that together and with God's help we can and will resolve the problems which now confront us.[8]

Other studies have also noted that Reagan displays liberal tendencies, despite the common belief that his position is "conservative." For example, W. Wayne Shannon writes that aspects of Reagan's inaugural are "deeply Lockean," and that, "Aside from 'supply-side' economics, there is nothing whatever in it [the Reagan perspective] that anyone with a decent memory or any knowledge of American history ought to regard as new."[9] So liberalism has been a great unifying and pervasive force in American history, spanning more than two hundred years and strongly bringing together both business liberals and reform liberals in pursuit of common, transcendent liberal goals.

Although liberalism has been the focus of American ideology, there have been two prominent, relatively conservative forces in American history: the Federalists, who had some fear of the masses, and the Antebellum Southerners, who were motivated by the desire to maintain their lifestyle and their peculiar institution of slavery. These two groups came close to putting more emphasis upon the "wisdom of the ages," as embodied in tradition, than upon individual judgment. The Federalists were dealt a severe blow with the bloodless Jeffersonian revolution of 1800, which proved their fear of the masses to be unfounded, and they were finally laid to rest after their ill-fated opposition to the War of 1812. The conservatism of the Antebellum South as a force in foreign policy existed until the Civil War, when its desires were actively frustrated by the rest of American society. In time, both conservative forces were destroyed by the dominant liberalism in America. The behavior of liberals had been modified only slightly by conservatives, and after 1865 this tempering force was weak, although it has occasionally played a part in American policy because of the deficiencies of liberalism. Since that time, challenges to the American liberal ideology have failed in large part because conditions that in other countries brought about the formation of competing ideologies did not exist at the same time in the United States.[10]

Hartz believes that if American liberalism is to be modified in the current era, it is most likely to result from American contact with foreign governments at a time when liberalism has shifted to an extreme.[11] This demonstrates that development of the foreign policy implications of American liberalism is important to the study of liberalism in general, as well as to American foreign policy.

LIBERALISM AND FOREIGN POLICY

Liberalism has been identified by Samuel P. Huntington in his 1957 book, *The Soldier and the State,* as having several characteristics that influence foreign policy actions and tend to give Americans a marked commonality in foreign policy thought. Of particular importance to mood/interest analysis are the following Huntington observations:

1. "Liberalism normally either denies the existence of power, minimizes its importance, or castigates it as inherently evil . . . [and] tends to assume the existence of . . . national security."
2. Although "the liberal believes that the natural relation is peace," he "will normally support a war waged to further liberal ideas," either business or reform.
3. The liberal is normally uninterested in national security affairs and, when forced to consider them, will apply his well-developed and change-oriented domestic policy values.[12]

Edward Weisband's 1973 analysis argues that United States justifications for its foreign policy actions have been based largely upon three fixed characteristics of the American ideological tradition derived from Lockean liberalism: self-determination, self-identification, and self-preservation.[13]

While in domestic policy, reform liberals and business liberals can and often do balance each other because of conflicting immediate goals, liberal interest in foreign policy is irregular, and a liberal consensus can be attained more easily. The unrestrained desire of reform and business liberals to alter social conditions and seek improvement is particularly well evidenced in international affairs. Humankind has been unable to reach its often repeated goal of peace in any permanent sense. The natural reaction of the liberal is to urge change of the political nature and military manifestations of the system in order to obtain lasting peace.

When Americans disagree on specific foreign policy issues, it often is in terms of the appropriate application of the liberal ideology. President Woodrow Wilson, leader of the Wilsonian internationalists, and Senator William E. Borah, leader of the hard-core isolationists, held similar nationalistic views; the difference between them being that internationalist Wilson saw an arrangement like the League of Nations as conforming to American national principles,[14] while isolationist Borah did not.[15] In this instance, Borah represented an introvert application of liberalism while Wilson represented an extrovert application. Hans J. Morgenthau ascribes a similar lack of realism to both antileague "isolationists" and Wilsonian "internationalists."[16]

The Wilson-Borah disagreement occurred during a time when the public mood was changing, which happens every two to three decades. Most Americans agree on a mood at any given time, but similar backgrounds can lead to different views at different times. For instance, many admirers of the reform liberal La Follette movement were critical of McCarthyism, but one analyst found "continuity between the isolationist wing of the La Follette movement and the strongest pro-McCarthy counties in 1952."[17] This apparent incongruity appears less striking when it is remembered that liberalism has both introvert and extrovert extremes.

Despite many similarities, the two liberal variants may affect different aspects of American foreign policy. The profit motive, which is at the root of business liberalism, is an important reason for continuing United States interest in international economic opportunity. Likewise, the humanitarian concern, which is inherent in reform liberalism, helps to explain the constant United States interest in humanitarian affairs. However, in a complex world situation, many matters, primarily those of a politico-military nature, cannot readily be identified as being clearly economic or humanitarian concerns. Thus, these matters are particularly subject to alternation between two distinct foreign policy moods.

On the one hand, both types of liberals may shy away from an activist politico-military policy as too costly in economic and human terms, especially in a war situation. A business liberal with a firm belief in economic betterment can decide that the laissez faire example of a strong and prosperous United States is more influential than the threat of armed force and that trade is more powerful than weaponry. Similarly, a reform liberal emphasizing a strong belief in human betterment can determine that the example of a free society is more persuasive than threatened violence. Thus, both business and reform liberals can tend toward minimum international politico-military involvement, or introversion, for quite understandable reasons.

On the other hand, a society using an example-setting strategy can be ignored in the rush of international events. Perhaps instruction of other countries in the American free enterprise, humanitarian, and democratic traditions is necessary to bring about international change. Perhaps American trade needs physical protection or an initial boost to get started. With these rationales, both the reform and business liberal have natural extrovert positions.

The American liberal is periodically torn between introversion and extroversion, two possible expressions of his liberalism. Business liberals and reform liberals have usually acted in concert when dealing with foreign policy. On some occasions, both groups have chosen to become actively involved in international affairs, and on other occasions, both groups have chosen to remain relatively aloof, preferring to set an example. The fact that the reform liberal is torn between being an example and providing direct instruction is well documented, perhaps because most academic observers in the United States are sympathetic to the reform liberal viewpoint. The ambivalence of the business liberal is less recognized because of the easy equation of business with the military, from which is stimulated the belief of many that the business community is consistently extrovert. However, instances in which business has been noted to have deviated from the expected promilitary extrovert position call the generalization into question.

The diversity of business liberal thought is a particularly important consideration. Extrovert manifestations of the business liberal frequently have been noted, as exemplified by business liberal support of a strong navy during most of the nineteenth century and support of much of the American involvement in twentieth-century international politics. Introvert manifestations are noted to a much lesser degree, but are nevertheless significant. For example, at the same time business liberals pushed for a strong navy, they also formed a substantial part of the opposition to the War of 1812, the Mexican War, and the Spanish-American War. In the twentieth century many business liberals opposed Theodore Roosevelt's foreign policy assertiveness,[18] Franklin Roosevelt's indirect aid to the Allies prior to 1941,[19] and early commitments in the cold war.[20] Recent documentation of the many sides of the business liberal can be found in a 1975 study by Bruce M. Russett and Elizabeth C. Hanson.[21] It must be concluded on this point that business liberals are more complex than is normally believed and that they do not simply follow the dictates of a "conservative" ideology. One distinction that can be drawn between different types of business liberals is the difference between a business liberal involved in international trade and the business liberal involved in national and local trade. The multinational business liberal is most likely to appear extroverted, while the national and local business liberal may only make this a consensus when public mood is fully extroverted.

One illustration of the desirability of using the division of terms reform liberal/business liberal, as opposed to the traditional liberal/conservative dichotomy, is the 1950 foreign policy stance of Herbert Hoover, who cannot be fully understood if he is simply labeled a conservative. Hoover is far better understood as a business liberal. In 1950 he made some foreign policy warnings which were contrary to the later reputation of conservatives and which were to become popular with increasing numbers of liberals some two decades later. His now famous Gibraltar Speech warned against a United States commitment on the Eurasian mainland, which he maintained would be very difficult to sustain. Instead, he believed that the United States should become the Gibraltar of Western civilization, retaining appropriate naval and air capabilities.[22]

Walter Lippman, from 1919 until his death, pointed the way for business and, particularly, reform liberal orientations even though his distrust of popular opinion in policy-making could be called classically conservative. Beginning in 1919 with the Treaty of Versailles, he was continually ahead of liberal ideology on foreign policy. In 1969, with his "blue water" strategy,[23] Lippmann took a stance close to that advocated in Hoover's Gibraltar Speech given nineteen years earlier; the introvert tenor of this Hoover-Lippmann viewpoint has gained support since 1969, though its specifics make it infeasible.

Both Hoover and Lippmann, taking liberal introvert positions, advocated an American defense perimeter that stopped in the "blue water" off the Eurasian mainland. Hoover stressed problems of expense in a business liberal fashion, whereas Lippman stressed quality of life in a manner especially appealing to reform liberals. Lippmann went so far as to state that Ameica's whole way of life had been distorted by excessive American involvement on the Eurasian mainland starting before the Korean War. Thus Lippmann, who appeals especially to the reform liberal community, agreed with Hoover's earlier warnings to the same effect: America was too activist. Certainly, to call Hoover simply a conservative is inappropriate.

The Whig platform of 1852 expresses introvert sentiments of the type now popular in the United States. "Our mission as a republic is not to propagate our opinions, or impose on other countries our form of government by artifice or force; but to teach, by example, and show by our success, moderation and justice, the blessings of self-government, and the advantages of free institutions."[24] However, this was the last time the Whigs competed in a presidential election as one of two major political parties, for one of their major problems was that they expressed the introvert, example-setting viewpoint during a time of increasing extroversion.

A well-known, early supporter of the introversion that now characterizes the United States was Senator J. William Fulbright. In 1966, when Fulbright was chairman of the Senate Foreign Relations Committee, he expressed his viewpoint in the book, *The Arrogance of Power.*

If America has a service to perform in the world—and I believe she has—it is in large part the service of her own example. In our excessive involvement in the affairs of other countries we are not only living off our assets and denying our own people the proper enjoyment of their resources, we are also denying the world the example of a free society enjoying its freedom to the fullest.[25]

A recent example of this viewpoint, in keeping with the current introvert mood, is contained in President Carter's statement that "No other country is as well-qualified as we to set an example."[26]

A comparison of the 1852 Whig platform, Fulbright's 1966 book, and President Carter's 1977 statement indicates historical continuity in introvert American foreign policy thinking. Such continuity can also be seen in extrovert foreign policy orientations. In contrast to periods of liberal introversion, periods of liberal extroversion have grown in terms of the geographic scope to which they have applied, although essentially they remain the same with regard to ideological rationale. During extrovert phases dating back to the early 1800s, both reform and business liberals have sought active United States involvement in certain international politico-military situations.

Business liberals expressed a type of extrovert thinking in the 1864 Republican platform:

Resolved, That we approve the position taken by the Government that the people of the United States can never regard with indifference the attempt of any European Power to overthrow by force or to supplant by fraud the institutions of any Republican Government on the Western Continent and that they will view with extreme jealousy, as menacing to the peace and independence of their own country, the efforts of any such power to obtain new footholds for Monarchical Government, sustained by foreign military force, in near proximity to the United States.[27]

President William McKinley, speaking of the Philippines around the turn of the century, expressed another form of extroversion when he said: "We could not leave them [the Filipinos] to themselves—they were unfit for self-government . . . there was nothing left for us to do but to take them all, and to educate the Filipinos, and uplift and civilize and Christianize them. . . . and I told him [the cartographer] to put the Philippines on the map of the United States."[28] Comparison of this statement with the 1961 inaugural address of reform liberal John F. Kennedy in the latest extrovert phase evidences continuity and growth of extrovert liberal thinking. Kennedy proclaimed: "Let every nation know, whether it wishes us well or ill, that we shall pay any price, bear any burden, meet any hardship, support any friend, oppose any foe, in order to assure the survival and success of liberty. This we pledge—and more."[29] These statements are derived from the common philosophical basis of American liberalism. The differences which can be noted in this sampling of liberal statements are due more to increased United States capabilities than to philosophical conflicts.

In extroversion, as in introversion, when a business-liberal/reform-liberal alignment does occur, the effect on American foreign policy is marked. Bruce Russett and Elizabeth Hanson make observations in this direction: "Economic interest and ideology—whether of the "liberal messianist" [reform liberal] variety or of a conservative anticommunist [business liberal] sort—might therefore combine, in the American case, to produce a more powerful impetus to an assertive, activist foreign policy than either could produce alone."[30] This reference of Russett and Hanson is to a convergence on extroversion. An example of such unity on introversion, on the other hand, occurred during the late 1930s when the isolationist coalition included both business and reform liberals.[31]

Further insight into the two-sided nature of American liberalism as it relates to foreign policy is given by Samuel P. Huntington in his 1981 book, *American Politics: The Promise of Disharmony*. As in his 1957 book, Huntington maintains the Hartzian idea of the predominance of liberalism in America, but he adds, "If one had to apply one adjective to them [American ideals], 'liberal' would be it, but even this term does not convey the full richness and complexity of the amalgam." This amalgam is better described, says Huntington, as the American "creed," which is a conglomeration of elements, including medieval legalist ideas, seventeenth-century Protestantism, Lockean and Enlightenment ideas, and others. Although many of these elements are inherently contradictory, Huntington points out that the basic creed has remained essentially unchanged for two hundred years.

The point here is that these inconsistent elements of the American creed have regularly contradicted each other in American foreign policy as well. Huntington notes the historical fluctuations in the different American liberal ideals that the public has called on our foreign policy institutions to support, citing the "new realism" of the 1950s and '60s and the "new moralism" of the 1970s as examples.[32] In relation to the mood/interest theory, then, this illustrates how the same basic American liberalism can equally support contradictory ideals, such as introversion and extroversion, depending on predominant moods.

Therefore, American liberalism is apparently much more than a simple conglomeration of ideological statements. It also lends itself well to an interpretation of American foreign policy history based on moods, since at least one dominant trait of the American liberal is that he or she is never satisfied with the present situation. How, then, is the impact of this liberalism felt in American foreign policy?

FOREIGN POLICY MOOD ALTERNATION

Both reform and business liberals are constantly dissatisfied with, and therefore continually endeavoring to change, the realities of international politics. American liberals have alternatively embraced two methods of change, choosing either a tendency toward introversion or a tendency toward extroversion, reaching an extreme in one before abandoning it for the other. American foreign policy, suggests the mood/interest theory, has fluctuated in this manner since 1776.[33]

Frank L. Klingberg's 1952 article, "The Historical Alternation of Moods in American Foreign Policy," delineates the mood swings fundamental to the mood/interest theory.[34] However, little was heard or said of Klingberg's long-range perspective until about a decade and a half later when his indication for the end of the fourth extrovert phase uncannily became fact. A serious look at mood, to include its current implications, is long overdue. The mood/interest theory works toward that end, relating long-term fluctuations of foreign policy to the shifting liberal moods of the American public and the leaders who respond to the public.

Klingberg divided United States foreign policy history into four "extrovert" and four "introvert" phases.[35]

Introvert	Extrovert
1776–1798	1798–1824
1824–1844	1844–1871
1871–1891	1891–1919
1919–1940	1940–

By extension of the extrovert phases averaging twenty seven years and introvert phases averaging twenty one years, one can approximate the end of the 1940 extrovert phase to be near 1967 and the end of the current introvert phase somewhere in the late 1980s. The 1968 date can be documented as the end of the last extrovert phase, but future dates remain a matter of pure conjecture.

Klingberg's article provides extensive statistical documentation to support his phases. In his research, he tallied the number of wars, armed expeditions, and annexations—the most prominent indicators of extroversion—and found them to be situated overwhelmingly in extrovert phases. He studied inaugural addresses, annual presidential messages, and major party platforms and determined the percentage of each which was devoted to foreign policy, especially positive American action beyond its borders. He then charted the results, which further supported his mood analysis. Other indicators that Klingberg studied were treaties, diplomatic warnings, annual naval expenditures, and election results. These, too, were in agreement with his theory.[36]

Klingberg's analysis and the fluctuating liberalism of the mood/interest theory must be understood as long-range perspectives. A consideration of the difference between long-term mood and short-term opinion should facilitate this understanding. The mood/interest theory necessarily concedes that short-term fluctuations may occur within a long-term mood phase, and that individual indicators may deviate from the composite mood. Klingberg notes that "any study of the American mood for a short period of time will probably find the temporary fluctuations of opinion more impressive than its stability or consistency."[37] Thus, while "public opinion" can be useful in understanding "public mood,"[38] the mood/interest theory emphasizes the underlying mood of the American public rather than momentary opinions.

The underlying mood, in introvert phases, is typified by the concern to prevent development or expansion of American political and military concerns beyond its own borders. George Washington's statement gives an excellent indication of such an underlying mood of the American public during introvert phases: "So far as we have already formed engagements, let them be fulfilled with perfect good faith. Here let us stop."[39] There is little politico-military assertiveness during introvert phases as compared to extrovert phases, which are characterized by a tone of expansion and extraterritorial political involvement. Each phase contains a period during which the extremes of introversion or extroversion are in conflict with the foreign policy interests of the nation. Introvert phases are characterized by a basic reluctance to do all that might be necessary to protect American interests in the world political arena; this reluctance grows in intensity during the phase. Conversely, an extrovert mood can grow to the point that the United States can do too much for her best interests;[40] each major American war since the Revolution has started during an extrovert phase.

Klingberg's mood analysis is worded carefully and does not place moods into a definite framework other than to establish introvert and extrovert phases with appropriate academic caveats. The mood/interest theory asserts that Klingberg need not have been so modest, for his analysis did in its own careful way project a major change in American foreign policy not foreseen by scores of analysts who relied on more conventional tools. Most often, the conventional tools examine the world situation and conclude that American leadership can meet the challenge on a continuing basis and that the public can be sold on a course of action if the case is well presented.

The contention of the mood/interest theory is that the study of American foreign policy is best served by drawing Klingberg's moods into a more definite and, hence, less defensible form to see what it might mean to American foreign policy study. A number of American foreign policy analysts acknowledge a certain validity in the Klingberg analysis.[41] However, analysts are usually optimistic on the question of whether Americans will outgrow the undesirable aspects of mood fluctuations: they commend the public for checking previous excesses of American policy and predict the public's ability to see the need for a still active, though more restrained, American role.[42] This type of analysis often merely tends to explain Klingberg prior to proceeding to other courses of analysis. In fact, one analyst whose post-1870 dates of changes in foreign policy thought are similar to Klingberg's, nevertheless rejects the idea that precise numbers and dates can be used in studying foreign policy trends. He concludes that, "as social scientists, of course, we do not accept the notion that God plays numbers games with United States foreign policy."[43]

Klingberg gives various indications as to how moods operate. He says that there are several up-and-down fluctuations within a mood and notes that this is what might explain why analysts of short periods of time have difficulty understanding moods. Later, he states that a change from one phase to the next takes place over a several year period and that moods tend to grow over a period of time.[44]

The material developed below builds on considerable evidence that those minor fluctuations that occur within a larger phase do, in fact, follow an overall pattern which increases in intensity. Thus, the growth and the several year change-over receive the greatest emphasis in this study. Indeed, a widespread shift takes a number of years if for no other reason than that old policies and attitudes cannot be changed at once. At times of change-over it is possible to have a new introvert mood as old extrovert policies are being modified. The steady growth of each individual mood phase is indicated by the tendency of extreme actions to be taken toward the end of a phase and not at the beginning.

Paths to the Present, by Arthur Schlesinger, Sr., supports fluctuating moods in domestic politics. The book suggests that "the electorate embarks upon conservative policies till it is disappointed or vexed or bored and then attaches itself to liberal policies till a like course is run." In comparison, the pre-1948 dates in Schlesinger's analysis do not correspond to Klingberg's pre-1948 dates. Schlesinger suggests that 1947–1963 will be conservative and that the next conservative "epoch" will be due "around 1978."[45] Hindsight in the 1980s provides more support to Klingberg than to Schlesinger, but Schlesinger's portrayal of the public tendency to go to one mood extreme before abandoning it for another is a valuable illustration of mood fluctuation.

Granted that human behavior during two hundred years cannot be represented in mathematically precise terms, the mood/interest theory suggests that an undulating curve (like a sine curve) may *roughly* represent the regular mood fluctuation of the Americn public as manifested in their liberalism. For simplicity of presentation and stimulation of thinking, the undulating curve illustrating the Liberal Moods Proposition has been pictured in figure 2 (page 4). At the apexes of the curve are the dates at which extrovert phases become introvert, and at the nadirs of the curve are the opposite transitions. At this point, certain mathematical conceptions must be abandoned for the sake of clarity. While sine curves are normally products of charting points on a graph, this diagram is not meant in that way. For example, the turning point at 1798 is not mathematically the same as the turning point at 1891. The curve is only an attempt to indicate that a change in public mood and policy action occurred in the same direction at each of these points in time. The mood curve is manifested in liberalism, and liberalism appears necessary for its operation. That does not mean that it is caused by liberalism though this could be the case. The terminology "American liberal mood curve" will be used for purposes of a short descriptive reference.

It must be stated that as an expression of overall mood or policy, this representation does not reflect the momentary changes which naturally occur in day-to-day, politico-military activity. Rather, it is an attempt to show a mood over time, a mood that is dominant in public thought and in United States diplomacy. The implicit argument is that because American public mood is so predictable and consistent in its shifting, it must be the predominant influence on policy; too many different variables and events impinge on policy for it to shift so predictably or regularly on its own. Hence, that regularity of shift is provided by public mood unless the regularity also coincides with another variable.

The curve shows the dominant general mood in public thought and in United States diplomacy over time. The regular repetition of history implied by the curve is at variance with the American liberal belief in a constant progression of history. The mood/interest theory argues that this belief, characteristic of liberal writings and suggesting that America has outgrown its moodiness, needs to be balanced by some argument that it has not.

Indeed, the mood shift following the Vietnam war has produced a considerable amount of writing which stresses that the American public has thrown off the simple internationalist/isolationist (or extrovert/introvert) dichotomy. As one study notes, "There is general agreement among analysts that the uni-dimensional, internationalist-isolationist continuum was a casualty of Viet-nam."[46] The argument, generally, is that the Vietnam war was a formative experience whose lessons divided the public into several factions, thus eliminat-ing the possibility of any widespread public consensus comparable to that of the cold war era. After looking briefly at a few of the writings to this effect, a number of considerations will be raised to support the mood/interest contention that this is the kind of analysis that allows the cyclical pattern to continue; the public has not outgrown the introvert mood, it has merely outgrown the novelty of that mood.

Ole Holsti and James Rosenau, in their article "Vietnam, Consensus, and the Belief Systems of American Leaders," write that the only consensus on foreign policy in the post-Vietnam era is that we should learn from the lessons of Vietnam; there is no such agreement as to what lessons should be learned.[47]

Regarding foreign policy beliefs in a more general context than only those responses to the Vietnam experience, Ole R. Holsti metaphorically describes America as the "Three-Headed Eagle." By this, he is referring to the three "clusters of belief" in America in recent years: cold war internationalism, post–cold war internationalism, and isolationism. The basic difference between the two internationalist categories, according to Holsti, is that the cold war internationalists emphasize the East-West division and argue that most signifi-cant global problems are related to that division, while the post–cold war internationalists perceive the world as a complex, interdependent system where U.S. efforts to promote global stability are necessary and where the Soviet threat is more dispersed than during the cold war era. The isolationists, as in most analyses, stress that the importance of U.S. activity is overemphasized, and that the problems needing action are mostly domestic.[48]

Another article, by Michael Maggiotto and Eugene Wittkopf, divides the American public into four categories, each representing roughly the same percentage of the public: isolationists (20%), who oppose both militant interna-tionalism and cooperative internationalism; accommodationists (27%), who support cooperative but oppose militant internationalism; internationalists (30%), supporting both cooperative and militant internationalism; and hard-liners (23%) who support militant internationalism while opposing cooperative internationalism. By these figures, Maggiotto and Wittkopf argue that the American public is overwhelmingly internationalist (80% supporting some international activity), but that any consensus on the form of internationalism to be taken is lacking.[49]

Michael Mandelbaum and William Schneider similarly argue that the American public is basically internationalist, but that a sharp distinction exists between what they term liberal (reform liberal) internationalism and conservative (business liberal) internationalism. The former, according to these authors, is more concerned with moralistic issues, while the latter is concerned with politico-military interests. Mandelbaum and Schneider also recognize the non-internationalists, but the argument is still towards predominant internationalism lacking consensus as to form and primary interests.[50]

The mood/interest theory, on the contrary, argues that the conclusion of Vietnam marked the beginning of a new introvert phase much like previous introversion. First, an introvert mood need not be characterized by an "isolationist consensus." Other authors, such as Selig Adler and Manfred Jonas,[51] have noted the complexity of previous introvert phases. Jonas, for example, delineates five isolationist categories: foreign-oriented, belligerent, timid, radical, and conservative.[52] Thus, lack of consensus on specific aspects of introversion does not eliminate the possibility of an introvert mood. Indeed, in foreign policy matters a lack of consensus signals introversion since positive action in the Amercan political system usually requires consensus.

Second, most recent studies do not take into account the fact that the United States can pursue a portion of its interests to some degree while still being basically introverted.[53] The attitude of maintaining only outright commitments can preserve the illusion of international activity while actually neglecting less obvious, yet important interests, as is characteristic of introvert phases.

Similarly, the so-called internationalism suggested by some does not always account for differences between politico-military, economic, and moralistic interests. For example, Mandelbaum and Schneider do distinguish between moralistic and politico-military interests, but look at these as divisions within a basic internationalism.[54] On the other hand, the mood/interest theory contends that politico-military interests are of primary concern and historically are what have divided introverts from extroverts, while economic and humanitarian interests are secondary and characteristically are emphasized in both introvert and extrovert periods. Thus, introversion is not characterized necessarily by a lack of international activity; rather, it is characterized by a failure to adequately address politico-military interests abroad.

Adding to the likelihood of this confusion is the fact that, unlike any previous introvert periods, the United States is now very much in the center of international political activity. Common-sense observation shows the degree to which our nation is involved, and this is also illustrated by George Modelski's theory of long cycles. According to his theory, the United States is currently occupying the position of dominant power in global politics, and the need for action in protection of our interests may be greater than recognized. Modelski sees America's current position as a provider of hope for conciliatory measures, such as arms control for the prevention of global (nuclear) war; other dominant powers in the past have enjoyed relative peace when they have been at a similar point in the period of dominance.[55]

Much power used in American diplomacy implies the threat of force; such a threat is important for a leader and a dominant power. It is not always publicly supported, but without it politico-military interests risk neglect. On this point, James L. Payne writes: "If we are to avoid such tragedy [of unnecessary and catastrophic war], we must grasp the relationships between American action— or inaction—in the present and the indirect and future consequences of that action. The focus for understanding these relationships is our nation's most powerful foreign policy instrument: the American threat of war."[56] In this regard, President Reagan's 1983 actions regarding Grenada could be particularly important insofar as they demonstrate an assertiveness which in a period of introversion is likely to be noticed by others.

Finally, a possible reason for underestimating the need for American action to protect its politico-military interests is the feeling that attempts at promoting these interests are generally unsuccessful. However, Samuel Huntington, in *American Politics: the Promise of Disharmony*, points out the little noticed value of U.S. actions abroad. He contends that right-wing "fascist" dictatorships, which have received U.S. support, are historically more stable, less repressive, and more susceptible to U.S. and Western influence than left-wing dictatorships; the U.S. almost single- handedly established the largest expansion of democracy in history by the inauguration of democratic regimes after World War II; U.S. influence in Greece and Italy helped stem communist expansion during the cold war era; and American involvement in Latin America has corresponded with the advancement of democracy in the area.[57] Conversely, it is easy to see how a lack of American activity abroad can lead to the decline of American interests.

So, recent literature stressing that the United States has changed since the Vietnam war, in that the past isolationist-internationalist dichotomy is now obsolete, seems to help perpetuate the liberal ideology by assuring experts that we have changed from the past when we have not. The mood/interest theory, on the other hand, stresses that current American foreign policy actions in relation to American politico-military interests indicate the current existence of an introvert phase.

INDIVIDUAL MOOD PHASES

The mood/interest theory incorporates many of the indicators Klingberg utilized to detail shifts in American foreign policy moods. Presidential messages, inaugural addresses, and major political party platforms since 1844 are helpful indictators suggested by Klingberg's study.[58] He also used statistics on naval expenditures, which were subsequently gathered for the mood/interest theory, along with key congressional votes to study shifts in support of naval expenditures during periods of introversion and extroversion.[59] Analysis of these data, in conjunction with the works by Louis Hartz and Samuel Huntington, aids the tracing of liberal tendencies on foreign policy through the early years of American history.[60]

A study of major territorial expansion since the Revolutionary War, which was also suggested by Klingberg's article,[61] showed that such expansion occurred exclusively during extrovert periods. After the United States could no longer feasibly expand its territorial borders, mutual defense treaties (considered a form of extroversion) operated as a surrogate for territorial expansion. A total of eight mutual defense treaties were signed by the United States after 1945 covering about 16 million square miles, close to 30 percent of the world's land mass.

Information was gathered on instances of the use of U.S. armed forces abroad from 1798 to 1970, as well as major United States armed actions overseas with relevant congressional action from 1789 to 1970.[62] United States armed forces overseas were used more often and more violently during periods of extroversion than during periods of introversion. This, too, supports the assertions of the mood/interest theory. The above sources, and others, contributed to the following general historical account of each American foreign policy mood phase.[63]

The First Introvert Phase: 1776–1798

The initial goal of the Revolutionary War was the establishment of more congenial ties with America's ruler, Great Britain. Territorial ambitions were also apparent in the invasion of Canada during the first year of the war,[64] but by late 1776 the primary motivation of the American patriots was an introvert desire for independence from foreign rule. Therefore, the continuing Revolution signified the beginning of the first introvert phase.

During this phase, the Federalists, who combined business liberalism and conservatism in their ideology, were an important force in America. Although they were generally in favor of a strong central government, the more agrarian, states' rights reform liberals prevailed after the Revolution with the adoption of the weak Articles of Confederation. After their failure, a stronger constitution was adopted to replace them. Business liberals were interested in foreign trade, while reform liberals were concerned with the development of the frontier.

Although conservatives had influence through such men as Alexander Hamilton, and to a lesser extent George Washington, liberals were continually asserting themselves as the introvert mood grew in intensity. Armed forces were maintained at weak levels. The Militia Act of 1792 reserved all authority over the state militias to the states during times of peace. Conservative Hamiltonian plans for a professionalized military were frustrated, and a peacetime navy was not created until 1794.

In 1793, toward the end of this first introvert phase, President Washington issued his famous Neutrality Proclamation with regard to the conflict between

England and France. The position of a neutral nation desiring trade with both sides was difficult to maintain. Reform liberal opposition to his conservative/ business liberal foreign policy position increased with resentment of the behavior of major European powers, particularly Great Britain, toward the United States. Some long-standing commercial, shipping, and territorial differences with the British were settled by the 1794 Jay Treaty, but many points were questioned by the American public and the compromise barely passed the Senate 20–10 in 1795. In 1796 President Washington gave his Farewell Address, calling for the United States to have as little political connection as possible in extending its commercial relations. Washington's address was reflective of the cautious, low-key foreign policy positions of the time, which aimed at insuring national survival. From 1795 to 1797 the United States pragmatically agreed to tribute treaties with three of the Barbary states. However, New England business liberals became disturbed at the increasing violation of their commercial interests by foreign powers. In 1798 came a gradual American liberal mood change from introversion to extroversion.[65]

The First Extrovert Phase: 1798–1824

The French response to the Jay Treaty was a firmer policy against neutral American shipping. Americans were unhappy, and there was soon enough liberal support to fight a limited, undeclared naval war with France from 1798 to 1800. An extrovert phase had begun, necessarily modified by the need for American diplomatic reality and the competitive presence of the Federalist conservative elements. However, with the election of reform liberal Thomas Jefferson and the peaceful transfer of power that ensued, conservative fears of mass rule, which had provided much of their cohesion, were reduced, and the Federalist conservative elements began to fade from the American scene.

As American resentment against payment of tribute to the Barbary pirates increased, President Jefferson initiated armed action. He also established the United States Military Academy at West Point in 1802, but altered it from a military institution of the type supported by Hamilton to a scientific-technical institution.[66] Reform liberals concentrated much of their efforts on territorial expansion during this mood phase, and in 1803 Jefferson negotiated the purchase of the Louisiana Territory. During the early years of this phase much business liberal effort went into supporting naval expansion; reform liberals also gave the navy limited support, but the product of this support was, for the most part, relatively ineffective gunboats.[67]

The indecisive War of 1812 was fought against Great Britain from 1812 to 1814. Evidently, less liberal support for such a war existed earlier in the phase since considerable British provocation (for example, the 1807 Chesapeake-Leonard Affair) was answered short of war. Apparently, the liberal extrovert mood had not gained sufficient intensity to support a war effort until 1812. Still, there was considerable business liberal opposition to the War of 1812, although it was not hard-core antimilitary because many of these opposition business liberals had supported naval expansion. Conversely, many war supporters were reform liberals who had opposed naval expansion. This merely illustrates that the business liberal/reform liberal convergence on extroversion was not yet complete. Although the war did not result in territorial gain, its outcome did increase international respect for the American position in North America and to a lesser extent on the high seas. Significantly, Federalist opposition to the War of 1812 contributed to the downfall of their party later in the phase.

Following the War of 1812, there was sufficient congressional support to permit the establishment in 1815 of a Board of Naval Commissioners which increased the power of the professional navy.[68] Some conservative leaders of the South also showed signs of significant vitality during this time. One representative of the group, John C. Calhoun, served as President Monroe's secretary of war from 1817 to 1825. Although he demonstrated innovation and initiative, the ever-dominant liberals frustrated most of his proposed educational changes for the military. Calhoun, however, did manage to establish an artillery school at Fort Monroe and improve military administration.[69]

Reform liberal support for territorial expansion continued with the acquisition of Florida in 1819. However, with the proclamation of the Monroe Doctrine in 1823, the United States clearly stepped beyond its capabilities.[70] If the Monroe Doctrine seemed to be effective, it was due to the complementary interest of Great Britain and the protective insulation that its strong navy afforded the United States. Europeans were at peace and posed a decreasing threat to America, while in the United States there were important internal problems to address. Business liberals lost interest in this unilateral proclamation while continuing to pay attention to their relations with foreign trading partners. Reform liberals, influenced by the peaceful international scene and the complicated responsibilities implied in Monroe's proclamation, also became less interested in an extroverted politico-military foreign policy. This overbearing position yielded to a combined liberal mood of introversion beginning around 1824.

The Second Introvert Phase: 1824–1844

A general contentment with American survival characterized American foreign policy during the 1824–1844 introvert phase. As in other introvert phases, the United States did not retrench as much as it solidified advances made during the previous extrovert phase. This phase started under business liberal President John Quincy Adams, but the reform liberals soon found their own spokesman in President Andrew Jackson, who, contrary to what could be expected from his aggressive actions in Florida, carried the country even further into introversion. Typifying the liberal aversion to the military, Jackson more than countered what few measures Calhoun had been able to implement toward professionalization of the military. Jackson thoroughly democratized the army, tried to assimilate it into the civilian sector, closed Calhoun's artillery school at Fort Monroe in 1835, and even opposed Jefferson's West Point.[71] Naval construction during this period did not keep pace with modern developments, although the situation improved near the end of the phase. Americans were busy settling territory acquired during the previous extrovert phase.

In 1836 Texas achieved independence after a bitter struggle with Mexico. The undeclared neutrality of the United States was pro-Texan in practice. Still, the liberal mood of the United States was introvert and, despite the desires of many Texans, annexation was not forthcoming. United States-British tensions grew when Britain indicated some willingness to protect Texan independence, while United States-Mexican relations worsened with Mexico threatening war should the United States decide to annex the fledgling nation. United States-British tensions were further increased over activities by individual Americans during various insurrections in Canada; yet the United States endeavored to enforce official neutrality. The United States and Britain also experienced boundary conflicts, particularly in Maine and Oregon. In 1842 an agreement was reached over the boundary of Maine. Many Americans were both embarrassed and enraged by the terms of the compromise settlement, but it did pass the Senate. The feeling that perhaps the United States had not been active enough during this introvert mood grew. The business liberal outlook was again manifest in the area of naval expansion while reform liberals were oriented toward territorial expansion. As the introvert mood weakened, support for both types of expansion grew.

Despite the disappearance of the major vestiges of New England conservatism, conservatives in the South continued to rationalize and romanticize their lifestyle. This produced enough internal cohesion to maintain themselves as a viable force within the predominantly liberal society and to secure the continued existence of the institution of slavery. At some points during this introvert phase and the extrovert phase which followed, this competing ideology served to modify the liberal tendencies of the larger society, but did not prevent the intensity of foreign policy moods from increasing according to normal patterns.

The Second Extrovert Phase: 1844–1871

The second extrovert phase featured a favorable settlement in 1846 of the Oregon boundary dispute with Great Britain, in contrast to the less favorable Maine settlement four years earlier. Under the leadership of reform liberal President James Polk, the United States entered into war with Mexico beginning in early 1846 after Polk sent American troops into disputed territory. As with the War of 1812, much of the opposition to the Mexican War came from the business liberal community. This opposition intensified when the ambiguous circumstances under which the war had commenced became obvious. However, the favorable war settlement featured a substantial transfer of territory to the United States.

After the war, as the extrovert phase grew in intensity, reform liberal opposition to naval expansion softened, as did business liberal opposition to territorial expansion. Americans spoke of their "Manifest Destiny." There was serious talk about the acquisition of Cuba, and a treaty was signed with Britain concerning a possible Central American canal. Commodore Perry visited Japan and some naval improvements were achieved. However, naval development and territorial expansion in this phase were complicated by the growing domestic sectional tension over slavery. The extrovert characteristic of territorial acquisition, involving the increasingly bitter argument as to whether new land would be slave or free, led in part to the Civil War.

At the war's end, southerners had been divested of their human property and southern conservatism was eliminated as a strong, ideological force in America. The United States no longer had major ideologies other than liberalism to consistently compete for public support, and thus fewer forces to modify extreme liberal tendencies.

After the Civil War, the United States became assertive about French actions in Mexico. A large, sparsely inhabited region called Alaska was purchased from Russia in 1867. Americans pressed for financial settlement of claims against Great Britain for British subjects who built and sold to the American Confederacy ships which subsequently inflicted costly damage on the Union. Business liberals were upset over these financial losses; reform liberals were upset as a matter of principle. As the negotiations were protracted, frustration and intolerance grew. By 1869 American demands reached unrealistic proporions. The chairman of the Senate Foreign Relations Committee implied that the British debts could be cancelled by the cession of Canada to the United States. The United States, however, was in no mood for a conflict with Great Britain. Moves to annex the Dominican Republic and Virgin Islands met with a decided lack of enthusiasm. The American public, now composed of an even greater proportion of liberals, tired of war, and realizing the height of the American extrovert position, settled with Britain and began a mood swing toward introversion.

The Third Introvert Phase: 1871–1891

The reasonable Treaty of Washington with Great Britain in 1871 heralded the beginning of the third introvert phase. Business liberals continued their support of the war hero and Republican unification figure, Ulysses S. Grant, in the presidency. However, another scaling down of American foreign policy objectives took place when Grant's unrealistic efforts to annex the Dominican

Republic were frustrated by the Congress. Typical of American liberalism, the military establishment had been drastically cut back after the Civil War. Army expenditures were cut from over $1 billion in 1865 to just under $36 million in 1871.[72] Business liberals viewed large defense expenditures as a drain on economic growth. In fact, this entire introvert phase was characterized by tremendous internal industrial growth as emphasized and stimulated by business liberals. Reform liberals directed their attention toward the settling of the West and improving the living conditions of workers victimized by American industrialization.

The Spanish seizure in 1873 of a gun-running ship illegally registered in the United States and the execution of the partially American crew provoked no decisive call to arms. Efforts by a French company to build a canal in Panama produced only mild American reactions, especially in comparison to American actions in the same area during the following extrovert phase. Without the challenge of southern conservatism, business and reform liberals emphasized particularly their domestic distinctions; the resulting domestic controversies allowed the generalized liberal introvert foreign policy mood to drift further, increasing the intensity of the mood. The United States Senate took an assertive role in curbing extrovert foreign policy manifestations and "ratified no important treaty between 1871 and 1898."[73]

Throughout the 1871–1891 introvert phase, the United States maintained a low profile as European powers became more assertive throughout the world. The navy was weak throughout most of this phase; in fact, in 1881 "it was suddenly realized with alarm that several South American republics had been acquiring warships, any one of which single-handedly could probably destroy the entire United States Navy."[74] The United States therefore took some measures to improve its navy in the latter part of the phase and established the Naval War College in 1884. Despite this effort and a relatively consistent disinterest in world affairs, European imperial assertiveness indicated that neglect of American interests was more pronounced toward the end of the phase than toward the beginning. This European assertiveness, combined with America's relative weakness, moved liberals to support a more active international role for the United States. As was the case in previous shifts from introversion to extroversion, business liberals were interested in naval expansion. Reform liberal interest was directed toward perceived injustices on the international scene. A phase of combined liberal extroversion began around 1891.

The Third Extrovert Phase: 1891–1919

The third extrovert phase can be characterized as an abortive effort at launching the United States as a major world power. The reform liberal President Grover Cleveland, an introvert during his 1885–1889 term in office, took a strong stand against the United Kingdom in the 1895 Venezuelan boundary crisis. The Spanish-American War, which began in 1898 over reform liberal concern for oppressed Cubans, resulted in the acquisition of Puerto Rico and the Philippines and an increasingly active role in world affairs. Business liberals had been skeptical of the 1898 war effort until the possible benefits of imperialism and the new economic opportunities resulting from the war were perceived.[75] Hawaii was soon annexed and the "Open Door" to China proclaimed.

It was during this phase that a group advocating some nonliberal policies emerged in American history. The neo-Hamiltonians combined aspects of earlier American conservatism with aspects of liberalism. Like the conservatives, they could pursue national interest by means of power politics and, like the liberals, they could be assertive adventurers who rationalized policy in liberal terms.[76] Theodore Roosevelt provided a good deal of political leadership. Army and navy modernization throughout this phase was inspired by the writings of such neo-Hamiltonians as Admiral Alfred Thayer Mahan and General Leonard Wood. President Theodore Roosevelt sent the Great White Fleet around the world and the United States power abroad increased. The United States participated in the Hague Court and entered into a large number of arbitration treaties. The assertive Roosevelt Corollary to the Monroe Doctrine dates from this period, which also saw the completion of an American canal across Panama, a new nation which had gained its independence from Colombia with American assistance. Since territorial expansion was now limited, American extrovert emphasis had shifted to the expansion of politico-military influence.

Although American liberals followed the neo-Hamiltonians' foreign policy position, they did so mostly by default since no liberal alternative was made available. President Taft's "Dollar Diplomacy" was an effort to popularize extroversion for business liberals. In Woodrow Wilson, liberals finally found an alternative to the power politics of the neo-Hamiltonians. Wilson's moralistic efforts to affect the course of Latin American and later, European affairs, capped this extrovert period and carried America to the extreme of liberal extroversion. His over-involvement in the affairs of Latin American and Europe, tied to his strong vision of a new world order, was unrealistic for his time. Wilson's moralistic emphasis in foreign policy, however, hurt the neo-Hamiltonians and destroyed the potential for this quasiconservative force to obtain an enduring place on the American scene. With the displacement of the neo-Hamiltonians, liberals gained strength in the Republican party and, feeling the strains of Wilson's comprehensive world commitment, began to move to another mood of introversion.[77]

The Fourth Introvert Phase: 1919–1940
The fourth introvert phase began with the liberal defection from Wilson after World War I. The Treaty of Versailles, which included provisions for the League of Nations, was rejected by the Senate and a separate treaty of peace was later negotiated with Germany. The leadership of the reaction against Wilson

had diverse motivation. Some leaders, such as Henry Cabot Lodge, initially were interested in discrediting Wilson for partisan political purposes. Reform liberals, tired of extroversion, joined the ranks of those opposing Wilson's internationalism.[78] Some powerful ethnic groups also contributed to the launching of this phase.

As the 1920s progressed, the introvert movement intensified and gained support from business and reform liberals. America, however, was not ready to pursue extreme introversion this early in the phase. The administrations of Harding, Coolidge, and Hoover inched toward introversion while straddling the fence between introversion and extroversion.[79] The United States was active in East Asian affairs, participated in disarmament conferences, helped initiate the Kellogg-Briand Pact outlawing offensive war, and cooperated with the League of Nations; however, growing introversion prompted the United States refusal to join the league because of the commitments it might entail and also prompted its failure to adhere to the World Court because of intense congressional opposition.

Not until after Franklin Roosevelt took office in 1933 did America become entrenched in introversion. The four Neutrality Acts of 1935–1939 were an extreme manifestation of American introversion dictated by public mood and were an unrealistic answer to the dictates of world events. The circumstances leading to Ameirican involvement in the Second World War demonstrate the costs of such a policy. Reform and then business liberals joined in support of another extrovert orientation, belatedly realizing the necessity of an active United States participation in world affairs to insure its security.

The Fourth Extrovert Phase: 1940–1968

In the early years of the fourth liberal extrovert phase, Americans were absorbed in World War II. After the war's conclusion, reform liberals were particularly vocal on the need for continued American extroversion. The United States spearheaded the effort to establish the United Nations. Business liberals, increasingly supportive of extroversion, still were reluctant followers of the reform liberals in foreign policy; and since the reform liberals were not fully prepared to assume extrovert responsibilities, conservatives were again in some positions of responsibility. The naturally conservative military was given a significant role in the governing of occupied territories, and a number of military men were appointed to civilian foreign affairs and defense posts after the war.[80] Conservative realist George Kennan formulated the doctrine of containment in 1947. American liberals soon became concerned about the "communist menace" and set out on an anticommunist crusade. Economic aid was used to bolster friendly nations in Europe and other parts of the world. The United States took the initiative to form broad alliances like the OAS, NATO, and later SEATO. Under President Harry Truman, the United States became involved in a frustrating limited war in Korea, which was eventually ended by President Dwight Eisenhower. Eisenhower, however, also followed the extrovert mood and sent United States forces to Lebanon. America developed an impressive nuclear arsenal under business liberal Eisenhower and joined the space race. Reform liberal President John Kennedy emphasized a diversified conventional defense strategy and began the Peace Corps.

Kennedy took office near the height of the cold war against communism. The administration had a mixture of liberal and conservative beliefs, as did the turn-of-the-century neo-Hamiltonians.[81] As often is characteristic of times with some conservative influence, the military was modernized through improved management techniques which met with mixed public reaction. America became involved in another limited conflict in Vietnam, which continued under reform liberal Lyndon Johnson. At its zenith Vietnam was to have 543,500 United States troops committed to the conflict,[82] at an annual cost of $28.8 billion.[83]

Vietnam, by the apex mood year of 1968, was seen as an area in which the United States was overcommitted and overextended. Business liberals became wary of this extrovert foreign policy because of the costs of such an extensive network of commitments. Reform liberals shared these frustrations and found a need to first deal with domestic problems, such as equality for minorities, as well as to change the thrust of their world reform efforts from direct involvement to example-setting. As was the case in 1919, a particularly important role in the 1968 mood shift was played by a group of reform liberals who formerly supported an extrovert, Democratic president's policies. The stage was set for a joint liberal swing back to another period of introversion.

The Fifth Introvert Phase: 1968–

Evidence indicates that the current introvert phase was firmly established and grew in intensity during the 1970s. An early portent of the mood shift to introversion occurred with the decidedly introvert reaction to the July 1967 crisis in the Congo.[84] The Vietnam Tet Offensive in early 1968 was the prelude to a political year characterized by a marked lack of support for President Johnson and his extrovert Vietnam policies.[85] The business liberal Richard M. Nixon was elected, at least partially and significantly, on his pledge to end the war in Vietnam.

The current introvert phase has seen policy responses such as the conclusion of the American role in Vietnam, a decline in military spending as a percentage of gross national product, and termination of the draft. In 1973 the Congress passed the War Powers Act restricting the ability of the president to engage in prolonged extroverted politico-military activities without congressional involvement.

The year 1976, finding the United States fully in its fifth introvert phase, saw

President Ford and his secretary of state unable to obtain a commitment for even indirect support for one faction in the African nation of Angola in the face of large-scale Soviet and Cuban intervention on behalf of an opposing faction. The introvert mood of the American public was expressed in its election of an inoffensive introvert leader, Jimmy Carter. President Carter expressed this introvert rationale in his inaugural address:

> Our Nation can be strong abroad only if it is strong at home, and we know that the best way to enhance freedom in other lands is to demonstrate here that our democratic sysem is worthy of emulation. . . . We will not behave in foreign places so as to violate our rules and standards here at home, for we know that the trust which our Nation earns is essential to our strength.[86]

In 1977 and 1978, despite the strong examples of France, Belgium, and Morocco, the United States minimized involvement in struggles in the African nation of Zaire. A 1978 study notes that President Carter operated under more than seventy congressional foreign policy constraints and advocated repealing only three of them.[87]

At the same time that the United States was minimizing its politico-military role in the world, the Soviet Union was building its strength. To be sure, a reduction of the United States role in parts of Asia was feasible because the Sino-Soviet split created a more multilateral power balance. However, the U.S.S.R. did not share the American desire for a reduced politico-military role, and the world moved toward a dangerous power imbalance.[88] Toward the end of the 1970s, the American public mood became more self-interested than earlier in the decade. However, there was no return to the "missionary zeal" of the 1960s.[89]

The 1970s saw a steady growth in the importance of the Middle East/Persian Gulf area to the United States. A number of United States foreign policy adjustments were required to achieve even an Israel-Egypt settlement not supported by most Arab states. By the end of the decade, the importance of the Middle East/Persian Gulf had increased because of the continued political necessity of insuring Israel's survival and the economic necessity of importing Middle Eastern oil. The Shah of Iran's 1979 replacement by a theocratic regime added to regional instability.

It is possible that such instability, combined with indecisive United States policies, made the difference in the Soviet decision to invade Afghanistan during the winter of 1979–1980. Such Soviet behavior alarmed the United States, which started to increase its military spending, expanded cooperation with the People's Republic of China, and sought nonmilitary means of communicating dissatisfaction to the Soviets. Whether these events are but a phase in the development of an introvert mood, as indicated by history, or indications that there might be an earlier than expected return to extroversion can only be determined with time.

The extrovert-sounding rhetoric of President Ronald Reagan also gives an appearance of a return to extroversion, but it should be noted that Reagan's actions to date have failed to match his rhetoric. Perhaps a Congress with introvert ideas and realization of American weakness helped restrain Reagan's hand, but policies toward situations in Poland, El Salvador, and even Lebanon evidence a U.S. policy of restrained action. Even the strongest Reagan actions, such as those in Central America and the Caribbean, have come in a geographic region of long-standing American strength. Cuba is allowed to do in Africa what it is not allowed to do in Grenada. If anything, the Reagan adminstration seems comparable with that of former President Franklin D. Roosevelt, where foreign policy problems were realized but viable options for dealing with them were very much limited. Also, both FDR and Reagan faced significant domestic problems demanding action, so their attention was diverted from foreign matters. Again, historical perspective will clarify the situation.[90]

2. Alternate Methodologies and Foreign Policy Concepts

If the mood/interest theory is a valid interpretation of American foreign policy, it is reasonable to expect that other analyses relating to public moods and foreign policy activity could be related to it. The first part of this chapter, then, will deal with several long-range studies and how they relate to the mood/interest theory. Later in the chapter, other prominent descriptions of American foreign policy and their relation to liberal moods will be discussed.

U.S. FOREIGN POLICY MOODS APPLIED
TO PRESIDENTIAL PERSONALITY
by Robert E. Elder, Jr., and Jack E. Holmes*

In order to reinforce the linkage between foreign policy moods and actual foreign policy behavior, this section will examine several long-range studies and their relation to the mood/interest theory: a Library of Congress survey of military actions abroad from 1798 to 1970, David McClelland's work on the human motivations of affiliation and power as they relate to war, David Winter's studies of the power and affiliation motivations of American presidents as expressed in presidential inaugural addresses, James David Barber's categorization of American presidents, and Arthur Schlesinger, Sr.'s 1948 and 1962 and Robert Murray and Tim Blessing's 1983 compilations of presidential rankings.[1]

These comparisons show that discernible patterns of behavior in American foreign policy do exist. Such patterns may occur because of changes in motive level on the part of large segments of our population. Evidence of these motive shifts may be discerned through changes in the motive imagery expressed in popular literature and in presidential inaugural addresses. Regular changes in public mood influence the types of presidents elected to office, the prestige granted to presidents in the years following their departure from office, and the degree to which a president's experiences in office are likely to be positive or

---

*Adapted from papers prepared for the 1982 and 1983 meetings of the International Studies Association.

negative. Foreign policy mood cycles also appear to operate in conjunction with a public policy cycle that alternates scandal and political reform with social and economic reform and war.

Congressional Study of Uses of Force Abroad

The mood/interest theory holds that public mood greatly influences shifts in American foreign policy from periods of introversion to extroversion and back. This proposition fits neatly with documented events in American political history. As table 1 suggests, virtually all of our major wars and land annexations have taken place during extrovert periods. (Tables begin on page 169.)

A closer survey of uses of force abroad from 1798 to 1967, done by the Library of Congress for the House Committee on Foreign Affairs, suggests that extrovert periods also far surpass introvert periods in regard to instances of force used abroad (see table 2).

The mood/interest theory suggests that aggressive or expansive activity fluctuates in accordance with immediate past events as a liberal public interacts with a power-oriented international environment. An introvert phase starts as a reaction to excessive extroversion, and uses of force should gradually decline as the introvert phase continues. Toward the end of the introvert phase, however, the international environment should begin to stimulate an increase in activity that becomes dramatic as the phase changes from introvert to extrovert. Extrovert phases should feature a gradual increase in activity abroad that begins to slow somewhat as the international environment starts to force a decline of American activity into introversion. There also should be some tendency toward a mid-phase balance, sometimes seen as a decline in activity in middle stages of introvert and extrovert phases, since American activity is most in accord with the immediate demands of the international system.

An examination of uses of force abroad by stages of introvert and extrovert phases indicates that patterns projected above are most obvious when the stages of all introvert and extrovert phases are added.[2] Counts for uses of force abroad within the three stages of individual introvert and extrovert phases are believed to be subject to variables affecting only a single phase. Thus, the analysis centers on cumulative totals. Table 3 documents use of force in first, second, and third stages of extrovert and introvert phases for which the congressional study data are complete.[3] Twenty-one-year introvert portions of each cycle were divided into three seven-year stages, and extrovert phases, which average twenty-seven years, were divided into three nine-year stages. Short years were taken from the second stage, while extra years were placed in the third stage. This method was designed to minimize variations in the length of stages.

Table 3 indicates that first thirds of introvert periods are likely to exhibit force that represents a continuation, albeit with gradual deescalation, of the excesses of the previous extrovert period.

The last thirds of introvert periods feature an increase in use of force, and thus reinforce the mood/interest theory's claim that because interests have been ignored, foreign policy makers belatedly start to compensate for their previous unwillingness to protect national interests. The public has the least difficulty with the expression of its introvert mood during the second stage of introvert periods, as indicated by the greater use of force at either the beginning or end of these periods. Extrovert periods, on the other hand, exhibit less second-stage balance and feature a gradual rise in uses of force which tapers off during the last two-thirds of a phase. Table 4 gives a generalized picture of the stages in policy orientation toward uses of force across history.

That the mood/interest theory identifies a pattern that persists across time is difficult to dispute. But why do such patterns occur? The theory suggests that in addition to mood acting in relation to immediate past events, swings in public mood trigger policy changes that may or may not lead to other events in the long term. Only when mood is at an extreme do events act to force a mood change. As has been stated, the mood/interest theory proposes that mood swings are best expressed by the changing nature of Lockean liberalism and its aversion to excessive concentrations of power. This, in combination with a lack of strategic restraints such as those experienced by most other world powers, has allowed mood to fluctuate pretty much as a liberal public would dictate.

McClelland's Study of Low and High Power Motives

To say that liberals are change-oriented does not address the question of what makes them predisposed to certain types of change; nor does it explain why such changes occur in historically discernible patterns. Events are one possible explanation for these shifts, but at times the patterns seem to occur with no discernible relationship to events. Another possible explanation dealing with forces affecting public mood has been suggested by the studies of psychologists such as David McClelland, who explained changes in terms of shifting balances of human motives. In this regard McClelland successfully isolated and measured three distinct motives shaping human behaviors: the need for power, the need for achievement, and the need for affiliation. The desire for power involves the need to have status above, or control over, others; the desire for achievement involves the need to accomplish concrete measurable results; and the desire for affiliation normally deals with the need to have the affection or approval of significant others.[4]

McClelland later applied techniques used on economic development to American political history. He coded literature in mid-decade years and found a relationship between high power/low affiliation scores and war.[5] He suggested that these wars occurred in decades that began fifteen years after the high power/low affiliation years.[6] Our studies suggest a more immediate relationship. The United States has had seven major foreign wars. The mid-decade year prior to

World War I was not scored. For the other foreign wars, high power/low affiliation literature was found in the last mid-decade year scored prior to the war's start in five out of six instances.

Table 5 compares the second stage periods in extrovert and introvert cycles with McClelland's high and low power years. It would be expected that second-stage periods would correspond to McClelland low power years, because during second stages American moods correspond best to short-term interests, indicating a power/affiliation balance.

The two studies coincide on six of eight chances for a relationship between second stage periods and a power/affiliation balance; one instance fits in part and another does not fit. The partial fit occurs because the 1835 low power year, while within the 1831-1836 second stage, is at the very end and thus does not allow for the lead time posited by our analysis. The suggestion that second stages are periods of strategic balance and show less tendency toward overreaction seems to be matched by McClelland's measurement of the relationship between the motives of power and affiliation during these periods.

How good a measure is McClelland's motive theory as an explanatory variable for shifts between introvert and extrovert periods? It would be expected that high power/low affiliation literature would occur in swing decades (the last five years of an old phase and the first five years of a new phase), because a stronger power motive is needed in order to reverse the excesses of the previous phase when U.S. interests were not properly maintained.

High power years occur in swing decades in 6 of 7 chances when swings occurred and data were available (table 6). Although the samples are quite small, the coincidence between the mood swings and McClelland's shifts in motivational balance tends in the direction of the mood/interest analysis.

Power Divergence Scores and Affiliation Ratios

If a relationship is definable between high power/low affiliation literature and wars and various other power-related forms of behavior, and if the balance between these various motives measurably shifts across time, what of the motives of our chief architect of foreign policy, the American president? David Winter measures the motives of American presidents through a content analysis of their first inaugural addresses. Winter argues that of all the speeches a president makes only his first inaugural allows for the free expression of dreams and aspirations. The president is on a honeymoon and has not yet become enmeshed in the rough world of presidential politics.[7] In such a situation, Winter suggests, and we concur, the president's dominant motive is most likely to show through.

In analyzing inaugural addresses, we first compiled each president's total motive score—the number of times he referred to the themes of power, affiliation, and achievement per thousand words. The number of times each type of motive imagery was referred to was divided by a presidential total motive score to yield a percentage for each individual motive. The affiliation percentage was then subtracted from the power percentage to provide a power divergence score (PDS).[8]

Our thought was that a high power divergence score would indicate power dominance of the sort against which McClelland warns. Low or negative power divergence would indicate a power/affiliation balance less likely to produce aggressive behavior. Comparisons were made between extrovert and introvert, as well as between second-stage and first- and third-stage presidents. We thought that if the McClelland and mood/interest theses were to be reinforced, the inaugural addresses of presidents occupying office during extrovert periods would exhibit a high PDS. Presidents in office during introvert periods would be more likely to register a low PDS. Presidents in both extrovert and introvert second-stage periods would have a closer balance between affiliation and power than presidents at the beginning or end of extrovert and introvert periods. Finally, presidents in introvert second-stage periods would have the lowest PDSs of all.

Table 7 provides achievement, power, affiliation, and power divergence scores for all elected presidents who served at least one year in office from Polk through Reagan, as well as presidential PDS averages for second-stage-only (SSO) presidents and non-SSO presidents in introvert and extrovert periods.

Although the SSO and non-SSO differential for the third extrovert phase is an exception, the findings in table 7 essentially confirmed our prediction. Note that the average PDS for SSO presidents is less than a third that of non-SSO presidents and that the difference increases considerably when non-SSO presidents and SSO introvert presidents are compared.

A further relationship between the mood/interest theory and power divergence scores is illustrated in figure 5. The lowest average PDSs for introvert and extrovert phases occurred in the second stages. This drop reflects the proximity of public mood to perceptions of national interest; yet as would be expected, the average score of the extrovert phases is higher than that of introvert phases. The figure demonstrates that PDSs often fluctuate with the mood curve.

If one looks at the ratio of affiliation motive to total motive score for the presidents studied, nine presidents have had ratios of 1:4.9 or below (see table 8). Three of the four peacetime presidents with a ratio of 1:4.9 or below (Cleveland [second term], Theodore Roosevelt, and Taft) served during the third extrovert phase (1891–1919). During this phase, all presidents except McKinley had 1:4.9 ratios or below. The robust and self-confident aura of 1891–1919 perhaps accounts for the low ratios of the period. The president who is the exception, McKinley, found himself practically pushed into the Spanish-American War by the "yellow journalism" of the period. (Zachary Taylor, a Mexican War hero elected in 1848 but constrained by regional difficulties, was the other peacetime president with a low ratio.)

Figure 5.   Fluctuating Average Power Divergence Scores and the Mood/Interest Curve

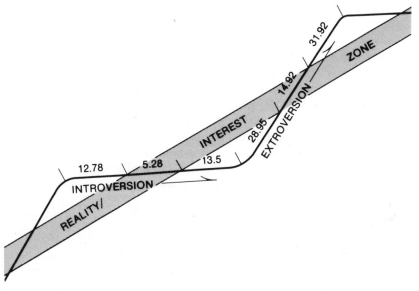

	1st Stage	2nd Stage	3rd Stage
Introvert	12.78	5.28	13.5
Extrovert	28.95	14.92	31.92

Sources: Figure 5 is derived from table 7 and the mood/interest curve.

Indeed, with the exceptions of McKinley and Taylor, table 8 shows a tendency for wartime presidents to have lower ratios than the peacetime presidents in the same eras. In the second extrovert phase, two of the three lowest presidents were Polk and Lincoln. The third extrovert phase is the exception although World War I president Wilson was tied for the second lowest ratio. During the fourth extrovert phase, the highest ratio was Eisenhower, the president least associated with the start or escalation of a war.

A clear-cut difference is visible in the ratio of motive imagery between extrovert and introvert periods with the exception of the fourth introvert period. This exception would not be the case if one excluded Franklin Roosevelt. From his scores, one would expect Roosevelt to be war-prone. He was moving toward military build-ups to meet a growing German-Japanese threat; more important, he was fighting an economic war for the survival of the nation—a war in which strong, decisive leadership was necessary.

Ronald Reagan, elected in 1980, has a 1:4.65 ratio, the tenth lowest ratio.

Reagan has moved toward substantial increases in military expenditure as did Franklin Roosevelt in a similar period. Should this be cause for alarm? In a strictly statistical sense, one cannot tell since Franklin Roosevelt's ratio is much lower and Reagan's ratio is close to that of several peacetime presidents. However, Reagan's ratio is lower than those of other presidents in his period.

Comparing Franklin Roosevelt to Ronald Reagan, one notes that each followed a lower power divergence president who had difficulty coping with large issues (Hoover and Carter, respectively). Each also down-played his foreign policy concerns to gain support for domestic policy. It was eight years after Franklin Roosevelt's inaugural before direct American involvement in World War II started, but Roosevelt fought to increase defense expenditures and respond decisively to the growing German and Japanese threats during most of his first two terms in office. As Reagan emphasizes the need for a strong foreign and defense policy, he looks like a man who is on time in terms of cycle theory.

McClelland Compared to Winter

Having established a relationship between the data of the mood/interest theory and Winter, we measured the degree to which power divergence scores correlated with McClelland's years of high and low power. We hypothesized that a presidential inaugural in a decade following a high power year would be more likely to reflect the mood of the literature of the period or the president involved would be less likely to be elected. To establish some basis for comparison, we constructed a table of the presidential first inaugurals nearest to the dates content analyzed by McClelland in his study of American literature. The findings presented in table 9 partially confirm our hypothesis and the exceptions to the rule are limited in significance.

In twelve chances, eight presidential inaugurals nearest in time to the twelve years content analyzed by McClelland had a power divergence rating corresponding to McClelland's rating for their period. Eight in twelve chances (67%) is a solid indication of a noncoincidental relationship. It is also interesting to note that in three of the four cases where motive in literature and presidential PDS did not coincide, a president's death had resulted in giving a vice president the incumbency power necessary to win the office. (Perhaps this was against the original inclinations of party and public?) The fourth case, McKinley, involved a president with a conciliatory inaugural following a divisive election.

Behavior in Office and Inaugural Addresses

Do presidential inaugurals also relate to actual behavior in regard to use of force? The ten presidents with the highest PDSs and the ten presidents with the lowest PDSs were selected and scored in terms of number of forceful actions per year in office. The findings are in table 10.

With one exception, the presidents with highest PDSs are extrovert presidents. The one exception is Coolidge, who has a marginally high PDS and is a successor president. There is also a strong indication that low-PDS presidents once in office are less predisposed to take forceful actions to protect American interests abroad. High-PDS presidents averaged 1.35 actions per year in office in comparison to the low-PDS president's average of .87 actions per year in office. Table 11 compares second-stage-only presidents for both extrovert and introvert periods from the second, third, and fourth mood cycles with first- and third-stage-only extrovert presidents from the same cycles in regard to their likelihood to use force.

Although second-stage-only presidents have just over a quarter the power divergence scores of their first- and third-stage-only extrovert counterparts, there is no decisive indication that their slightly lower levels of force are the result of lower PDSs. However, six of the seven major American wars since 1845 started under the ten first- and third-stage-only extrovert presidents, whereas none of the wars started under the six second-stage-only presidents. As suggested earlier, once momentum toward action builds in an extrovert period, it may be difficult to slow regardless of presidential motivations.

Only when the second-stage-only introvert presidents were sampled was strong support found for our hypothesis that power divergence scores and forceful actions per year should relate to stages. Presidents classified only in the second stage of introvert periods had quite low PDSs and were less inclined to use force than were presidents at either end of an extrovert period. Thus, in these instances, motive scores and likelihood to take forceful action do relate. Note the PDSs of Hayes and Hoover, in comparison with their counterparts who were classified only in the first and third stages of extrovert periods.

As is indicated in table 12, introvert second-stage-only presidents have less than one-tenth the PDSs and forceful actions per year as their extrovert first- and third-stage-only counterparts, suggesting a relationship between PDSs, use of force, and mood stages.[9]

Barber's Categories of Presidents

The thesis of James David Barber's book, *The Presidential Character: Predicting Performance in the White House,* is that character is of prime consequence in presidential performance. This character is manifested in either high energy or passivity (active or passive), and enjoyment or lack of enjoyment of the job of being president (positive or negative). Although Barber suggests that situational context and ideology are also considerations, he believes that character is the prime determinant of behavior in the oval office.[10]

Our thought was that situation and ideology are of equal importance to early childhood experiences in forming a president's character. Public mood may dictate not only what presidential policy will be, but may even decide which candidate is elected. Table 13 lists presidents under Barber's categories, whether they occupied the presidency during an extrovert or introvert period, and their party affiliation.

Active-positive presidents, with the exception of Rutherford B. Hayes, tend to be found in extrovert periods. They also tend to be Democratic, a party affiliation associated with an activist rather than a passive caretaker concept of the presidency. Active-negatives appear to follow the same general pattern. Note that passives, both positive and negative, are mostly introvert (55%) and either Republican or Whig (91%).

Taken alone these results seem to suggest that circumstances are influential in shaping character. However, in support of Barber, it is still possible to suggest that Americans during introvert periods favor presidents with passive predispositons. If this is the case, democracy is working very well indeed and the public appears to be getting exactly what its mood dictates.

Before proceeding further in our analysis, it was decided to classify each president by the stage or stages corresponding to his presidency. Table 14 lists presidents from Polk to Carter and how they are classified by stages of mood phases.

Carrying our investigation one step further required the checking of "bridgepoint presidences," or presidencies that fall within a year of the transition year between phases in the mood cycle. A mood-oriented viewpoint would argue for a greater amount of uncertainty and thus negativity during bridgepoints between periods, because mood transition demands a style of behavior different from that of the preceding period. Table 15 lists all bridgepoint presidents and provides their Barber type.

Examination of table 15 reveals that Franklin Roosevelt and James Polk are the only major exceptions to the suggestion that occupation of the presidency during one of the bridgepoint years is not a pleasant experience. James Monroe's first term was considerably easier than his second, which spanned a period of transition. If he is rated as a passive-positive, it is largely because of the "era of good feeling" with which his presidency began.

Because these results fit well with our speculations, it was decided to determine the degree to which second-stage presidents differ from their first- and third-stage extrovert counterparts. The thought was that because second stages exhibit more balance between power and affiliation, presidential style would be more passive in these than in extrovert first and third stages. In addition, the authors speculated that because of Republicans' concept of limited governmental power, they would be more likely to be elected to office during second stages than would Democrats. Since foreign policy moods and interests are most in harmony during second stages, the authors hypothesized that second-stage presidents would be a bit more positive than their first- and third-stage introvert counterparts, as second stages have less of the tension that can produce negative behavior.

Table 16 shows that second-stage presidents tend to be more passive (45%

vs. 23%) and Republican (64% vs. 38%) than first- and third-stage extrovert presidents. Second-stage presidents also tend to be slightly more positive (55%) than first- and third-stage introvert presidents (43%). Thus, table 16 essentially confirms the preceding speculations.

Barber Compared to Winter

Barber's findings correspond to mood cycle periods and stages, but do they also mesh with Winter's method of categorizing presidents?

Robert Elder (1981) suggested that a relationship appeared to exist between Barber and Winter, and that integration of the two approaches could provide a basis for examining the underlying motivations of presidents as they were entering the office, as well as their actual behavior as presidents.[11] Table 17 provides summary averages of Winter ratings of presidents from Polk through Carter by Barber category and mood/interest phases. The force indicator levels are calculated on the basis of numbers of uses of force abroad, major wars, and major war casualties per year each of the four Barber types occupied the presidency.

Table 17 suggests a degree of complementarity between specific Winter motives and Barber behavioral categories. For example, active-positive presidents appear to be distinguishable from all other Barber types in having a closer balance between power divergence and achievement. Presidents who are passive-negatives are least likely to serve in extrovert phases. Active presidents are much more likely to be involved in major wars, and are also most likely to occupy the presidency during periods when these wars involve heavy casualties.

Active-negative (and to a lesser degree passive) presidents are distinguished from active-positive presidents by an imbalance between their achievement and power divergence scores. McClelland suggests that high achievers have a strong desire to see results but do not like taking high risks to realize their aims.[12] This description fits the active-negative. In a highly politicized broker-rule environment which necessitates compromise, tangible results are more difficult to realize. This achievement/negativity hypothesis may be a possible explanation for Barber's and most historians' perceptions of active-negatives as having greater unhappiness and perceived ineffectiveness in the oval office. It is interesting to note that the last two sets of bridgepoint years between extroversion and introversion (1918–1920 and 1967–1969) have been occupied by three of the eight active-negative presidents. Seven of the eight occupied the presidency during very trying times, as can be seen from certain events: Taylor—Compromise of 1850; Buchanan—Southern Secession; A. Johnson—Reconstruction; Hoover—Great Depression; Wilson—World War I; L. Johnson and Nixon—Vietnam.

Passive presidents are distinguished from active presidents by a greater need for affiliation and low power divergence scores. Passives are involved in substantially fewer wars with fewer casualties than their active counterparts.

Passive-negatives most often are elected in introvert phases or second stages of extrovert phases.

Possibly the least expected result in the chart is that active-positives and passive-negatives have the lowest average numbers of uses of force abroad per year in office. The highest number of uses of force per year is scored by passive-positives, followed by active-negatives. However, as noted above, when one calculates major U.S. wars and especially battle casualties in major wars, the results are closer to those expected: active-positives appear the most likely to get involved in major military conflict, and this would be especially true if the table were modified to include Civil War figures. Thus, intensity as well as number of uses of force is important when considering Barber types. Indeed, some of the previous results could have been more impressive had the researchers weighted the uses-of-force-abroad formula to take greater account of intensity.

That Barber's presidential categories correspond closely to the data on moods and presidential motivation is clear. The question that needs to be answered, however, is whether a president's behavior is influenced more by circumstances he faces in office, his ideology, or his character.

Certainly the relationship noted earlier between bridgepoint years and negativity, even when high power divergence, generally a signal of a positive character, is present (e.g. Wilson), indicates that events or time periods may occasionally overshadow character as a cause for negativity in the oval office.

Second-stage extrovert and all introvert presidents have been found to have a greater tendency toward passivity and affiliation than their first- and third-stage extrovert counterparts. Does this mean that presidents act passively because the mood of the electorate gives them no other choice, or are they elected during these periods because their character predisposes them toward passive-affiliative behavior? A single conclusion is not readily apparent.

One enticing possibility noted earlier is the achievement/negativity hypothesis: high achievers may become frustrated in a broker-rule political environment, and, if achievement is their dominant motive, they may end up as active-negatives. High achievement and negativity are present in presidents L. Johnson, Nixon, Buchanan, and Hoover. Striking a blow against the achievement/negativity hypothesis is the clear exception of McKinley, who was a high achiever with a very low PDS. Although he did not complete his second term in office, McKinley must be scored as passive-positive as of the time of his death. It also seems possible for an electorate to perceive and elect high or low energy presidents depending on popular mood at the time of an election. Considering all of this, it appears to us that situation and mood of the electorate is as likely to trigger negativity in the White House as character.

Posterity Ranking and Public Mood

To what degree does the time period that a president is in office influence his posterity ranking? At least five studies have ranked presidents in terms of effectiveness in office.[13] An accomplishment poll and best/worst studies have also been done. The combined average rankings of three of these studies are listed in table 18. The studies considered in obtaining these presidential posterity rankings included surveys of historians by Arthur Schlesinger, Sr., in 1948 and 1962 and by Robert K. Murray and Tim H. Blessing in 1983.[14]

Table 19 gives a summary average for presidents by rank, Barber type, Winter power divergence rating, party affiliation, and foreign policy mood. Our prediction was that in general the higher a PDS and the more forceful actions a president has taken, the higher the president's rank will be in the eyes of posterity. McClelland had linked high power to both reforms and wars, the items most written about by political historians. It seemed likely that extrovert presidents would attract more attention than their introvert counterparts. Unlike Bailey, who found that historians have a bias toward Democrats,[15] the authors found Republican and Democratic presidents distributed in accordance with PDS average and Barber type.

As is indicated in table 19, a president's ranking is affected by his personality type. Active-positives clearly have the highest posterity rank and a correspondingly high power divergence score. Of the other three categories, active-negatives rank highest in the eyes of historians. Table 20 lists presidents by stages in the Klinbgerg-Holmes mood cycle and points to the fact that rank and mood stage also correspond. The average number of actions during each of the six stages of mood cycle across the three periods for which data are available is included, as is the average PDS per cycle stage.

Table 20 basically worked as expected. The average posterity rank for extrovert periods was significantly higher than that for introvert periods. The one finding that needs elaboration is that one of the higher posterity rankings of the six stages is accorded third-stage introvert presidents. By the third stage of introvert phases, Congress has grown quite influential in foreign policy matters and a president who begins to reassert presidential authority prior to a new extrovert phase can look quite good in retrospect.

This table provides students of public policy with an emerging pattern of the interaction between presidential personality, public mood, and the making of foreign policy.

Possibility of a Combined Cycle

The mood/interest theory implies that foreign policy moods may determine political behavior. However, moods labeled extrovert and introvert may be part of a public policy cycle that includes patterns of reform and scandal, as well as wars and territorial annexations. Frank Klingberg has done suggestive work in this area[16] and David McClelland's work was a valuable catalyst in suggesting the link between reform, war, and higher power divergence, and between affiliation and scandal.[17]

The relationship between reform cycles in American history and data presented earlier further confirms McClelland's hypothesis. Introvert periods are often associated with scandal and political reform. Although the public shows more concern with propriety during the first two stages of introversion, presidents who allow or are involved in major scandals are often found during the first stage.

First-stage introvert presidents also tend to slightly above average affiliation scores (table 7), low power divergence scores, and low posterity rankings (table 20). Second-stage introvert periods are characterized by political reform and an attempt to clean up the mess created in the first stage: a "His Honesty" Hayes,[18] a political outsider like Hoover, or an "I'll never lie to you" Carter. Average affiliation scores for presidents following scandals usually begin to rise as the public elects presidents who flaunt their honesty and nonpoliticized orientation. Third-stage introvert presidents tend to be more predisposed to initiate reforms of a more meaningful nature (Roosevelt and his "New Deal," Reagan and his "New Federalism"). During the last introvert stage and the first stage of extrovert periods, the socioeconomic, reform-war portions of the public policy cycle become more evident. Abolition, Populism, the New Deal, and New Federalism were all born in the last-stage introvert/first-stage extrovert thirds of the mood cycle.

Extrovert periods appear to alternate reform with war (Mexican War, abolition, Civil War; Populism, Spanish-American War, Philippine Insurrection, Progressivism, World War I; World War II, Korea, civil rights, War on Poverty, Vietnam).

Each of the extrovert periods under consideration concludes with a war followed by a period of political scandal, reform, and quiescence. This cycle is repeated three times during the period covered by this study. These relationships are summarized in table 22.

In conclusion, a comparative survey of the mood/interest theory and the survey of uses of armed forces abroad by the Library of Congress, the studies of David McClelland, David Winter, James David Barber, and the presidential rankings compiled by Arthur Schlesinger, Sr., and Robert Murray and Tim Blessing indicate a high degree of congruence between mood cycles and the findings of the other five studies. In extrovert periods, wars, actions to protect interest abroad, and territorial expansion are more likely to occur. Extrovert periods are likely to begin with, end with, and be immediately preceded by high power/low affiliation imagery in American literature and presidential inaugurals. Extrovert periods are also dominated by energetic presidents who like their jobs and are most often Democratic. Introvert periods, especially during the second stages, are significantly lower in actions taken, force invoked, and power imagery in literature and presidential inaugurals; such periods evidence a high need to affiliate and achieve, and a relatively low power drive. Accordingly, introvert periods are more likely to feature passive presidents.

The data in this comparison suggest that the work of authors analyzing similar phenomena using different methodologies can be related in a meaningful manner. The fact that they can be related reinforces each of the works by indicating that others rendered similar conclusions by different methodologies. In addition, it suggests that American foreign policy analysts would benefit by paying greater attention to long-term trends.

The easiest way to see the relationship between these studies and the mood/interest theory is to fit the findings of these studies into the basic fluctuation of mood from one extreme to the other and the first, second, and third stages of each introvert and extrovert period.

It is difficult, however, to summarize the work of David McClelland in this manner; his limited number of dates does not lend itself to specific agreement with individual introvert or extrovert cycles. McClelland is most applicable in pointing out the difference between all second stages, whether introvert or extrovert, and all first and third stages. In this respect, McClelland's analysis of literature supports the mood/interest theory. McClelland's low power/high affiliation years correspond with second stages, when activity on the international scene is quieter than before or after. McClelland's high power years correspond with swing decades when the United States, at a mood extreme, is furthest from its national interest and high power tendencies are needed to redirect activity.

During the first stage of an introvert period, the public mood points back toward the nation's realistic interests but is not yet there. In this stage, the use of force abroad is less than the extreme of the third-stage extrovert; yet it has not decreased to the point that it will in the second-stage introvert period when the public mood is very near to realistic national interests. An analysis of Winter's scoring of inaugural addresses indicates that the average first-stage introvert president has a power divergence score that is lower than his more active third-stage extrovert predecessor, yet higher than the following second-stage introvert president who is nearer to the realistic short-term interests of the nation. Most first-stage introvert presidents are passive, negative, and Republican. The fact that they are passive agrees with the idea that they are in the process of turning the nation away from its extreme extroversion, and the fact that they are Republican, with that party's concept of limited government, coincides with their job of limiting activity and returning to national interest. Posterity ranks first-stage introvert presidents quite low, because they do not appear as dynamic as their extrovert counterparts and may be seen in retrospect as tempering the nation when it appeared to be most powerful on the international scene.

The fewest uses of force were found in the second-stage of introvert periods and can be explained by the fact that the nation is still compensating for its extreme extroversion. The United States is at a point where short-term national interests are being fulfilled. Other nations are unwilling to seriously challenge us because of memories of the last extrovert phase. However, our deepening introversion is noticed by the world, leading to renewed challenges in the third stage. Presidents during second-stage introvert periods have the lowest power divergence scores, possibly because the nation is on its way into deep introversion and presidents of this stage still are reacting against the power used during the preceding extreme extroversion. Second-stage presidents, whether introvert or extrovert, are more passive than first- and third-stage extrovert presidents. This may be because they are in office during a period nearer the nation's short-term interests, and thus have a better balance between power and affiliation. Posterity ranks second-stage introvert presidents quite low, in part because of their relative passivity and lack of forceful actions abroad.

Third-stage introvert periods appropriately have more uses of force abroad than the preceding second stages. Although the nation is in its deepest introversion, other countries are presenting the United States with greater challenges, some of which cannot be completely ignored. (Uses of force in third-stage introvert phases appear less severe than in other stages in terms of casualties and duration, but more research on this relationship is needed.) This third-stage introvert period naturally uses far less force than the following first-stage extrovert period when the nation has fully turned toward exerting itself on the international scene. Likewise, third-stage introvert presidents have higher power divergence scores than those presidents of second-stage introvert periods because there is a bigger difference between the nation's interests and its actions during the third stage that forces the presidents to speak of power rather than affiliation. First- and third-stage introvert presidents were more negative than second- stage presidents, thus reflecting the greater tension between short-term national interest and public mood during first and third stages. As would be expected, first- and third-stage introvert presidents are more passive than their extrovert counterparts in the process of exerting the nation on the international scene. Third-stage introvert presidents received quite a high posterity ranking, which may reflect history's positive view of their efforts to reassert themselves against a Congress that has grown strong in international affairs during the earlier part of the introvert phase.

As would be expected when the nation returns to extroversion, a marked rise in uses of force abroad compared to the preceding third-stage introvert period is seen. First-stage extrovert periods rise in the use of force, but not to the point that they will rise to later in the extrovert period when the nation has become committed on the international scene. Accordingly, first-stage extrovert presidents have an average power divergence score that is more than double that of the preceding third-stage introvert presidents. Their scores are also higher than second-stage extrovert presidents because of the greater tension between short-term national interest and public mood in first-stage extrovert periods. According to the Barber ratings, first- and third-stage extrovert presidents were the most active presidents, which is reflected in their drive to assert the nation on the international scene, whether or not in discord with national interest. First-stage extrovert presidents had an average posterity ranking of 16.3, which is higher than average and illustrates history's positive opinion of their efforts to reestablish the United States as an active international power.

Second-stage extrovert periods feature a gradual increase in uses of force abroad compared to first stages reflecting the pressure on the United States to continue its international commitment. Like second-stage introvert presidents, second-stage extrovert presidents have low power divergence scores, demonstrating the nearness of public mood to the short-term national interest. A majority of second-stage presidents are positive, perhaps because of the lack of tension they feel during a period when short-term national interest and mood are congruent. The posterity rankings of second-stage extrovert presidents drop, possibly reflecting the lull in new international activity due to the proximity of mood and interest and therefore leaves the increasingly extrovert public with perceptions of presidential ineffectiveness.

As one would expect, the use of force abroad is highest during third-stage extrovert periods when the mood reaches the extreme of extroversion and the United States is its most active in the international arena. Presidents serving in these stages have the highest power divergence scores, showing their extreme use of power language in accordance with the nation's international role. First- and third-stage extrovert presidents are the most active presidents, which indicate increased commitments abroad. Presidents of third-stage extrovert periods receive the highest posterity rankings, which reflects history's positive view of their active role in pressing the nation further into extroversion.

In the process of analyzing introvert and extrovert moods by thirds, the authors become ever more aware of the distinction between long-term and short-term considerations. Conflicts between moods and interests have been analyzed, referencing specific points in time. It is quite possible for an action dictated by mood to be within the American interest at the time it is taken, but to set the stage for future challenges by other nations and future U.S. actions not in accord with interests.

Our analysis makes the point that long-term considerations deserve increased attention. Should the authors not then take the long-term view of deviation from interests? The answer is yes if enough information is readily available to project the long-term consequences of actions. However, for purposes of this analysis, the authors thought it best to start with commonly identified short-term consequences.

A next step after the mood/interest conflict is acknowledged would be to look at actions that do not in and of themselves violate interests, but probably lead to later violations. For example, using such a framework it would be difficult to argue that second-stage actions are in accord with interests if they lead to third-stage problems. Rather, it would be entirely likely that second-stage actions (or lack of actions) set up difficult third-stage challenges that mood prevents the United States from meeting until events have forced a mood change. Certainly any attempt to avoid the extremes of mood must take such lead time into account.

It would seem that the people get approximately what they desire in a president. As Walter Lippmann implied in *The Public Philosophy,* the public in a democracy may have too much influence over foreign policy, sending foreign policy (often belatedly) on an emotional roller coaster that may make little sense in terms of real strategic interests.[19] What can be done about the situation? The public can attempt to control events and motives rather than be driven by them. It can attempt to respond to events with an awareness of the period the United States is currently in, treading heavily when the predisposition is too affiliative, more lightly when it would be too likely to use the "big stick." A more balanced approach to the making of long-range foreign policy is needed, but perhaps in a democracy like the United States this is more than can be expected.

OTHER FOREIGN POLICY CONCEPTS
AND LIBERAL MOODS

The contention that alternating U.S. foreign policy moods are manifested in liberalism can be challenged by assertions that other considerations are of equal or greater importance. However, the mood/interest theory sees these forces as operating within the general context of liberalism. Therefore, liberalism must be considered more significant than these other forces: (1) pragmatism, (2) moralism, (3) conservatism, (4) elitism, (5) circumstances unique to America, and (6) world events. While study of these concepts can improve understanding of American foreign policy, it must be emphasized that the mood/interest theory maintains that liberal moods are of foremost significance.

Pragmatism

Americans (whether reform or business liberals) want flexibility in their choice of actions, in part because their liberalism is firmly grounded in the American pragmatic tradition extant since before the founding of the republic.[20] The pragmatic liberal American may have his preferred methods of changing the international system, but will support even an opposite orientation if it appears to be appropriate to the circumstances and is rationalized in such a way as to seem consistent with liberal values.

A true pragmatist objectively evaluates *every* possible course of action in order to determine which will work best. Most Americans believe that they conform to this definition and that they, perhaps uniquely, have the capacity to choose the most rational course of action. Therefore, they perceive themselves to be pragmatic in deciding foreign policy, as in other issues. The mood/interest analysis asserts, however, that while America has a pragmatic tradition, its pragmatism in foreign policy is related more to the fluctuating liberal mood than to national interest or universal inherent pragmatism. Americans cannot be pragmatically objective because their perceptions are distorted by the liberal public mood that envelops most of the society.

As mentioned, the pragmatic tradition in America makes the appearance of a rationally pragmatic choice very important to Americans. If most Americans are in a dominant introvert or extrovert mood, though, how is the appearance of pragmatism maintained? The answer lies in the fact that "dominant" mood does not mean "unanimous" mood; deviations from the dominant public mood by nonrepresentative minorities offer alternatives on both sides of the dominant mood, which are needed to make the dominant public mood appear pragmatic. Thus, nonrepresentative viewpoints have a sort of bracketing effect: by representing extreme views, they counterbalance one another and make the mainstream public mood appear less extreme and more rationally pragmatic.

An analysis of United States senators and their voting patterns on major issues illustrates this point well. Such an analysis is based on the fact that there are nationally visible figures outside of the mainstream of American thinking who can supply the diversity needed to propagate perceptions of "pragmatic" decision-making. In the case of United States senators, it is easy to see how some senators, namely those of the sparsely populated states of the West and Great Plains, can give the appearance of strong opposition to the public mood while not representing a large portion of the American public.[21]

A brief study of some of the important issues in recent foreign policy history and of the Senate's response to them shows that senators advocating a foreign policy different from the mainstream of American thinking have most often come from the sparsely populated states of the West and Great Plains. It is argued that the viewpoints of these senators are related to the constituent make-up of their states in that important characteristics of these states, such as the relatively small population per square mile and the propensity of constituents to take pride in their senator, produce less sophisticated balances of interest than are produced in most other states. In earlier times, when communications were less developed and election to the United States Senate less direct, senators holding extreme positions were more likely to come from a variety of states than is now the case.[22] Still, the effect is the same: senators representing views outside the public mood help the public mood appear pragmatic.

A senator with fewer interests and constituents to be concerned with is allowed more freedom of action and greater amounts of time to work on substantive issues. Also, a senator from such a state is frequently given more leeway by constituents who, due to geographic isolation and fewer constituents per senator, form stronger loyalties to their "person in Washington." The result is a United States Senator who does not need to tread as many thin lines between opposing constituent interest groups—a senator who is more likely than others to deviate from the overall mood in foreign policy decisions.

Liberal Americans are by nature likely to have some leaders who are ahead of the mood simply because of zeal to sell the public on a new position. Usually some leaders with a more complex position than the current mood can be heard. What is most difficult to find are leaders who have fallen behind a mood or who state a clear position at one extreme; in this regard, senators from the sparsely populated states of the Great Plains and West are important. These senators practically ensure that the pragmatic American will be able to find national leaders more introvert and more extrovert than the current mood. In this manner, the mood of the country at large can seem to be a pragmatic compromise whether it happens to be extremely extroverted, extremely introverted, or somewhere in between.

Using Manfred Jonas's study on isolationism, *Isolationism in America 1935–1941*, the twelve major isolationist senators of the 1930s can be selected.[23] Seven of these senators were from sparsely populated western and Great Plains states.[24] These extremely introvert senators were sometimes balanced by senators from their own states who held opposing viewpoints. For example, Edward R. Burke, a colleague of isolationist George Norris from Nebraska, in 1940 introduced controversial legislation to reinstate the draft.[25] In this case, with isolationist leaders even more introvert than the dominant mood phase, as well as some persons less introvert than the dominant mood, an extreme introvert position, reluctantly reinstating only a quite limited draft in the face of great national danger, could be perceived as a pragmatic balance between the opposing forces. Still, the world situation at that time would indicate that such an American balance was indeed extremely introvert.

An analysis of senators opposing NATO in 1949 provides further substantiation of the point that sparsely populated states of the Great Plains or West are more likely to produce views outside of the current mood. The vote in the Senate committing the United States to the NATO alliance on July 21, 1949, was 82 to 13. Eight of the thirteen senators voting against NATO were from sparsely populated states of the Great Plains or West.[26] These opposing senators were balanced by other leaders ahead of the mood who stressed the need to meet the challenge of communism and a vote for the NATO alliance easily could be perceived as pragmatic, a perception that would have been impossible before World War II when the United States was in an extremely introvert mood.

A vote analysis of a version of the proposed Bricker Amendment of 1954, which aimed at subjecting treaties and executive agreements to increased constitutional and legislative scrutiny, shows that senators from the Great Plains and West were more likely than other senators to lend it their support. Proponency of the Bricker Amendment indicated an introvert position because of the stringent limitations it sought to impose. The Senate failed to refer a version of the Bricker Amendment to the states by a vote of 60 to 31 on February 26, 1954. Only five opposing senators, or a little less than one-sixth of the opposition, were from sparsely populated states of the Great Plains and West.[27] Since states of the Great Plains and West with small populations compose just less than one-third of the entire Senate, one may assume that senators from these states were more likely to vote in favor of the amendment than senators from the remainder of the country. This support effectively added to the introvert position, which in turn made the extrovert position that eventually defeated the amendment appear more pragmatic.

Another example indicating that senators with a less demanding constituency are most likely to be inordinately introvert or extrovert is found in the support given the introvert National Commitments Resolution of 1969. The resolution passed the Senate by a vote of 70 to 16. Nine of the sixteen opposing senators were from sparsely populated states of the Great Plains and West.[28] Opposition senators did not carry the day, but certainly served to express an extrovert view at variance with the existing public mood. This view, balanced with those of strong introverts ahead of the mood, served to convince the public of its pragmatism.

In the 1981 Senate vote concerning President Reagan's proposed sale of weapons to Saudi Arabia, which included a number of Airborne Warning and Control System (AWACS) radar planes, the 52 to 48 vote supporting the sale depended on support from the sixteen sparsely populated states of the Great Plains and West. Twenty-four of the fifty-two votes supporting the sale came from the sixteen states named, whereas only eight of the forty-eight opposing votes came from these states. Also, those eight votes came from seven different states; in only one of the sixteen states, Oregon, did both senators vote against the sale. Interestingly, one of these two senators, Senator Packwood (R-Oregon) was the major Republican party leader of opposition to the sale; this further emphasizes the ability of these senators to take diverse positions. Without the support of these senators who had the freedom to vote contrary to the predominant introvert sentiments, the sale would never have been approved.[29] In this case the flexibility allowed these senators gave President Reagan the chance to carry out what could be argued as a truly pragmatic policy in an introvert mood. Acting outside of the public mood would rarely be possible for a president without such support.

Less than average susceptibility to presidential foreign policy lobbying, tendency to extremes, and latitude in foreign policy stances are frequent characteristics of senators from sparsely populated states of the Great Plains and West and were also manifested in the 1978 vote on the Panama Canal treaties. While senators from these states are less than one-third of the Sente, they cast over half of the votes in opposition to the treaties, again strengthening the pragmatic appearance of the final outcome of the votes.[30] Interestingly enough, two senators who assumed leadership roles in support of the treaty were from sparsely populated western states. Senator Frank Church from Idaho was the floor leader in favor of the treaties and Dennis DeConcini of Arizona played a leadership role in formulating reservations and understandings.

When nationally articulated extreme positions of some senators are balanced by positions in the opposite extreme, the general public may conclude that middle positions must be moderate and therefore reasonable. The Gulf of Tonkin Resolution affords another example. The two-vote opposition to this resolution by senators from sparsely populated western states[31] and the strong extrovert measures concerning Vietnam advocated by Barry Goldwater (Arizona) helped to convince the country that President Johnson's 1964 actions were, indeed, reasonable and proper; Johnson was portrayed as a moderate. Only with the perspective of history can this portrayal be viewed as inaccurate. President Johnson, in reality, was not acting according to interest but rather in an extremely extroverted manner according to mood.

Table 23 (page 000) summarizes the points made above by comparing Senate votes with votes from the sparsely populated West and Great Plains states. By calculating what the West and Great Plains vote would have been if it were proportionate to those states' percentage of the entire Senate vote, and then comparing this to the actual votes from these states, the bracketing effect in regards to the appearance of pragmatism can be seen, with the general public mood being situated between widely diverse views.

This American desire to have at hand a variety of alternatives from which a "reasonable" course of action can be selected is also illustrated by the presidential elections of 1964 and 1972 in which senators Barry Goldwater of Arizona and George McGovern of South Dakota, respectively, were overwhelmingly defeated. Goldwater carried the torch of strong extroversion in the face of a slightly less extrovert public mood and lost the election. Likewise, McGovern was ahead of the 1972 mood in that he was more introvert than the general public which chose the more moderate Richard Nixon.

Americans, who perceive themselves as pragmatic partially because of the presence of these nonconformist leaders, fail to see that their foreign policy stances are becoming extreme (either introvert or extrovert); this in turn enables a mood to escalate with minimum restraints. It must be noted, however, that if America's stance becomes too extreme, that pragmatic element of American thought will force a decisive shift in mood. Americans believe that if one course of action fails, perhaps the opposite course of action might succeed. When the force of world events periodically dictates such change, America's unique pragmatic impulse helps to generate it.

Moralism

Moralism is seen by many foreign policy analysts as having a significant bearing on American foreign policy and it operates as an inherent set of political values within the broader liberalism. In the United States moralism can many times be equated to religion, since most American leaders base their morality on their religious background. The impact of religion on American morals can be traced back to the early settlers who came to America for religious reasons. America's consistent humanitarian concern, reflected in its overall morality and policy, demonstrates American adherence to the idealistic and universal demands of religion. United States foreign policy has often been observed as having a stronger moralistic tone than is found in the foreign policies of other nations.[32]

More specifically, the idealistic viewpoint of foreign policy reflected by moralism states that nations should do what is "right." A nation is only as strong as its morality and sense of purpose. Moralism demands consistency of action toward a set of idealistic goals. Once one of the liberal foreign policy orientations is adopted, be it introvert or extrovert, it must be pursued consistently with little attention to the other liberal foreign policy orientation. When the adopted orientation begins to fail to correspond to reality, the moral demand for consistency results in a temporary increase in the intensity of that particular orientation or mood. When this orientation finally reaches an extreme, the pragmatic demand for workable change and the consequences of unrealistic foreign policy force a reversal in foreign policy by both reform and business liberals. Thus, moralism motivates Americans to allow a mood to run rampant before changing it, but when it is changed the moralist wants to change it completely. After the change, moralism requires consistency in the opposite direction until another extreme is reached, and so on.

Similar introvert or extrovert moral traits in presidents can appear at similar points in the development of separate introvert or extrovert phases. For example, both presidents Hoover and Carter, whose terms fell in the middle of introvert phases, evidenced a strong humanitarian concern and support for arms control and disarmament. Presidents Theodore Roosevelt and Harry Truman each served toward the beginning of an extrovert phase and sold the public on moral requirements that necessitated increased American foreign policy activity.

Moralistic and religious opinions regarding foreign policy vary with the general public mood. Moral arguments rarely give clear and constant guidance to the moralist in foreign policy matters. In an April 1978 interview Henry Kissinger noted: "You have to know how to go from your values to your security, your world structure, or whatever it is you are aiming for. You cannot simply do it in a fit of moral enthusiasm."[33] An American moralist's sense of purpose can lead to strong disdain for war or to zealous support for a particular war, but rarely in between.

A look at some leading national statesmen reveals that positions by persons of similar religious background can vary considerably. Senator William E. Borah, a strong opponent of the Treaty of Versailles, came from a midwestern Calvinist background.[34] President Woodrow Wilson, supporter and negotiator of the treaty, was the son of a Presbyterian minister. Richard Nixon liked to refer to his Quaker background; for example, during the 1970 Middle East crisis he said, "There is an old Quaker saying, 'the most important quality in a crisis is peace at the center.' "[35] Curiously, much of the hard-core opposition to his Vietnam policies came from Quakers. Joseph Kennedy, the father of the first Catholic president of the United States—John Kennedy—took a vastly different viewpoint toward the U.S. role in Europe from that of his son.[36] The Reformed Church in America has had two of its members serve as president of the United States: Martin Van Buren, who was a careful introvert, and Theodore Roosevelt, who was a strong extrovert.

During the 1920s and 1930s, there was religious support for disarmament and opposition to the munitions makers. A crusade against an atheistic communism received religious support in the 1950s and early 1960s. Much religious concern has been shown with the destructive nature of modern weapons and the inability of nations to resolve differences during the late 1970s and early 1980s. An example of disagreement between American foreign policy analysts arguing from a Christian perspective during the same time frame is provided by authors Robert L. DeVries and Ronald Kirkemo. DeVries argues that decreases in birth rates come with economic prosperity and that the United States should promote minimal economic rights for each person in the world. Kirkemo says that exports of food reserves could be contingent upon the developing countries starting "family planning programs to begin slowing the population boom."[37]

This same point is also illustrated by the current split in Christian viewpoints in America. On one side, the mainline Protestant denominations in America support a mostly introvert position regarding foreign policy, with an emphasis on arms control. The argument is that the destructive power of modern weapons works against God's will and threatens everyone and everything and should be strictly controlled. On the other side are some Christian-oriented organizations like the Moral Majority, sometimes called the "New Right."[38] Since communists actively oppose Christian values, these organizations advocate a more extrovert foreign policy than their mainline counterparts and a strong military deterrent to communist expansion. Again, the point here is that American moral values, Christian values in this case, can support both introvert and extrovert foreign policies.

Due to the inconsistent guidance provided to American foreign policy makers by moral considerations, some observers argue that the country should follow a realistic point of view. The realist argues that the United States must do what is in its interest, since this is the way the international system functions. Realists maintain that wars can be caused by an unduly inflated sense of justice, that morality cannot be imposed by force, and that current military capabilities are too awesome to risk an unnecessary war over conflicting moralities. Idealists attack this realistic point of view as being unworthy of the aspirations of the American people.

In the end, the realist can be seen as having a position in between the two extremes of American idealism. He takes a more moderate view than many American liberals, such as Wilson, Borah, and Joseph or John Kennedy. While idealists as a group might be said to embrace an inconsistent idealism, which is disruptive to world peace and stability, the realist point of view at least affords a chance for a sustained American contribution to world order.

Conservatism

A third force that must be analyzed is the sometimes powerful impact of classical or Burkean conservatism on American foreign policy. Why is it that an overwhelmingly liberal country's conservatives have a significant impact on its foreign policy at certain times? Much of the answer to this question centers on the inability of the two varieties of liberalism to address the complexities of international relations.[39] The liberal, particularly at times of mood change, desires immediate and sweeping revisions of policies that take much time to change. The conservative more readily accepts the immediate realization of limited measures. In addition, since liberalism does not provide the tools for creative thinking on military matters, conservatives also can be instrumental in changes regarding military strategy and organization. For purposes of this analysis, the conservative who is reconciled to foreign policy realities can be compared to the realist.

The mood/interest theory argues that the American public rules foreign policy and indicates that American foreign policy is liberal, since the perspective of the realist or conservative is foreign to American public thinking. The reason the realist or conservative point of view has been supported by many influential Americans is that many times liberals have unrealistic expectations of foreign policy. Sometimes they adopt an introvert stance, sometimes an extrovert stance; sometimes the only feasible alternative is in the middle range where lies the consistent position of the realist or conservative. Thus, at many times the conservative position coincides with the only feasible options available to frustrated liberals. The conservative can be viewed as farsighted in that he is consistently within the boundaries of the interest zone. At the start of a new mood phase, liberals of both varieties and conservatives can find themselves in general agreement, such as the conservative-realist agreement from 1940–1947, with increasingly extrovert liberal idealists, and from 1968–1972, with increasingly introvert liberal idealists.

Both George Kennan and Henry Kissinger can be described as foreign policy realists or conservatives who place emphasis on major power balances in world politics. Both believe the public can be sold on wise policies. In the tense atmosphere of 1947, Kennan advocated the need for containment of the Soviet Union.[40] The liberal public bought Kennan's policy, but later militarized it to what he considered an unacceptable degree.[41] In 1969 Kissinger joined the Nixon administration as a foreign policy advisor who advocated balance-of-power policies consistent with American capabilities.[42] Kissinger was able to execute his policies through secret, personal diplomacy. However, the public became restless for liberal rationales and methods of the kind later provided in the rhetoric of President Jimmy Carter in such areas as human rights, arms control, and a general advocacy of humane purposes for American foreign policy.

During Kennan's time (1947), the United States mood was below the interest zone, but moving in an extrovert direction. In 1969 with Kissinger, the mood was above the zone but moving in an introvert direction. Kennan and Kissinger were influential in their respective eras because they provided rationales to move American policy in a direction favored by the public. The public listened less to Kennan and Kissinger as time progressed and further movement in the direction of the then current mood was believed desirable. Though realists such as Kennan and Kissinger might be correct in their policy arguments, the mood/interest analysis indicates that the liberal public can be sold only what it wants to buy and sees balance-of-power positions largely as temporary measures.

Important contributions by civilian conservatives have also been made in the realm of military affairs. Federalist Alexander Hamilton's ideas about the military were more conservative than his peers and had a rough time in the American political system. Conservative southerner John C. Calhoun made some important contributions when he was secretary of war under President James Monroe from 1817 to 1825. After the Northern victory in the Civil War, civilian conservatives were not particularly influential in military affairs until the turn of the century, when neo-Hamiltonians such as Theodore Roosevelt, who thought in a mixed liberal-conservative manner, were instrumental in the development of a modern general staff system and in securing recognition of modern naval strategy.[43] The Kennedy administration can be identified as another influential group that thought in a mixed liberal-conservative manner.[44] Robert McNamara, Kennedy's secretary of defense during the last part of the 1940–1968 extrovert phase, brought some sweeping innovations to the United States military establishment in planning and organization. However, the time that Calhoun, the neo-Hamiltonians, and the Kennedy administration remained in power was limited, as was the execution of their policies.

Elitism

Most analyses of American foreign policy either implicitly or explicitly endorse the proposition that an elite group determines American foreign policy and then persuades the public of its appropriateness. Indeed, foreign policy has often been a concern involving few Americans. Wise actions in foreign policy require a knowledge of other governments, which an elite can most easily acquire, and in which the electorate has little interest. In essence, therefore, the elite can be said to make foreign policy decisions and suggestions which the public, with little knowledge of alternatives, will accept.

Elitist theory is an attractive perspective for a number of reasons. Foreign policy is indisputably the province of the elite in most countries of the world and scholars are therefore conditioned to think about elite control. Foreign policy writers, whose credentials naturally depend on analytical ability, are less likely to experience the power of the public than is the politician who must compete for the public's votes in order to win and retain office. Writers with governmental experience who emphasize the importance of their actions while in government also contribute to the illusion of elite rule. Another important reason for adherence to elite rule doctrines is that people naturally believe their own activities and perceptions of reality are superior to those of others. Thus, a person can easily assign failures to an elite who does not listen to him. If the public were held to be the supreme authority, the responsibility would force all Americans to take a much harder look at themselves.

The elitist perspective has merit and can even be a basis for some mood analyses. In the early 1970s Graham Allison argued that the foreign policy attitudes of elite young Americans contrasted sharply with those of their elders,[45] and Michael Roskin noted the importance of shifting elite generational paradigms in foreign policy.[46] Indeed, mood swings are easier to explain if an enlightened elite, rather than the entire public, is assumed to periodically shift directions.

One shortcoming of elitist analysis is that it fails to give sufficient attention to other considerations. Placing mood shifts within an elite context makes it difficult to grasp the underlying importance of mood because the elitist analyst naturally emphasizes modification of elite behavior to check moodiness. Such emphasis all too easily by-passes the possibility that public moods are deep, underlying, recurring, and not easily changed. Elites may influence public mood and express new opinions, but the mood/interest theory argues that these elite influences will not stand in the long term if they attempt to contradict the general public mood.

Many adherents to elitism make the debatable assumption that elites can guide the public mood and change policy when they believe appropriate, while it often fails to explain the reverse—that the public can ably restrain or temper elitist policies. For instance, the elitist orientation fails to explain how a leader like Lyndon Johnson, who followed his foreign policy consistently, could lose his ability to govern effectively in the face of the public reaction against American involvement in Vietnam. As had also been the case with the Korean war, the long-standing mass opinion that one fights a war right or not at all ultimately won out over arguments by many in the elite concerning the necessity of coping with the complex challenge of limited war in the nuclear age. The mass public had its way in Vietnam as American policy began a shift in 1968 that led to the termination of direct American participation in the war by 1973.[47] The liberal aversion to limited wars is again becoming accepted policy.[48] President Carter appeared reluctant to commit the nation to another limited Asian land war and indicated that "South Korea would be protected by U.S. nuclear might—and the implication that it would be used 'if necessary'—after the withdrawal of American troops."[49] While a delay of United States troop withdrawal was announced in 1979, it is clear that the elite neither wins every argument nor shapes long-term opinion.

A 1982 survey of the public and leaders identifies gaps between the two in significant areas. The public is presently less prone than leaders to support an active role in world affairs, foreign economic aid, foreign military aid and sales, free trade, actions against South Africa, previous U.S. actions in Vietnam, relations with Cuba, use of military force in the event of invasion of countries allied with the United States, increased relationships with the Soviet Union, and arms control.[50] These choices basically outline policies now being followed by the government with the exception of willingness to use military force in the event of invasions of allies. Thus American foreign policy generally is closer to opinions expressed by the public than to those of elitist leaders.

The mood/interest theory accepts elite influence on foreign policy formulation, but emphasizes that the elites regularly alter policy according to the public's demand. Elitist theory too often fails in the matter of identification. Who is the elite? How did they become the elite? Why are they listened to in preference to others? The mood/interest theory argues that elites are chosen by the public from among a large body of potential elites. One elite can be replaced with another elite.

Although the public cannot comment daily on matters of foreign policy, the public does set the parameters within which the political leadership must act. The mood/interest theory admits that elites make foreign policy decisions and influence the public over the short term. Over the long term, however, an elite must remain inside the parameters set by the public or risk being replaced by a new elite. In cases of conflict, mood clearly prevails over the desires of an elite leadership. Presidents throughout history have had their foreign policy limited by prevailing public mood. Even aristocratic John Adams, while trying to adhere strictly to his conscience, would yield in the face of irresistible public pressure.[51] Presidents who have not adjusted to change in mood have found themselves in losing positions like those faced by Woodrow Wilson over the League of Nations and Lyndon Johnson over Vietnam. Others, such as Franklin Roosevelt during the extremely introvert 1930s, have conformed to public mood on foreign policy to gain domestic objectives.

The "public mood" discussed in this analysis refers more to that of the mass public than to that of the elite or attentive publics.[52] In general, the mood/interest theory asserts that a combination of the mass mood and world events sets the boundaries within which the elite and attentive publics must maneuver if they are to be effective.

Many analysts of American foreign policy underestimate the role and intelligence of the mass public.[53] Often it is criticized for being uninformed, pessimistic, and supportive of unwise policies. Gabriel Almond's 1950 book on foreign policy moods contained implied criticism of the mass public for tendencies toward military solutions and isolationism.[54] The implicit idea in all of this is that informed individuals can lead the mass public down the right path.

The mood/interest theory suggests that the mass public can be more indicative of ultimate policy than the elite or attentive publics. Since Almond wrote his book, two trends unexpected by many of the foreign policy elite emerged in American foreign policy. The first was the "militarization" of American foreign policy which became more popular[55] as extroversion, particularly that directed toward containing communism, grew in intensity. The second was the late 1960s shift to introversion.[56] Thus, the tendencies toward military solutions and isolationism that Almond saw in the mass public both found their way into American policy. The "pessimism" that Almond criticized in the mass public was not characteristic of his own work, as he was optimistic that some of the past American moodiness could be overcome.[57] Perhaps the mass public's alleged pessimism deserves greater attention and consideration by foreign policy analysts interested in future implications for American foreign policy.

The criticism of the mass public as being uninformed about foreign policy is well documented, but uninformed does not necessarily mean unintelligent. The mass public is simply more concerned with the domestic matters affecting them directly. As Almond determined in his studies: "It is not the foreign or domestic character of the issue which determines the accessibility of public attention, but the intimacy of the impact. From this point of view, foreign policy, save in moments of grave crisis, has to labor under a handicap; it has to shout loudly to be heard even a little."[58] Because American liberalism is constructed primarily to deal with domestic issues, the mass public does not have many ideological tools to comprehensively consider problems of foreign policy. However, the mass public's lack of information could mean that it is less likely to be caught up in a momentary mood than is the elite or attentive public, which endeavor to lead the mass public. Elite decision-making may be action and reaction, whereas the public has general perceptions that will give them a consensus for a period of time.

A more suggestive method of breaking down public thinking than into the standard mass, attentive, and elite public categories might be into the consistent, leadership, and mass public categories. The consistent group, diverse and composed of members of the public least prone to fluctuation, represents all the feasible options that can be used in a policy-making situation. Members consistently occupy one of the points on an introvert- extrovert continuum. The leadership public decides which members of the consistent public shall have their viewpoints put before the mass public. The very zeal of the leadership public in attempting to give the mass public the choice it desires makes the leadership public the most prone of the three to fluctuate. The actions and rhetoric of the leadership public, in its attempt to "sell" the public on a certain policy direction, can contribute to the normal momentum of a mood swing, but cannot alter normal changes in international direction (as witness the cases of presidents Wilson and Johnson). The mass public, the final arbiter of American foreign policy, does fluctuate, but only within definite boundaries. If the leadership public's persuasive zeal were tempered by an acknowledgment of the mass public's intelligence (as opposed to knowledge), perhaps the elites would be less likely to oversell certain policies and create unrealistic expectations, making it less likely for moods to be carried to illogical extremes.[59]

Bernard C. Cohen, usually an adherent to elite perspectives, says this about Klingberg's public mood perspective: "a policy making system which has mastered all the modes of resistance to outside opinion nevertheless seems, from a long-run perspective, to accommodate to it."[60] The foreign policy arguments advanced by the mood/interest theory are pluralistic. Acknowledging the significant role of elites in foreign policy determination, the theory maintains that the role is circumscribed by the desires of the public, which regularly shift according to mood.

It is recognized that there is no definitive way to prove whether an elite leadership or the public mood ultimately determines foreign policy. Since most analyses support an elite rule argument, however, the impact of public moods on foreign policy has been insufficiently identified and analyzed. This analysis maintains that the powerful elite retains its position only so long as it remains true to public mood. The elite makes many decisions, but wisely makes most of them within parameters set by the public. The mass public has many tools with which to contain and influence elites. More research is needed to identify the exact dynamics of group interaction and influence. The relationship may be somewhat dialectical with the elite offering pragmatic decisions and the public continuing along its steady path to one extreme or the other. The argument here, however, is that a first step is the recognition that the mass public may be more influential than commonly thought.

Fortunate Circumstances and Modern Technology

A fifth consideration that helps explain the operation of American liberalism in the foreign policy realm is the role of fortunate circumstances and modern technology. American circumstances have been so fortunate that moods have been able to predominate over foreign policy interests to a much greater degree than is possible in most other countries. America's dominant liberal ideology has flourished without strong internal opposition, insulated from the international consequences of basing foreign policy on that liberal ideology. Such consequences have been felt strongly only every two to three decades, when the cumulative force of world events helps stimulate change from introversion to extroversion or vice versa.

European nations, often bordered by a number of strong potential rivals, are unable to deviate so far from a realistic foreign policy approach. Germany simply cannot follow liberalism from extreme to extreme and still hope to survive. The United States, with its weaker neighbors to the north and south and expansive oceans on the east and west, can do so and has. Japan might not have to worry about immediately powerful neighbors, but its freedom to act is restricted by a dense population and dependence upon trade. Its economic interests must be given a higher priority than is the case in the United States, which has considerably more natural resources and less dependence on trade. Thus, the United States has the ability to shape short-term events to a much greater degree than other major powers.

One can argue that modern technology has stripped away America's insulation from world politics by making Americans and the rest of the world more interdependent. However, as one of two super-powers, the United States is more militarily independent than previously. Unless absolutely necessary, no nation will stand in the way of a strong United States desire to be introverted or extroverted. The United States is powerful enough to stand apart from a number of world events if it so desires, and the United States is not inhibited from taking an active role in many world events if this is in accord with the prevailing public mood. Military super-power status also can compensate for some of the leeway lost by other changing circumstances, such as strong Third World concerns or spreading nuclear arsenals.

When the military super-power status is combined with the momentum gained from a two-hundred-year cycle of fluctuation, fortunate circumstances and modern technology can be seen to have allowed and will continue to allow the changing liberal moods of the public to conflict with foreign policy interests at the extreme.

Events

The regularity in moods advanced by the mood/interest theory might actually be a recurrence of certain types of events that require similar United States responses. Some foreign policy literature identifies regular patterns in international events. Warfare and violence do not occur on an entirely random basis; patterns of some sort do exist. Such patterns do not correspond exactly to the dates of American liberal mood phases, which occur with greater regularity;[61] yet there can be no denial that world events affect U.S. foreign policy and probably do so increasingly as the United States plays a larger role in international politics. Events also have a particularly strong impact upon policy when mood phases have gone to such an extreme that U.S. policy is very unrealistic; at such times, events can contribute to a mood change insofar as the deficiencies of the existing mood are demonstrated by events. However, the mood/interest theory argues that usually United States reactions to events are conditioned more by American foreign policy moods than by the nature of the events.

To illustrate this point, the mood cycles developed in Chapter 1 can be compared to the Small and Singer analysis of all international war. Table 24 (page 188) shows the average nation months of war under way per year in each of the comparable mood phases described earlier.

It is evident from this perspective that the international war pattern has a limited relationship to American liberal moods prior to 1919. Similarly, comparison of interwar intervals of nations which fought in three or more interstate wars shows that the United States mean interval of 24.2 years is the highest mean interval, and is nearly twice the average mean interval of the nineteen other nations listed.[62] Also, even as one of the largest and most powerful nations, the United States ranks only tenth in Small and Singer's rank order of nations by war experience indicators.[63] The indication of these two points is that despite its size and influence, the United States is not consistently involved in international wars.

Finally, Small and Singer suggest that involvement in international wars does fluctuate in somewhat of a cyclical pattern, with peak periods about twenty years apart.[64] Although this pattern might be said to support some general idea of a cyclical theory of international politics, the cycles identified by Small and Singer do not correspond to the American liberal mood cycles. The conclusion to be drawn from these several indications is that the American mood fluctuations defined by this theory are somewhat independent of the influences of international events, and that these moods do determine the foreign policy response to such events to a greater extent than the reverse.

While American foreign policy moods are different and more regular than world events patterns, it is obvious that world events affect American foreign policy moods, especially when moods reach extremes. American extrovert periods do correspond to periods of more international violence than introvert periods, though the difference was not dramatic before 1919. Alternative patterns of world events with less regularity than American foreign policy moods have been hypothesized. Detailed research on American mood patterns in the context of alternative theories regarding world event patterns could reveal relationships that would improve understanding of the mood/interest theory.

Some analysts of American foreign policy go so far as to argue that each event is different when analyzed in detail, as is the American response to each event. However, patterns do exist and identifying them is valuable as long as it is done with appropriate attention to detail.

The American's liberal ideology tells him to be introverted or extroverted. Within this encompassing force his pragmatism tells him to choose thoughtfully a course of action from among those which confront him; only at extremes, however, does such pragmatism lead to a change in his extrovert or introvert orientation. Moralism tells Americans to pursue an orientation consistently until it has clearly failed; then moralism prompts them to try the opposite mood orientation. The few conservatives in American history have had a strong influence on foreign policy at certain times, but only within parameters allowed by liberalism. Elites, likewise, have some influence, but there are several potential elites at any given time and the mass public gives its ear to the one it chooses. Fortunate circumstances will probably continue to permit American foreign policy to fluctuate, although world events will continue to present challenges. At the root of all these considerations is a strong American liberalism very much related to public mood and its conflict with foreign policy interests.

3. American Foreign Policy Interests: Their Moody Relation to Policy

The forces behind United States foreign policy moods and United States foreign policy interests are in basic conflict, periodically causing American foreign policy to deviate from interests. This basic conflict cannot be analyzed until both sides have been identified. Liberal foreign policy moods, including their relationship to some other foreign policy concepts, have been delineated. On the other side of the conflict are the politico-military interests the United States needs to pursue in the international system.

POLITICO-MILITARY INTERESTS

Karl W. Deutsch said that, generally speaking, "the foreign policy of every country deals first with the preservation of its independence and security, and second with the pursuit and protection of its economic interests."[1] This being so, discussion of interests centers on matters of a political and military nature.

The foreign policies of individual nations are necessarily linked together. A powerful nation must take more actions than weaker nations. Thus, action required to achieve American interests has expanded with the growth of American power. This growth has enveloped more geographic areas, required greater United States activity, and necessitated increasing adaptivity to changing circumstances. In extrovert phases, the United States has expanded its politico-military activity and ultimately done too much in pursuit of its interests. In introvert phases, the United States has endeavored to avoid new politico-military activity and ultimately has not done enough to protect its interests.

Although liberal American thinking contains an aversion to the use of power, the complexities of international relations frequently require it. The world does not share the liberal American's ideology, nor the Marxist's ideology, nor any single ideology; but most nations understand and appreciate the realistic functioning of power politics. Further, they understand that some use of power politics may be necessary to maintain politico-military interests to a greater extent than does the United States.

Within the gamut of political and military interests lies a wide range of viable actions, and as the world situation changes, the nature of such actions changes. Thus, in 1793 it was appropriate (in the United States interest) for President Washington to issue a proclamation of neutrality, and in 1950 it was equally appropriate for President Truman to send troops to Korea. In the former example, the need for internal development was more important for maintaining independence than was the need for involvement in European disputes; in the latter example, United States security interests were better served by the United Nations action than by the issuance of a neutrality statement. One should note that these policies are the results of human perceptions of the international situation and the nature of American interests at a given time.

America's most basic interest, preservation of its territorial integrity and well-being, has been directly threatened at various times. The outcome of the Civil War prevented the dismemberment of the nation. In a much less dramatic sense, Florida Indians in the early 1800s and some Mexican nationals in the early 1900s threatened internal placidity in border areas and were pursued beyond United States borders. Japanese aggression in the Pacific eventually posed a definite threat to American territorial integrity and was countered by the United States entry into World War II. Since 1945, basic preservation has also entailed the prevention of a destructive nuclear, biological, or chemical exchange.

America's interdependence with other nations requires a degree of freedom of the seas. In early years, America went to war (declared and undeclared) with France from 1798 to 1800, certain Barbary states from 1801 to 1805 and 1815, and Great Britain from 1812 to 1814, in part to protect this basic interest. The United States' displeasure over British actions regarding construction of Confederate commerce raiders during the Civil War also demonstrates American concern regarding freedom of the seas. German attacks on American shipping were a major consideration prompting American entry into World War I.

The primary interests of United States foreign policy include more than just these basic concerns with territorial integrity and freedom of the seas. In the complex world situation, the United States has specific interests in extraterritorial geographic areas. Events in one part of the world have had an increasing impact on other parts of the world. Because security is not easily divisible, a nation must seek to realize politico-military conditions outside its immediate boundaries. These can, of course, vary with the size and geographic location of a nation.

The mood/interest analysis rejects the argument that American interests are so global that regional variations are of questionable significance. Rather, an early point in the identification of a viable set of interests is the recognition of regional variations. Bernard Gordon, in his book *Toward Disengagement in Asia,* has classified three levels of geographic interests for the United States.[2] Those interests in the first level are of such importance that the United States is willing to intervene militarily to protect them; activities in areas of level-two interest are of concern to the United States but do not necessarily require a military commitment; and those activities in the third level can be most easily ignored because they least threaten American national security. The focus of the mood/interest theory is three geographic areas of level-one interest: Europe, the Western Hemisphere, and East Asia.

One interest of a first level nature is the prevention of one-nation (or coalition) dominance in Europe.[3] The early opportunity of the United States for internal development was the result not only of the neutrality proclamation, but also, and more importantly, of the factional nature of European politics which kept a single, powerful European state from turning its attention westward toward the not yet powerful, but wealthy, American continent. In this century, both world wars were fought in large part to prevent a German hegemony in Europe. In the post-World War II period, United States efforts have been directed against a threat of Soviet hegemony in that area.

A second important geographic concern of the United States has been to preserve its dominance among major powers, first in North America and later in the entire Western Hemisphere.[4] The North American interest is one of survival since the United States has a larger population than its North American neighbors and is the naturally dominant power. Origins of the interest in the Western Hemisphere can be traced to the Monroe Doctrine and to the turn of this century when the United States assumed from the United Kingdom the dominant politico-military role in the Western Hemisphere.[5] Internal disputes in Latin America have not threatened United States dominance simply because no Latin American state has had big-power status; therefore, internal disputes in that area cannot be considered a level-one interest.[6] The fact that the United States sometimes has intervened when it was not necessary is indicative of an unrealistic public mood or an attempt to compensate for weakness elsewhere in the world. In terms of level-one interest, United States politico-military involvement is essential only when necessary to prevent politico-military domination of Latin American areas by extrahemispheric forces. A recent example of the pursuit of this interest is the willingness of the United States to go to war over the placement of Soviet missiles in Cuba. If a Latin American nation, such as Brazil or Mexico, were to acquire major power status as long-term trends indicate might be possible, United States interests would require dominance in North America and an appropriate balance of power within Latin America. This discussion of past and possible future changes in United States interests in the

Western Hemisphere indicates that interests can change in accordance with changing situations.

Another level-one United States interest is the prevention of one-nation (or coalition) dominance in East Asia (China, Japan, Korea, and Southeast Asia).[7] United States interest in this area developed gradually and was openly articulated near the end of the last century as the "Open Door" policy. In the late thirties and early forties, Japan's threat of dominance eventually led to American intervention, and in the early sixties, a major change in the Southeast Asian situation was perceived as possibly leading to Sino-Soviet hegemony.

Sources other than Gordon can be cited in support of this statement about Europe, the Western Hemisphere, and East Asia as priority areas of geographic interest.[8] The need to prevent one-nation dominance in these areas is still crucial to the United States, but it has been modified recently to include the dominance of a single ideology, such as communism or fascism. As noted earlier, American interest since World War II has required consideration of the world's ability to destroy itself with nuclear, biological, or chemical warfare.

American interests in the Western Hemisphere, Europe, and East Asia require a certain degree of American interest in other geographic areas which Gordon identifies as level-two interests. For example, the economies of Western Europe and Japan are particularly dependent on oil from the Middle East, and although it was once definitely an area of level-two interest, the Middle East has moved closer to being an area of level-one interest. Conflicting pressures on the United States have increased the danger of America being drawn into any clash between Israel and the Arab nations. On one hand, American sympathy for Israel and commitment to Israel's existence have remained constant when other governments have abandoned that nation for reasons of political expediency; American involvement on the Israeli side in the Middle East has the potential to promote Soviet involvement on the Arab side. On the other hand, Soviet involvement in Arab nations and the need for oil from these nations have balanced United States sympathy for Israel. Thus, though the Middle East may not definitely be a level-one interest, it has moved in this direction during the last decade.[9] Indeed, because the Reagan administration has greatly expanded the Carter plans for a rapid-deployment force for Persian Gulf contingencies, the need for Persian Gulf oil may even be ahead of the U.S. priority in East Asia.[10] However, one must keep in mind that East Asia is a long-standing interest where the United States happens to have flexibility because of a current power balance, and the current situation in the Persian Gulf happens to have put pressure on the United States.

South Asia has moved closer to joining Africa in level three, mostly because of leeway provided the United States by the Sino-Soviet split. These two areas have been of distinctly limited interest to the United States. During the period of European colonial rule, the United States regularly regarded these areas as being under European dominance. Flurries of U.S. interest were evidenced during the 1940–1968 extrovert phase but weakened at the start of the post-1968 introvert phase and are even weaker today. Currently, United States interest in South Asia and Africa is probably limited to maintaining accessibility.[11]

American wars and near wars can be related to the above interests. Whenever such conditions threaten, America becomes war prone because of the demands of interest. Despite fluctuations in public mood and in the nature of United States foreign policy, Gordon would argue that interests generally have been consistently pursued during this century.[12] Nevertheless, nations do not always act or think in terms of their best interest. Gordon does not analyze specific actions at specific times in terms of public mood, and he seems to view foreign policy makers as somewhat apart from public mood influence. Mood, however, is also involved: it emphasizes specific enemies, acts for ideological reasons, and influences the proneness to war.

THE MOOD/INTEREST CONFLICT

Successful pursuit of national interests implies the use of some degree of power. The American liberal orientation includes a distaste for power politics and, subsequently, for the notion of pursuing interests. Therefore, in order to make politico-military interests palatable to the public, American leaders have used what are today known as "Madison Avenue" techniques. Euphemizing interests in terms like "Manifest Destiny," "Anticommunism," and "self-determination" has not only allowed pursuit of interests, but has also produced popular slogans which have remained in the American mind after their usefulness has ended. Leaders, empowered by election, are forced to carry out policies that are not always in the American interest. Such "packaging" of interests and its resultant effects are prime motivators of the extreme fluctuations of mood and policy.

Prevention of one-nation dominance in Europe and Eastern Asia prior to World War II could be achieved through insuring that two or more viable political groups existed in both areas. In times of extreme introversion, such as the late 1930s, the United States did too little to maintain this interest. Since 1945, the United States has had to assume an active role in order to maintain the European and East Asian balances. Most of this action was during an extrovert phase, and by the late 1960s more was being done than was required. In the mid-1970s, the United States reached a desirable level of activity. However, the current continuing introversion involves the danger of disastrous neglect.

Perhaps the real problem lies in the demand of the public for clear images of ambiguous situations, images which are necessarily discredited by the complexity of world events. The argument of the mood/interest theory is not for a curtailment of democracy, but rather for citizen recognition of the conflict between their attitudes and the reality of international politics.[13]

The Mood/Interest Conflict Proposition of the mood/interest theory emphasizes this basic conflict. Each new mood phase starts as a justifiable reaction to the excesses of the previous phase. Time is required for the excesses to be corrected. Then the phase passes through a middle-range viable interest zone and finally concludes in unchecked excesses setting the stage for the opposite phase. In this manner the regularly undulating curve of the mood/interest theory is perpetuated.

When the fluctuating mood curve is superimposed on the ever-rising level of activity required to realize interests, the mood curve becomes one of extrovert rise and introvert plateau. It is important to realize that the mood curve taken alone follows a rise and fall pattern like other cyclical theories. Thus, in the largest sense, the United States has been forced to adjust to the ever-increasing level of activity that requires the world situation to meet interests. However, the introvert/extrovert mood curve dominates in the short-term and often forces the United States to act outside of its interest zone at the beginning and end of mood phases.

Such a pattern suggests that the turning points of the curve are possibly the necessary adjustments of a democratic society whose foreign policy activities and public mood must be somewhat compatible with the pursuit of national interests, a requirement for survival in the international system. Thus, during the brief period of time before each phase changes (possibly two to seven years), the prevailing mood has become powerful enough to prevent United States leaders from always acting within the national interest. The policy of the first few years after the phase change may also be in conflict with United States interest, because the actions and attitudes just preceding the shift must be corrected before the United States can again act realistically.

It is apparent that there are internal and external forces behind the mood fluctuation. The internal mood of the nation may cause the country to reach one extreme, but mood can vary only so far from external realities represented by the interest zone before it is forced to turn once again toward true interests. For example, during the 1930s public mood forced the nation deep into introversion, but the external realities of World War II represented by the later bombing of Pearl Harbor forced the mood to change. In such instances, external realities are an important force preventing even greater extremes.

When the rising level of United States national interest is added visually to the mood curve, the resulting illustration is figure 6. Both of these depictions represent an average from which there can be some individual variation. Changing American foreign policy moods are depicted by a line that undulates in an upward direction. A constantly rising zone of actions in accord with the United States' interests is reflected by the inclined shaded area. While the overall number of actions required to achieve the United States' national interest has risen steadily in the past and is continuing to rise, the number of required actions might level off or even decline in the future.[14] The conflict in the

Figure 6. The Mood/Interest Conflict

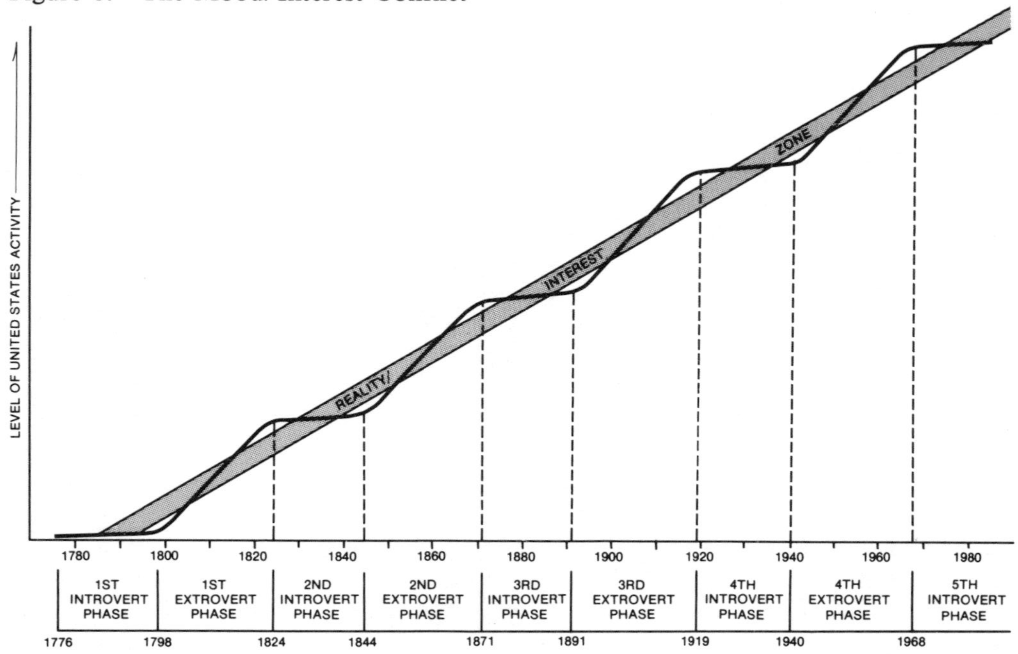

The curve represents the public mood, the fluctuations of which, over the course of time, reflect the alternating attempts of American liberalism to change international politics. The shaded area (reality/interest zone) represents the interim period during which liberal mood and politico-military interests are in harmony. The curve extended above or below the reality/interest zone reflects periods of excessive extroversion or introversion, respectively, demonstrating that a new introvert or extrovert phase begins at a time when overall mood leans strongly in the opposite direction.

diagram is basic: the American public with its changing mood curve is in opposition to the dictates of the international system, represented by the shaded area. Moods are sometimes in accord with interests, but periodically they are not.

Analysis even indicates that there is a lapse before the effects of neglect of interests is felt. If this is the case, the mood/interest cycle would be particularly difficult to overcome because actions causing problems can occur a few years in advance of the problems. Thus, during the 1919–1940 introvert phase, the weak U.S. response to the invasion of Manchuria in 1931–1932 could have set the stage for problems from 1935 to 1939. Yet this nation's overall policy in 1931–1932 could have been realistic. The same might be said of President Eisenhower's overall policy from 1953 to 1961, even though certain initial moves were made in Vietnam during those years. Operation of lead time could make it even more diffiicult to break the mood/interest conflict pattern.

INTERESTS, MOODS, AND WAR

A nation's wars are the most emphatic expression of its foreign policy. If the mood/interest theory's validity is to be advanced, American wars should fit into this framework, relating American wars to foreign policy interests and looking at both the wartime dissent and the results of war.

American wars and near wars can be related to the pursuit of United States interests which have grown in scope and complexity over time within the constraints of liberal public moods. Following a period of introversion and a difficult attempt at political and commercial neutrality, the United States entered its first phase of extroversion under the cautious John Adams, who directed an undeclared naval war with France from 1798 to 1800. During this same extrovert mood phase, the United States fought the Barbary State of Tripoli from 1801 to 1805, finally ending the Barbary nuisance in an 1815 war with Algiers.

Like most of the major military actions of this phase, the War of 1812 was directly related to America's interest in freedom of the seas. The United States contentions with Great Britain and earlier with France might also be related to the prevention of one-nation dominance in Europe. Many early American presidents had served as secretary of state and were adept at playing European powers against each other. Although probably not engaging in war with France or Great Britain specifically to combat one-nation dominance in Europe, America nevertheless seems to become war prone whenever such dominance is threatened. Whatever its motivations, the War of 1812 began amidst a public clamor for action, although war was declared by the narrowest margin ever.[15] The fact that it was even declared, the preceding large turnover in the Congress, and the strength of the War Hawks,[16] is indicative of this public clamor, especially since the United States and Great Britain were approaching a settlement on the major disputed issues. The dissent that existed had to be tolerated because of some regional concentration (New England) and the danger that undue suppression might have posed to the very existence of the young United States. The War of 1812, occurring during the middle third of an extrovert phase, ended with a virtual restoration of the prewar status quo. Liberal America had been too fixated on extroversion to easily negotiate a settlement, but became flexible enough over time to end conflict with no worse than a stalemate solution to a war which had involved a threat to its territorial integrity.

The second American extrovert phase had scarcely begun when war was declared on Mexico in 1846 with great popular and congressional support.[17] Prevailing American sentiment saw the territorial gains of the war as contributing to the fulfillment of America's "Manifest Destiny," but the war also maintained interests in North America. The liberal public, however, had not yet fully progressed beyond the confused period of mood phase transition, and dissent rose as the ambiguity of the war's beginning and other problems became evident.[18] Dissent was tolerated because, as in the War of 1812, there was some regional concentration of dissent in New England; because the public mood was not yet strongly extroverted; and because, after some initial military engagements, victory over Mexico seemed imminent. In contrast to the War of 1812, but perhaps as an adjustment to the introversion which had characterized American policy until 1844, the Mexican War was settled favorably for the United States under a treaty which provided for the cession of New Mexico and California in exchange for a Rio Grande River boundary between the United States and Mexico and monetary considerations totaling $18.25 million. Even so, the extrovert mood was still consolidating, and prolonged negotiations were undertaken before a treaty was submitted to and ratified by the U.S. Senate.[19]

The American Civil War, an internal matter obviously related to the territorial integrity of the nation, occurred near the end of the second extrovert phase. This war is unique because Americans were the only major participants, and yet mood still played a part in perceptions of it. Before the war, during the middle years of the 1844–1871 extrovert phase, the normal degree of extroversion was a bit subdued by the North-South conflict since both sections were concerned with the question of whether annexed territory would be slave or free. The Civil War engendered frustration and disillusionment as it dragged on, and its fury produced a strong postwar introvert reaction. One can speculate that some of the disillusionment regarding the war was taken out on the South during Reconstruction.

The 1891–1919 extrovert phase included the Spanish-American War, in which the United States intervened in the Cuban situation to protect its developing interest as the dominant indigenous power in the Western Hemisphere. Progress toward a peaceful settlement with Spain had been made only to be eclipsed by the sinking of the U.S.S. *Maine* in the Havana harbor under ambiguous circumstances. Reform liberal concern for the oppressed Cubans fueled a public clamor for revenge, and by a substantial margin, the Congress approved a joint resolution condemning Spanish presence in Cuba. Nineteen of the twenty-one Senate votes against the resolution were Republican,[20] indicating business liberal reservations. Indeed, business liberals on the whole did not favor the outbreak of hostilities with Spain.[21] Dissent was not an important consideration, however, because a swift military victory seemed certain, and, as with the Mexican War, the public mood was not yet overbearingly extrovert.

American victory did come after three brief months of war, and business liberals abruptly changed their attitude as they perceived economic opportunities arising from the American acquisition of Spanish territories.[22] This shift and the fact that a Republican was in the White House encouraged Senate Republicans to overwhelmingly endorse the peace treaty, which contained a provision for the acquisition of the Philippines. Reform liberals, conversely, were not yet so extrovert as to plunge decisively into imperialism. The treaty barely passed the Senate.[23] Many reform liberals continued to disapprove of the American occupation of the Philippines, especially of the efforts to quell Filipino insurrections. In fact, the 1900 Democratic platform included an anti-imperialist plank. However, growing extroversion and an improved military situation in the Philippines gradually minimized the effect of the dissenters. In the introvert 1930s, definite efforts to divest the nation of its major Pacific holding were made only to be delayed by the Japanese attack on Pearl Harbor.

The 1898 acquisition of the Philippine Islands from Spain can be related to the United States interest in preventing European dominance in the Far East. Americans viewed European nations as excessively hungry for colonies and not above banding together to shut the United States out of the Far East. By establishing a foothold in that area, the United States thwarted possible European domination and presaged the Open Door policy regarding China.

President Wilson's actions in Mexico during the years prior to America's 1917 entry into World War I, although inspired by an overly ambitious extrovert desire to help the Mexicans govern themselves, had some relation to the United States interest as the dominant power in the Western Hemisphere and, after a 1916 border raid, to United States territorial integrity. America entered World War I to make the world safe for democracy; the entry was also related to the U.S. interest in freedom of the seas and the prevention of one-nation dominance in Europe. There were numerous dissenters to American involvement in World War I, and they were not readily tolerated. Although the public was beginning to tire of the extrovert mood which started in 1891, the overall extrovert mood was still strong and dissenters had the misfortune of facing and bearing its wrath. World War I, like the Civil War near the end of an extrovert phase, was instrumental in creating a public reaction toward introversion. Perhaps this is because the liberal American public had become so fixated upon extroversion that the nation could not make the necessary adjustments to do no more than needed to maintain its actual interests. World War I, under Wilson's messianic leadership, created expectations that were not fulfilled despite military victory, and resulted in generalized public disillusionment. United States intervention in the Soviet Union after World War I can be ascribed to Wilson's desire for an active American world role and U.S. concern with prevention of one-nation dominance in East Asia. Japan, in contrast to its exhausted European allies, had been greatly strengthened by its World War I participation, especially in territorial gains in the Pacific. Japanese troops, with an eye on further expansion, were sent into Vladivostok, followed by smaller numbers of British and American troops. The American reason for intervention, supposedly to rescue Russian war material and anti-Bolshevik Czechoslovak troops, was actually "to thwart Japan's imperialistic designs in Manchuria and Siberia."[24]

After an introvert period of no effective opposition to Japanese designs on East Asia and German designs on Europe, America early in the 1940–68 extrovert phase entered World War II, acting to protect neglected interests in Europe and East Asia, as well as freedom of the seas. The war with Mexico and the Spanish-American War, also at the beginnings of extrovert phases, similarly were waged in part to redress previous extremes of introversion.

There were fewer dissenters during World War II than there had been during World War I, and there was greater tolerance of their views.[25] The mood/interest theory could be used to explain the numerical difference by observing that World War II posed a significantly greater danger to American security interests, because those interests had been neglected in the introvert years prior to the war to a greater extent than in the extrovert years prior to World War I. The smaller number of dissenters in World War II allowed Americans to be more tolerant. Many Americans also remembered their own introvert mistakes in the 1930s and therefore were tolerant of what they perceived as mistakes of others. A related consideration is that people ahead of the times in World War II were pushing the need for extroversion; their task was made easier by the Japanese attack on Pearl Harbor. As in the Mexican and Spanish-American wars, the American public was in a state of transition from introversion to extroversion, and the circumstances of the times did not necessitate intolerance of dissenters; during World War I the transition was occurring in the opposite direction.

Later in the 1940-68 extrovert phase, America sought to protect its interests in East Asia by entering the Korean conflict. The danger involved in the undeclared war, although less than that in the two world wars, was considerable in terms of possibilities for escalation. President Truman's limited objective of preventing a North Korean takeover of South Korea was foreign to liberal America's "all or nothing" mentality regarding wars, particularly at a time of growing extroversion. In fact, the American liberal public mood generally was more extrovert than the president's policy. Hence, the president's major problem was those who wanted the war fought in a more vigorous manner rather than those who opposed the war. In this atmosphere, antiwar dissent did not constitute a major problem. As with the War of 1812, liberal America was unlikely to negotiate an early settlement in the midst of an extrovert phase but was still flexible enough to settle for a compromise return to the prewar status quo.

In the last years of the 1940–1968 extrovert phase, the United States entered the Vietnam war to combat communist designs believed to threaten one-nation dominance in East Asia. Like the Mexican War, the Vietnam war was begun with a considerable degree of public and congressional support.[26] In both cases, a great deal of dissent was generated over time as it became clear that the circumstances at the start of both conflicts were more complex than had been indicated to the public. In the case of the Mexican War, however, dissent was abrogated by an intensifying extrovert mood and decisive military victory. Conversely, the Vietnam war began in the latter part of an extrovert phase and steadily lost support and gained dissenters as military victory was not forthcoming. American liberals became frustrated with the limited war situation which, like Korea, was contrary to their "all or nothing" war mentality. Dissatisfaction increased. Since the Vietnam conflict was increasingly perceived as posing no major danger to United States security, dissenters were generally tolerated. But like the Civil War and World War I, the Vietnam war produced bitterness, disillusionment, and a reaction toward introversion. American participation in Vietnam involved more than was needed to prevent one-nation dominance in East Asia, and because of the public mood change, it was brought to a frustrating conclusion in 1973, five years into the current introvert phase. After 1969, the real conflict within the United States was between those who wanted to withdraw slowly because of power realities, represented by President Nixon, and those who believed that a faster withdrawal was needed, as represented by many in Congress. The slow withdrawal school won, but at the political cost of a substantial rise in congressional power and a reaction against Nixon's realist methods.

Of particular significance in the history of American warfare is the lack of new politico-military commitments during introvert phases. In the long run, however, the reality of international relations overcomes the extremes of either American mood. After 1945, the United States had to assume an active role on one side of the power balance in both East Asia and Europe to maintain its interests. This eventually led to overinvolvement in Vietnam, and only in the last decade has the United States returned to a desirable level of international activity. Internal forces checking American politico-military actions are likely to be strong over the next few years, which should produce opportunities for the reduction of tensions. During this time American policy could become less realistic and more unilateral, particularly in a politico-military sense. On the surface, the value to other nations of reaching accommodations with the United States might seem questionable. However, a summary of past American wars in relation to extrovert phases indicates that more is to be gained by accommodation than by confrontation with the United States.

America has fought eight major wars since the Revolutionary War. The three wars occurring in the first third of an extrovert phase were not anticipated on the basis of United States behavior in the decade prior to the war, but all three ended positively for the United States. The Mexican War ended in military victory and large acquisition of territory; the Spanish-American War ended in military victory, big power status, and small acquisition of territory; World War II ended in military victory and superpower status for the United States. Such unexpected action on a small scale was experienced by the French and the Barbary states in the first third of the first extrovert phase. In summary, an introvert mood will change into an extrovert mood and there is fury in such a change. The most dangerous situation for an American adversary is strong American action whose thrust can be sustained over a long period of time, which is precisely what can be expected at the start of an extrovert phase. This alone is reason for a present or potential future adversary to be cautious in taking advantage of American introversion. The continued existence of nuclear capabilities makes this situation all the more crucial.

By contrast, the two wars in the middle third of an extrovert phase, the War of 1812 and the Korean war, ended in essentially the prewar status quo. The three wars occurring during the final third of an extrovert phase, the Civil War, World War I, and the Vietnam war, ended with varied military situations, but in each case disillusionment with the war was instrumental in a public reaction toward introversion.

It is apparent that the mood/interest analysis is readily applicable to wars: their justification, dissent toward them, and their resolution. American foreign policy interests at times in the past have required war for effective pursuit; but those interests pursued too laxly, or too zealously, can result in costly wars whose outcomes fail to benefit the United States. These interests need consistant attention, but the shifting moods of the American public manifested in liberalism can prevent it.

As has been asked with increasing frequency in recent years, is it not possible to rise above this balance-of-power situation and move toward a greater global interdependence and peace? A good deal of literature has arisen relating to this subject, some arguing in favor of principles involved in such a move,[27] and some emphasizing difficulties involved because of military power balance structures.[28] The conclusion drawn by the mood/interest theory is that global interdependence is a viable goal and one that the United States should work toward, but overly wishful thinking should not overcome the need to consider basic security. In previous introvert periods, emphasis on economic and humanitarian concerns has contributed to the tendency to neglect security. Perhaps a hard look at American diplomatic history can help avoid this possibility in the current introvert phase.

George Modelski's long cycle theory of dominant world powers must also be considered. Modelski argues that since around 1500 A.D., a cyclical pattern of international politics is discernible. In cycles of a little more than one hundred years, certain nations have held a position of dominant power and have evolved through four subphases, starting with world power and ending in global war. The last cycle, in which Great Britain was the dominant power, ended with World Wars I and II, at which time the United States assumed the dominant power position in a new cycle.[29]

The significance of this cycle theory is that the United States is now in the stage of the current long cycle which Modelski calls "Delegitimization." Thus, the stage known as "Deconcentration" has to pass before the threat of global war looms again. Comparing the long cycle theory with the mood/interest theory, the next American extrovert mood is not likely to occur in the most volatile stage of Modelski's international cycle. If, indeed, this long-cycle theory holds true, there is some hope that the next extrovert period will not be as violent as some past extrovert periods have been. On the other hand, the gradual deterioration of American dominance predicted by the long-cycle theory and the dangers of nuclear weapons suggest that adequate protection of American interests will remain important.

SECONDARY INTERESTS

Economic and humanitarian interests are important to the United States. Because these interests consistently appeal to the American liberal ideology, they receive a more constant attention than politico-military interests and are not subject to the fluctuations of public mood that determine politico-military foreign policy. Humanitarian and economic interests thus are less prone to the problems involved in the mood/interest conflict. Politico-military interests, necessary to the survival of the nation's people and territorial integrity, take precedence over economic and humanitarian interests in the hard world of international politics.[30]

Economic Interests

Economic interests are of secondary importance in the determination of American foreign policy and differ from politico-military interests in their relation to liberal public moods in America. Although ideologically disinterested in politico-military matters, American liberals, especially business liberals, have a constant concern for economic affairs. Economic extroversion, an important aspect of capitalism, is apparent in introvert as well as extrovert mood phases. President George Washington's Farewell Address states that "the great rule of conduct for us, in regard to foreign nations, is, in extending our commercial relations, to have with them as little political connection as possible."[31] Selig Adler's study of isolationism concludes: "Yankee willingness to offer sacrifices of profitable business upon the altar of non-entanglement has been the exception rather than the rule."[32] In 1975 an analyst noted that American isolationism "insofar as it has existed has been specifically political and military."[33] Some more recent sources do not emphasize this traditional distinction between economic-humanitarian interests and politico-military interests when discussing the degree of internationalism in the American public's foreign policy thinking. They do acknowledge, to some extent, a diminished desire for military intervention abroad but do not relate this directly to traditional introversion as does the mood/interest analysis.[34] Economic consistency, as seen by the mood/interest theory, can be explained in part by restraints of profit and loss, which make economic concerns less prone to fluctuations of mood than humanitarian or especially politico-military interests.[35]

Public perceptions of the relative importance of economic and politico-military issues are, however, subject to the prevailing mood. In extrovert phases, economic issues are overshadowed by those of a political or military nature; during introvert phases America directs more time and intellectual energy toward economic issues. This is a difference in relative attention more than an actual fluctuation of interests.

The United States has proved its ability to be economically assertive regardless of public mood phase. During the second introvert phase, President Jackson was quite aggressive in demanding payment of debts owed by the French. In the introvert phase following the First World War, the United States became known as the infamous "Uncle Shylock" who demanded that European governments repay their war debts. Later in this same phase the Congress passed the Johnson Act against governments which had defaulted on their financial obligations to the United States. The current introvert phase has seen a marked postwar resistance to assistance to Vietnam, Laos, or Cambodia. All of these actions can be attributed to an introvert desire to make a point regarding poor politico-military investments of the previous extrovert years: perhaps some money can be salvaged from these investments, or at least more money and lives will not be sunk into a situation regretted by an introvert public.

The operation of business, tariff, and price fluctuations apart from the regular foreign policy mood fluctuations also suggests that economic interests are of secondary importance to politico-military interests. This is not to say that economic considerations cannot have some influence on a mood phase, only that they are not the primary influence. If they were, economic interests would relate directly to moods.

Tariff changes, for example, usually are made in response to different sets of circumstances, rather than foreign policy mood changes. In the early period of economic and political nation-building, the tariff was used as a tool to promote unity, independence, and revenue. Once the danger of foreign attack on the United States faded in 1828, tariffs were reduced. With the outbreak of the Civil War, high tariffs were once again imposed until about 1913. Since the Civil War, "the United States has been in five wars: the Spanish-American War, World War I, World War II, the Korean War, and the Vietnam War, but in none of these wars, strangely enough, has the tariff been raised."[36] A comparison of dates and direction of tariff changes with those of the mood phases in foreign policy indicates that there is no strong relationship between tariff changes and the particular introvert or extrovert phase.

The lack of a definite relationship between business cycles and foreign policy moods is just as evident as the lack of a definite relationship to tariffs. Frank Klingberg observed in 1952 that there seems to be no decisive effect from depressions in stimulating the United States to undertake "foreign adventure." Further, he identified seven significant depressions that occurred during introvert phases and four during extrovert phases.[37] Since that time, there have been the recessions of the 1950s in an extrovert phase and the recessions of the 1970s in an introvert phase.[38]

One economic fluctuation whose dates might be compared to the dates of American liberal mood fluctuation is the wholesale commodity price index as measured by N. D. Kondratieff in 1926.[39] His dates are not the same as Klingberg's, but there are enough similarities from 1844 to 1919, when Klingberg's transition years fell within Kondratieff's six- to eight-year long wave turning points, to suggest economic considerations can contribute to a politico-military mood. One problem with comparing the Kondratieff cycles to American foreign policy moods is that his cycles apply to Britain and France, which have not experienced regular foreign policy mood fluctuations, as well as to the United States. Kondratieff's cycles also do not apply to prices of all commodities and are less regular than American foreign policy mood fluctuations. The later fluctuations continue to be important, but in view of the decline of the gold standard there is debate as to whether Kondratieff's cycles are applicable to the post-World War II period.[40] Work by Jay W. Forrester indicates that another Kondratieff cycle has been completed since 1920;[41] this could mean that the rough comparison with the Klingberg dates can be extended. However, W. W. Rostow argues that changes in the world economy in 1972–1976 might mark the first stage of a fifth Kondratieff upswing;[42] if so, this upswing does not correspond to American politico-military extroversion.

George Modelski has compared his theory of long cycles to the economic fluctuations described by Kondratieff.[43] His findings display a significant correspondence between Kondratieff's waves and the subphases of his long cycles. This leads one to ask whether or not politico-military interests and economic factors might be interrelated to the point that they are inseparable. The correspondence between Kondratieff's waves and Modelski's long cycles helped convince the latter that perhaps this was indeed the case.[44] The mood/ interest theory maintains that economic factors have high priority in the United

States, and emphasis during an introvert mood can make them appear even more important, but politico-military interests are characteristically most important in United States foreign policy.

Several researchers have carried Kondratieff's long waves to the present. One interpretation that has a suggestive relationship with the mood/interest theory is that of Jacob Van Duijn, a Dutch economist, who builds on concepts initially posited by Joseph Schumpeter.[45] Van Duijn divides Kondratieff's swings into periods of prosperity (including war), recession, depression, and recovery. Table 25 (page 188) gives the percentages of introvert and extrovert periods that are consumed by each of Van Duijn's four divisions, each of which is eight to fourteen years in length.

This table indicates that international prosperity phases (which include years designated as war by Van Duijn) usually occur in extrovert periods, while international depressions are exclusively an introvert phenomenon. International recovery tends to be concentrated in introvert times, and international recession is a little more evenly divided between the mood types, though tending more toward introvert phases. Thus, harsher international economic realities seem to accompany introvert periods, while better international economic conditions are present in times of extroversion.

Robert Elder, Jr., and the author have explored these relationships further, comparing mood subphases of American foreign policy with the Van Duijn subphases of Kondratieff. The degree of correspondence between the two was suggestive. It was also found that an American war preceded every international economic downturn defined by Van Duijn, with one, the Vietnam war, starting just before the downturn and continuing through a large part of it. An American war has occurred after every international recovery; but World War II, a war that the United States was, for the most part, forced to enter, was fought during a recovery phase. This Elder-Holmes research indicates that American foreign policy patterns are more regular than those of other countries, and suggests that internal considerations, such as those advanced by the mood/interest theory, are more important in the United States than in other countries.[46]

The world economy appears to have a closer relation to American foreign policy moods than does the domestic economy. This could be due to relationships between the world economy and world politico-military situations. As previously noted, the latter situation, as reflected in interests, ultimately affects mood. Since most other countries do not make as sharp a definition between politico-military and economic interests as the United States, it is unlikely that the world economy and world politico-military trends have as sharp a dichotomy as American trends. However, this does not mean that the internal American mood is a product of economic considerations except in a rather indirect sense. The United States continues to promote economic interests on a regular basis while its politico-military mood fluctuates.

The partial independence of these economic indicators from the fluctuations of foreign policy moods suggests a lack of primary importance of economic considerations in the making of American foreign policy. Indeed, the utility of a country's active world politico-military role as a means of inducting general economic prosperity can be questioned.[47] A recent relevant example is the well-known strength of the West German and Japanese economies as compared to the economies of some countries with more active politico-military roles. Similarly, a study published in 1977 indicated that from 1948–1967, a period of extroversion, "there was little or no correlation between intervention and U.S. business involvements during or after foreign crises."[48] A study based on research in the early 1970s notes that:

Even those [business executives] who would resist substantial cuts in the defense budget seem *unconvinced that such cuts would have important deleterious effects on the country*. . . . Just 33 percent thought such a large cut "would have an adverse effect upon the American *economy*," and only 38 percent thought "a retrenchment of U.S. foreign policy commitments would have a negative effect on U.S. *economic expansion abroad*." . . . we find that the businessmen evidence substantial readiness to see the United States retreat from many of the military and political commitments of world power.[49]

This lack of relationship between extroversion in economic matters and extroversion in politico-military matters is apparent in the ideology of Senator William E. Borah of Idaho, a staunch isolationist, who nevertheless criticized the 1922 Fordney-McCumber Tariff as building "a wall around the United States."[50] The paradox appears again in Herbert Feis's analysis of the 1919–1932 era, which notes that although Americans opposed the League of Nations, they were still "disposed to relieve [world] suffering, to rebuild its destroyed parts and to help it regain health and strength," and that the three Republican administrations of the era "were in favor of our foreign financial activity."[51] Later during this introvert phase, President Franklin Roosevelt successfully pushed for reciprocal trade provisions. The extrovert economics of Senator Henrik Shipstead of Minnesota also differed from his politico-military ideology; one of two senators to vote against United States membership in the United Nations, he still believed that American farm problems had to be treated as part of the world economy if they were to be solved.[52]

Conversely, Americans who tend toward politico-military extroversion may not be so extroverted in their economics. An example can be seen in the current priorities of American labor organizations. Although predominantly extrovert and anticommunist in its politico-military persuasions, American labor tends to favor further restrictions on international trade to compensate for certain difficulties in competing in an open world market. American farmers, on the other hand, while perhaps sharing some of labor's politico-military convictions, are better able to compete internationally and favor fewer restrictions on world trade.

A relevant finding is that of Bruce Russett and Elizabeth Hanson, who conclude that foreign policy beliefs of businessmen are influenced more by domestic ideology than by economic interests.[53] The mood/interest analysis does not deny the role of business leaders in the formulation of American foreign policy. Rather, it suggests that in foreign policy, business leaders, like other leaders, act first in accord with their liberal ideology. Business leaders also pursue economic interests.

The current liberal introvert mood shows the expected propensity for assertiveness in economic matters. President Carter displayed a desire to decrease arms trade and in the case of another oil embargo, to use economic weapons to combat the offending nations. President Reagan has been willing to increase American arms sales in several instances. Such willingness, however, has not been accompanied by a corresponding degree of politico-military assertiveness. This dependence upon economic rather than politico-military clout during an introvert phase is predictable, but rather than proving economic fluctuations, it indicates instead that politico-military answers to foreign policy questions have temporarily been shoved into the background.

Humanitarian Interests

It has been noted that American liberal ideology contains an inherent aversion to matters of a politico-military nature. A more constant concern—especially of reform liberals—has been humanitarian interests, not only in domestic issues but also in American dealings with other nations. Throughout American history, medical and religious missionaries have promoted these humanitarian interests. Humanitarian concerns are more variable than economic concerns whose variation can be checked by profit-and-loss considerations, as well as by ideology; however, both are less variable than politico-military concerns. Nevertheless, humanitarianism in foreign policy can vary in meaning and application in the introvert and extrovert mood phases.

During the second introvert phase, 1824–1844, Americans expressed humanitarian concern for the people fighting against authoritarian control by European governments. In 1830 President Jackson and members of his cabinet appeared at rallies supporting the July Revolution in France.[54] Later in the decade, Americans were sympathetic to Canadian insurgents fighting for greater rights against the British government. The third introvert phase, from 1871 to 1891, witnessed American involvement in the recently established International Red Cross and the 1882 signing of the humanitarian Geneva Treaty of 1864 by President Chester Arthur[55] at the same time that the United States was avoiding politico-military involvements. The fourth introvert phase, like those before it, saw humanitarian concerns remain constant when politico-military concerns had diminished. Although a marked lack of enthusiasm for international involvement characterized this period, Herbert Feis has pointed out that Americans were "pleased" by their humanitarian efforts to relieve suffering and to rebuild certain areas destroyed by World War I.[56] The Neutrality Acts of the latter part of this phase were not applied against China, the underdog, in its struggle with Japan. Considerable missionary influence was felt regarding China policy, and the United States consistently maintained a deep humanitarian concern for the welfare of the Chinese people, as well as concern about growing Japanese influence.[57]

Humanitarianism during extrovert phases is more likely to evolve into politico-military involvement than during introvert phases. Such was the case in the 1890s when humanitarian concern over the oppressed Cubans contributed to the outbreak of the Spanish-American War. Similarly, post-World War II humanitarianism was eventually translated into anticommunist support. Following the war, Americans expressed sympathy for the suffering millions of war-devastated Europe. Secretary of State George Marshall publicly suggested that economic assistance be given to all European countries willing to cooperate with others in self-help efforts. The Soviet Union was asked to participate but was not interested, nor did her satellites become part of the Marshall Plan. America's growing extrovert mood, stimulated by the February 1948 political coup that delivered Czechoslovakia to the communists, strengthened domestic support for economic aid, and the Marshall Plan was passed by Congress in April 1948. Economic constraints are of less concern to humanitarian-based foreign policy formulation during such extrovert phases than during introvert phases, such as the one following World War I when the United States demanded repayment of European war debts.

Politico-military considerations are particularly prone to override economics during extrovert phases; following World War II, most Americans grew to believe that economic aid would strengthen the anticommunist forces of the world through a prosperity which would stimulate "free world" military and political strength. However, military aid soon proved popular with an increasingly extrovert public because this aid could be used to directly resist communism, a humanitarian purpose to the American liberal thinking of the time. In fact, military aid became so popular that the military rationale was soon used as a reason for the United States to provide economic aid even to countries where a postwar emergency argument was not applicable. Such military rationale was usually able to carry the day against the many foreign aid opponents who worried about economy in government and attention to domestic needs. Thus, a genuine humanitarian concern evolved into a definite politico-military concern during an extrovert phase.

The Peace Corps was created during the height of the 1940–1968 extrovert phase under John Kennedy's administration. President Kennedy's purpose in establishing the Peace Corps was to foster beneficial personal relationships between American volunteers and nationals of foreign countries where Peace Corps workers were providing aid and skilled services. This was an impressive foreign policy innovation, which was intended to be free of other foreign policy influences and thus nonpolitical in nature. The Peace Corps, a humanitarian gesture by liberal America to the disadvantaged countries of the world, enjoyed wide support when it was initiated, worked well abroad, and was in full accord with the extrovert mood of the times rationalized in appealing humanitarian terms.

Changing desires of recipient countries, budgetary pressures, and other considerations have led to a reduction in the size of the Peace Corps, but it still enjoys widespread popular support among the liberal public. Volunteer applications have been on the rise and the program seems to be a vigorous, ongoing operation.[58] The continued support of this program in the face of an introvert mood is significant. It demonstrates the strength of liberal America's humanitarian concerns and suggests that a cause rationalized and sold to the public in humanitarian terms can be sustained independently of the effects of American foreign policy moods.

Interest in foreign aid delivered with a politico-military rationale has significantly diminished during the current introvert phase. The "military strength against communism" argument has weakened in relation to economy in government, humanitarian, and domestic concerns. United States official development assistance to foreign countries has declined as a percentage of Gross National Product and in relation to percentages of aid given by other countries.[59] The foreign aid that remains is rationalized more by humanitarian interests and less by politico-military concerns than was previously the case. President Carter, in particular, was interested in humanitarian aid to Third World countries.

Much politico-military aid in this introvert phase has been seriously contested. After the 1973 Paris agreements, Congress was ready to allow South Vietnamese military equipment levels to decline, and in 1974–1975 Congress enacted a troublesome embargo on arms to Turkey. High levels of American aid continue to the Middle East, however, in hopes of encouraging an Arab-Israeli settlement in that area.[60]

The American public's attitude toward arms sales has been generally negative. President Carter appealed to this sentiment during his election campaign, and while in office attempted to decrease military sales with limited success. The United States, no longer so concerned with strengthening anticommunist forces, is more willing to give aid for humanitarian purposes; but bilateral aid has recently been given more emphasis than multilateral aid.

Humanitarian concerns in the form of human rights have recently gained attention. President Carter's reform liberal emphasis on such matters was pursued to the detriment of amicable relations with the Soviet Union and some Latin American countries. Congressional enthusiasm for promoting human rights at times even surpassed that of the Carter administration during the consideration of foreign aid measures.[61] The recent humanitarian emphasis in foreign aid might serve to lessen resistance to such aid during this introvert phase in the same manner that the politico-military rationale lessened resistance during the last extrovert phase.

Frank Klingberg mentions a current "consolidation (idealism)," Western or possibly world, cultural cycle phase which indirectly affects American foreign policy. This idealism should add to the normal strength of humanitarian considerations in American foreign policy over the next several years and perhaps even spur resolution of other foreign policy issues. Thus, in Klingberg's opinion the next extrovert phase has the potential to be less violent than previous extrovert phases.[62]

Humanitarian interests appear more important during introvert phases than during extrovert phases because of reduced concern about politico-military interests during introvert phases. Yet, overall humanitarianism is a constant concern of United States foreign policy.[63]

In the end, politico-military interests are still the deciding consideration in American foreign policy, especially in relation to the mood/interest conflict. Other cyclical theories offer at least some hope for the prospect of relating foreign policy issues. George Modelski's theory of long cycles indicates a relatively calm period ahead and his cycles seem to relate to Kondratieff's economic cycles. Also, Klingberg's "consolidation" phase in the world cultural cycle indicates the possibility of a significant change in attitude. If the indications of these theories are valid, and if our foreign policy is managed carefully, the United States might be able to avert some of the past problems of extrovert abuses in the coming extrovert phase. However, the future of American foreign policy cannot be forgotten in terms of the mood/interest theory, because this theory does not conclude with the same optimism as the others and is the one which most emphasizes American actions and ideologies.

AN APPLICATION: AMERICAN FOREIGN POLICY ON SIX GEOGRAPHIC REGIONS

The following section applies the Interests Proposition and the Mood/Interest Conflict Proposition to six geographic regions. This application illustrates the utility of the propositions in analyzing and prioritizing American foreign policy toward North America and the High Seas, Latin America, Europe, East Asia, the Middle East and North Africa, and South Asia and Sub-Saharan Africa.[64]

Two measures were utilized in this analysis as a check against excessive selectivity. First, the number of times a geographic area was mentioned in a diplomatic history textbook from 1776 through 1967 was charted by region and by mood phase. The same source was used to prepare the event chart for each region,[65] which facilitated comparison among mood phases and regions and also helped to minimize observations made out of context. The results of this study are presented in table 26 (page 189).

A number of conclusions can be drawn from a quick overview of the table. Overall patterns show (1) a significant increase in the level of activity over the past one hundred fifty years, (2) a definite alternating up and down pattern in activity, both by raw figures and by average of actions per year in each phase, and (3) a relatively heavy amount of activity in the first fifty years, most likely due to the needs of settling a new nation (note that these actions take place almost exclusively in North America and Europe). By regions, the following can be seen: (1) U.S. actions regarding North America and Latin America most closely follow the alternating introvert/extrovert pattern, (2) U.S. actions regarding Europe evidence a steady drop between 1776 and 1890, followed by a very sharp increase through 1967, and (3) U.S. activity in the Middle East and North Africa, and South Asia and Sub-Saharan Africa all show an increase, primarily since 1940, whereas East Asia has basically seen a steady increase for more than two hundred years. These observations are generally supportive of comments raised in the sections on each region. A survey of a variety of literature on United States policy toward Latin America, Africa, and South Asia to determine the extent to which each of the propositions can be related to such literature supports the concept of a public-dominated inconsistency in United States pursuit of its geographic interests.[66]

North America and the High Seas

Foreign policy problems in North America and on the High Seas naturally posed a greater threat to the United States in its earlier history than today. The United Kingdom was responsible for a substantial portion of these problems, since it ruled Canada directly until 1867 and had considerable influence on the High Seas through the early twentieth century. Although earlier relations with France, Spain, Mexico, and Russia also related to the United States position in North America and on the High Seas, the emphasis here will be placed on the more important relations involving Britain's navy and Canada.

The Interests Proposition and the Mood/Interest Conflict Proposition can be seen throughout the history of the United States' dealings with Canada and Great Britain. The mood/interest conflict is illustrated by the fact that after American demonstrations of extroversion, settlements usually favor the United States; but after a demonstration of introversion, less favorable settlements are usually reached.

The 1794 Jay Treaty, barely ratified by the Senate in 1795 near the end of an introvert phase, settled a number of issues remaining from 1783 and the end of the Revolutionary War on terms less than favorable to the United States.[67] After the Revolutionary War, European powers were rarely in a position to threaten United States dominance in North America due to geographic distance. Nevertheless, the United States worked to preserve its continental dominance with particular intensity during extrovert phases. In 1802–1803 when France was contemplating actions in Louisiana, the United States was willing to act to protect its position. Likewise, British actions in Texas, Oregon, and Canada at times resulted in strong United States reactions. After displaying its extroversion in the War of 1812, the United States made favorable settlements in the "Friendly" Conventions of 1815–1818. President Adams fumbled on the West Indian trade question in 1825, but a more introvert United States under President Jackson was willing to settle the matter in 1830, essentially on the United Kingdom's proposed 1825 terms.

The Webster-Ashburton Treaty of 1842, which was a compromise containing the precise demarcation of the United States border with Canada in the area of Maine was signed just before the end of the 1824–1844 introvert phase. After demonstration of some extrovert assertiveness, the Oregon boundary with Canada was settled on more favorable terms in 1846. A ten-year recipriocity treaty was signed with Canada in 1854. The Alabama Claims settlement of 1871 settled many of the United States–British problems from the Civil War, but there was a legacy of unsettled problems with Canada during the 1871–1891 introvert phase. An 1893 arbitration settlement was reached concerning sealing in the Bering Sea.

After American extroversion in the Venezuelan Boundary Crisis of 1895 and the Spanish-American War, a number of other issues were settled. For example, fisheries and sealing settlements were made in 1909–1912. United States entry into World War I on the British side caused American foreign policy toward Britain and Canada to progress beyond the point where any real possibility of war existed. Still, fluctuations prove that United States-British and United States-Canadian relationships are influenced by the conflict between American moods and realistic, politico-military interests. For example, in the introvert year 1932 the United States Senate rejected the St. Lawrence Seaway Treaty, but in the extrovert year of 1954 an agreement was reached to construct it.

Today if the United States allows its mood to adversely affect its naval power, there is the threat of Soviet denial of freedom of the seas; indeed, during the last ten to fifteen years, the Soviet Union has dramatically increased her naval capabilities and assertiveness on the high seas.[68]

Latin America

Latin America is of considerable importance to the United States. Since World War I when the United States emerged as a world power, foreign policy toward Latin America has vacillated in the context of the overall mood/interest conflict. Perhaps unintentionally our Latin American policy has been used to balance extrahemispheric policies. Because of weakness elsewhere, United States ties with Latin America were strengthened during American introversion prior to World War II. After 1947–1948, as the United States increased involvement throughout the world, Latin America tended to be placed on the "back burner" and was not moved from that level of importance until it became essential to the American interest, particularly during the early 1960s.

Evidence suggests that the areas which receive a large share of diplomatic attention in introvert periods tend to be the same areas that received major attention in the previous extrovert period. Thus, as Latin America was a major focus of foreign policy during the 1891–1919 extrovert phase, it was also attended to fairly often in the 1919–1940 introvert phase. During the most recent extrovert phase, however, Latin America received relatively little attention compared to Europe and East Asia, suggesting that it might be less popular in the current introvert phase. Considering lukewarm support for some of President Reagan's attempted actions in Central America, this lack of popularity still seems to be the case. However, the strategic importance of Central America and the Caribbean has at times forced strong American action, as during the 1940–1968 extrovert phase and the post-1968 introvert phase.

One consistent pattern that the United States has exhibited toward Latin America is a greater willingness to become involved in the nations of the Caribbean and Central American region than in other Latin American nations. This is perhaps due to the idea that the Caribbean Basin is our "third border" and that the area has a significant bearing on United States affairs.[69] In any case, United States inconsistency in foreign policy has had a greater impact on the Caribbean and Central America.

During the 1776–1798 introvert phase America was more concerned with its own consolidation than with Latin America; the only exceptions occurred when events directly affected this nation, such as those related to the mouth of the Mississippi River. As the 1798–1824 extrovert phase grew in intensity, some Americans provided help to Latin American forces fighting for independence. The Louisiana Purchase was made early in the phase and Florida was obtained late in the phase. The Monroe Doctrine, asserting a strong United States role in preserving the noncolonial portions of the Western Hemisphere and pledging that the United States would not intervene in European internal concerns, was proclaimed in 1823 just before the 1824 return to introversion.

Bickering in Washington delayed the departure of the two American delegates to the 1826 Panama Congress of Latin American republics and neither delegate ever arrived. As mood would indicate, the Monroe Doctrine was not invoked against European actions during most of the 1824–1844 introvert phase,[70] and Texas was not annexed when the opportunity arose. However, the 1844–1871 extrovert mood phase saw the application of the Monroe Doctrine, American annexation of Texas, acquisition of the present American Southwest from Mexico, and a strong post-Civil War indignation over French actions in Mexico.

In the introvert year of 1873 *The Virginius,* a ship illegally registered in the United States and running guns to Cuba, was seized, and its crew and passengers, including eight Americans, were shot; yet public reaction was not decisive. The 1871–1891 introvert phase also featured a lack of congressional interest in acquiring territory in the Caribbean just before the phase, a relatively mild reaction to a French effort to dig a canal across Panama during the middle of the phase,[71] and sponsorship of a Pan-American conference at the end of the phase. These events were mild in comparison to the events in Latin America during the 1891–1919 extrovert phase, which featured threats of war with both Chile and Britain, and actual war with Spain resulting from Cuban problems toward the beginning of the phase; an active American effort to obtain an independent Panama to facilitate the building of a canal during the middle of the phase; and American intervention resulting in increasing numbers of "protectorates" during the middle and end of the phase. President Wilson's moralistic prodemocracy recognition policy was felt in particular by Mexican governments toward the end of the phase.

United States interventions in Latin America were gradually toned down and eliminated during the 1919–1940 introvert phase. The most significant events during this period were in Europe and Eastern Asia, but the United States mood prevented the application of measures to prevent one-nation dominance in these two regions. Perhaps to compensate for weakness in Europe and East Asia, the United States pushed for strong, unified Western Hemisphere defense. In the 1940–1968 extrovert phase, the burst of United States activity that had characterized the 1891–1919 extrovert phase in Latin America was felt in Europe and East Asia. During this period the United States position in Latin America was one of a low profile, although action was strong at such times as 1954 in Guatemala and after 1959 when communism began to appear in the Cuban government. The current introvert phase has seen a push for human rights in Latin America by President Carter with mixed results. This push was resisted by certain Latin American governments, and recent United States toning down of the human rights theme gives evidence of introvert America's reluctance to move decisively beyond rhetoric in foreign policy.

While President Carter did successfully negotiate the Panama Canal treaties, neither Carter nor Reagan has had much success in increasing politico-military ties to Latin America. As mentioned, Carter's strong human rights policies limited his ability to make politico-military advances in the area. President Reagan, on the other hand, has used a quieter and less forceful human rights stand while trying to form ties, but the American support for Britain in the 1982 Falklands conflict and the public skepticism about the president's Central American policies have so far prevented a great deal of success.

The immediate strategic importance of Central America and the Caribbean, as a geographic area close to one of two world superpowers, creates a residual danger of neglect when the fluctuating moods are focusing mostly on other areas. That residual danger was apparent in the development of the Cuban missile crisis in 1962. In that case, the U.S. had been too concerned with globalism to place a proper priority on its immediate geographic area until the Soviets had missiles placed in Cuba. In 1965, due to extreme extroversion, the U.S. probably reacted too quickly to events in the Dominican Republic. In 1983, during the current introvert phase, the U.S. acted to forestall Soviet-Cuban activity on the island of Grenada. In that instance, U.S. introversion had led the Soviets to think that such a move might be feasible. Because world peace is based on stable relationships, U.S. neglect of Latin America combined with later corrective actions could be dangerous.

Europe

Until 1940 Europe was the center of world politics and, as such, the object of a considerable amount of American indignation over its methods of conducting international political and military affairs.[72] Europe was a low priority area for direct American effort because American problems with European powers usually resulted from situations outside of Europe or on the high seas.

American involvement in Europe during the 1919–1940 introvert phase was concerned with the constant interests of economic or humanitarian issues and war prevention agreements. Americans were not interested in politico-military alliances that would entangle them in European affairs. Conversely, with the beginning of an extrovert phase and America's entry into World War II, the United States became more involved in European affairs. The formation of NATO and the Korean war answered the question of whether the United States would have a land commitment to the Eurasian continent.

Indeed, the growth of American involvement in Europe from 1940 to 1968 can be compared to the growth of American involvement in Latin America from 1891–1919. There is a striking similarity between the evolution of the United States stance in these two different geographic areas during two different extrovert phases. In the 1891–1919 mood phase, a change in Latin American policy was indicated by a firm United States stance on the Venezuelan Boundary Crisis in 1895, followed by the 1898 Spanish-American War. United States involvement in Europe from 1940–1968 started with a major war in Europe against Nazi Germany, followed by disagreements with the Soviet Union, a wartime ally. The bases for a firm stance in Latin America from 1891–1919 were United States interventions and the Roosevelt Corollary, which asserted the right to intervene. A number of moves, such as standing up to the Soviet Union and forming the North Atlantic Treaty Organization, provided a basis for a firm stance in the Europe of 1940–1968. Business liberalism was the inspiration for President Taft's dollar diplomacy in Latin America and President Eisenhower's cost-effective massive retaliation in Europe. Congress soon became extrovert in

Latin America as it passed the Lodge resolution, and the post-Sputnik Congress was critical of President Eisenhower for inadequate defense measures. The 1891–1919 extrovert phase in Latin America was capped by President Wilson's moralistic admonitions to the Mexicans about democracy during their revolution. Similarly, in the 1960s presidents Kennedy and Johnson were admonishing Western Europeans to join an Atlantic Community or at least to contribute more to their own defense. As Latin America continued to receive attention in the 1919–1940 introvert period, to the exclusion of some more pressing interests, so Europe seems to be continuing to receive attention in the current introvert phase.

The strategic relationship of the United States to Europe depends in part on the U.S. relationship to East Asia. Some strategic policy and Eurasian continent questions are best answered in this context. With this in mind, the most logical defense plan from the United States' viewpoint, considering American nuclear force capabilities, would rely on the United States to provide the strategic nuclear capability, accompanied by a conventional capability supplied by the Allied nations of the Eurasian mainland. This "massive retaliation" philosophy was first articulated by the Eisenhower administration. The United States could help in the defense of its areas of interest without maintaining costly conventional forces. The underlying liberal mood accepts the doctrine of massive retaliation in times of extroversion, because the public believes in doing it right or not at all. The public is never comfortable with limited war and in times of introversion would rather avoid conflict altogether. Eisenhower also talked about a presence in new parts of the world at an acceptable cost. As time passes, it is becoming more apparent that Eisenhower's message was tough in order to appease the growing extrovert mood. However, the mood had not intensified to the point that the public demanded action to back up Eisenhower's rhetoric. In practice, the Eisenhower administration did not evidence anticommunism so much as national interest.[73]

During the even more extroverted 1960s under the Kennedy administration, the United States developed a flexible response to counter Soviet aggression with a response comparable to the challenge. The rationale was that this would lessen the chance of the use of strategic nuclear weapons. Kennedy followed the globalist rhetoric of the Eisenhower administration, but was forced to pay a higher price with a costly flexible response capability.

During the Kennedy and Johnson administrations the United States appeared almost equally interested in Laos, Berlin, South Asia, Cuba, and Africa, which lessened the priority of Europe. While seemingly abandoning traditional geographic priorities for globalism, Kennedy and Johnson assured adversaries that American military responses would be equal to the level of the challenge. The responsibility for this extroverted policy, however, does not belong to presidents Kennedy and Johnson, or to other leaders of the period. The mood/interest theory would argue that Richard Nixon would have had a foreign policy as extroverted as that of John Kennedy if he had been elected to the presidency in 1960. If blame is to be placed, it would have to be on the extroverted, crusading, anticommunist mood of the liberal American public of that time.

Accordingly, in 1969 President Richard Nixon began a policy more in tune with the new introvert mood. Balance-of-power techniques were emphasized to lessen the tensions between the United States and the Soviet Union and China. The resulting lesser conventional capability could necessitate the earlier use of nuclear weapons. President Carter's move to the position of peace by example was an expression of the deepening introversion. President Reagan has placed more of an emphasis, in rhetoric at least, on containment of the Soviet Union rather than human rights.[74] However, even President Reagan's firmness over foreign policy issues has been responsive to public mood, as is evidenced by the evolution of his stand on arms control. His rhetoric has not helped our relations with Western Europe, though, as they see the Soviets as less of a threat than does Reagan.

A reversal of roles between the United States and Europe has occurred since the 1930s when America was doing too little to protect its interests as illustrated by the Neutrality Acts. Today, Europe is doing too little to protect its interests while the United States carries the burden of Europe's defense. Any military confrontation could escalate to the point that the United States itself would be destroyed. During the last extrovert phase the United States was too active in providing defense for Western Europe, and today could not abandon its commitment without creating dangerous instability.

The Eisenhower, Nixon, and Ford administrations tended toward meeting a military challenge in an all-or-nothing manner, which does not afford much flexibility in a given situation and can leave one with only two undesirable choices. The Kennedy, Johnson, and Carter administrations tended toward meeting a military challenge at the level at which it occurred, which can exhaust resources by allowing adversaries to probe specific weaknesses with minimum uncertainty and assuring allies that the United States will pick up the slack.[75] Even tendencies between the all-or-nothing and meeting each threat at the level at which it occurs have marked limitations.[76] President Reagan has been less clear about his position on this issue, but he is definitely concerned with building a range of nuclear forces and a sustained war-fighting capability. Reagan has, however, displayed a belief in linkages between different Soviet actions and is linking his policies in various areas together in response. Because this differs from the flexible response approach of the Kennedy, Johnson, and Carter policy, Reagan appears closer to the positions of the Eisenhower, Nixon, and Ford administrations, even though linkage need not involve massive retaliation.

Most American analysts believe that the doctrine of mutual assured destruction is operative to the point that the Soviet Union does not need to be matched in every capability. Persons accepting such an assumption can easily support a freeze of nuclear capabilities. However, the assumption is disputed by some analysts who argue that the Soviets believe in limited nuclear war or that a defense such as space-based laser weapons can be devised. If this is the case, the Soviet build-up of nuclear weapons must be viewed with alarm. Other analysts argue that a no-first-use of nuclear weapons doctrine, possibly combined with high technology conventional capabilities, would help in Europe.[77] Another solution advanced to the nuclear controversy is the high frontier strategy, which seeks to utilize United States superiority in space technology to create a spaceborne, antiballistic missile defense system, among other capabilities.[78]

Perhaps the solution to the problem lies in reducing the extent of the American commitment to the Eurasian mainland: a "Gibraltar" strategy like that adovcated by Herbert Hoover in 1950[79] or a "blue water" strategy like that advocated by Walter Lippmann in 1969.[80] Under either of these strategies there would no longer be an effective American military presence on the Eurasian mainland, and militarily the United States would only be concerned with what happened outside the mainland. This could force Eurasian allies to develop more military capability, reduce prospects for United States involvement in a nuclear war, and enable the United States to choose either a nuclear or other supplemental response with minimum risk of a protracted limited war.

The strategy, however, does not account for the effects of a United States withdrawal from the Eurasian mainland which would probably include a rise in varying proportions of Soviet, Chinese, Japanese, and German power. Note that Germany has been crucial to European power balances in this century. If the U.S. withdraws its approximately 200,000 troops from West Germany, that nation would be placed in the precarious position of having three nuclear powers (the Soviet Union, Britain, and France) in its immediate area. Further, the strongest of the three, the Soviet Union, is in control of East Germany. At the least, U.S. troops would need to be replaced. Should Britain and France grow leery of involvement in this situation, West Germany could be forced to increase its conventional power to the point of alarming its neighbors or becoming a nuclear power. The memories surrounding the start of World War I and World War II could be particularly dangerous to European and, indeed, world peace. A situation threatening one-nation dominance of Europe could possibly develop. The Gibraltar/blue water strategy might relieve the United States of some immediate responsibilities, but long-term difficulties are likely to change in form rather than intensity.

The mature Atlantic alliance is currently facing an uncertain future. It was formed with the idea of common sacrifice with a shared view of a Soviet threat. Progressively the alliance has changed into a defense with a disproportionate American sacrifice, in part because the U.S. sees a greater Soviet threat than do the Europeans.[81] This new situation points out that what one generation and what one country chooses as priorities may not be another generation's or nation's choice.[82] The question for the coming decade is whether United States mood swings and European-American differences of opinion can be modified and NATO revitalized.

East Asia

The conflict between American mood and realistic, rational interests has been apparent in United States policy in East Asia (China, Japan, Southeast Asia, and Northeast Asia). Historically, Europe has been a higher priority to Americans than has been East Asia. Most Americans are of European rather than Asian ancestry, and American policy regards the consequences of United States–European relations as more far-reaching than the consequences of United States–East Asian relations. However, Americans have a particular fascination with China and, before the current communist regime came into power, directed a considerably more enthusiastic humanitarian effort toward China than toward most of the rest of East Asia.

The second extrovert phase was characterized by Commodore Perry's mission to Japan. A continuing American presence in China was strengthened by treaties granting the United States most-favored-nation trading status, along with other privileges, especially in Chinese cities previously closed to Americans. During the third extrovert phase an assertive United States acquired Hawaii and the Philippines and proclaimed the Open Door policy toward China.

The introvert mood after World War I evidenced United States withdrawal from most world politico-military affairs. America did remain somewhat vigilant in East Asia, and Japan viewed this as a threat, but the American public saw no need for military commitments and lacked sufficient armaments and resolve to back a strong policy. At the same time, the United States was anxious to give the Philippine Islands independence. It is not surprising, considering the mood which dominated American thinking, that Japan attacked Pearl Harbor in December 1941.

The fourth extrovert phase began with World War II. American emphasis on European involvement rather than Asian involvement illustrates the priority that United States policy gave Europe over Asia. In 1949, with the defeat of Nationalist China, America's special fascination with China was transformed into a special dislike. The United States initially hoped that the Chinese brand of communism might balance the Soviet brand, but in 1949 this was not perceived as a realistic possibility.[83] The extrovert mood allowed Secretary of State Dean Acheson to establish a defense perimeter which included the nations of Japan, the Philippines, and Australia.

The apparent communist response to this perimeter was a North Korean attack against South Korea in June of 1950. The United States, in an intensifying extrovert mood, was the cornerstone of a United Nations effort to combat the attack. The North Koreans were pushed deep into their own territory until Chinese "volunteers" intervened and stalemated the war around the original 38th parallel dividing line between North and South Korea. A settlement was reached in July of 1953.

The American public mood grew increasingly dissatisfied during the two and one-half years of inconclusive stalemate, which cost the lives of 54,000 Americans. The liberal aversion to limited war held firm, even in the midst of an extrovert phase. However, the extroversion that predominated did not allow America to forget its military commitment. After Korea, American defense strategy changed to massive retaliation, indicating that the United States might respond with its nuclear arsenal to a communist challenge and did not intend to fight another limited Korean-type war. However, largely unnoticed by the public was the possibility that the United States might not respond at all or might again respond in a limited manner.

Soon the new American strategy in Asia faced a major test. By 1954 the French effort in Indochina was crumbling, and direct American assistance was requested. The Eisenhower administration, not wanting another situation like Korea, decided that indirect American assistance after French withdrawal might be enough to handle the problem. The 1954 Geneva Accords established a communist North Vietnam and a noncommunist South Vietnam with provisions for free elections in 1956. The United States soon began providing indirect military assistance to Laos and South Vietnam. Cambodia, governed by the unpredictable Prince Sihanouk, had an irregular interest in American aid. The United States had, in essence, taken a limited risk gamble that a limited commitment to Indochina would help prevent communist dominance in East Asia.[84] For numerous reasons, including the fact that the United States and South Vietnam did not sign the 1954 accords, the promised free elections were not held in Vietnam.

American policy in mainland Southeast Asia was more ambiguous than ambitious. American reluctance to get involved directly related to definite desires for peace in the area and a minimum commitment of American effort while still containing communism. However, direct support of the indigenous people of the area was necessary for a successful American effort. In essence, the United States had four potentially contradictory policies: containment, maintaining general peace, minimum effort, and indigenous support.[85] These four 1954 policies replaced earlier American policies of containment, peacefully resolving colonialist-nationalist disputes, avoiding direct American responsibility, and aiding the people of the area in a missionary/humanitarian sense.[86] The years 1948–1950 saw the containment of communism gain support as the situation in China continued to deteriorate.

The American extrovert mood gained such strength that containment could not be down-played prior to 1968. Simultaneously, the United States escalated all four 1954 policies until 543,500 American troops were in South Vietnam at a cost of up to $28.8 billion annually.[87] After 1968, the United States deescalated all four policies at once until communist military efforts decided the issue in 1975. This unintended situation can be viewed as the logical result of inconsistent American policies dictated by changing moods reacting to complex events. The business liberals who were naturally strong in the Eisenhower, Nixon, and Ford administrations tended a bit more toward the minimum effort than the indigenous support policy, while the reform liberals in the Kennedy and Johnson administrations evidenced a bit more interest in indigenous support than minimum effort. Still, all four policies were almost simultaneously escalated and deescalated in the Southeast Asia region.

The important question currently is whether the United States would be prepared to take a more active role if required by a changed East Asian power balance. If Japan, China, the Soviet Union, and India remain in their present configuration, the current degree of American introversion toward East Asia may be relatively harmless. But if the multipolar balance of power falters, America could be in a difficult position. Indeed, the United States has had numerous economic problems with Japan. Events and situations change rapidly, but the United States has so far had enough leeway in the current introvert phase to give limited politico-military attention to Asia. The danger is that an extreme introvert mood could blind Americans to events upsetting the current precarious balance, such as a Sino-Soviet reconciliation, a strong Japanese military role, or Russian preoccupation in European affairs accompanied by a strong Chinese air/sea capability.

Strong American introversion in a world where possibilities such as the above might materialize could threaten one of America's major foreign policy interests—prevention of one-nation dominance in East Asia. A very real potential for misunderstanding exists because of the vast differences between United States and East Asian cultures. The importance first accorded by President Carter to moving toward withdrawal of ground forces from Korea as opposed to moving toward settlement of the Taiwan issue is one example of how misunderstanding might have presaged ill will for America's future in this area. The unsettled Taiwan issue had the potential for a much greater challenge to United States interests than did maintaining ground forces in Korea.[88]

President Carter's December 1978 recognition of the Peoples Republic of China seemed to acknowledge this reality, but recent developments in Sino-American relations continue to demonstrate the possibilities for tense situations. Adding to the general volatility of the situation, of course, were Chinese difficulties with Vietnam and the Soviet Union. President Reagan at first made and then curtailed moves toward friendlier de facto relations with Taiwan, which are viewed very negatively by the Chinese. In general, Reagan has continued to pay some attention to American interests in East Asia, perhaps, as with Europe, because the area was of such great interest during the most recent extrovert phase.

There are several reasons why the Sino-American relationship has oscillated so much: America's fascination with China, complimentary and contradictory economic and strategic interests, differing views towards human rights and the role of government, the Taiwan situation, and different cultural values are among the most important. One certainty is that the United States cannot allow its moody fluctuation to neglect its interests for too long, for the relationship could possibly alter Soviet-American relations. The United States is also currently working indirectly with the ASEAN Organization (Philippines, Singapore, Thailand, Indonesia, and Malaysia), in part because Soviet involvement in Vietnam presents a problem. This relationship in turn keeps the United States from drifting too far from China, despite difficulties.

A weak American response based on a long-standing pattern of introvert phase actions to a challenge requiring a strong Ameican response could be particularly dangerous. This is especially true if "during the final third of the twentieth century, Asia, not Europe or Latin America, will pose the greatest danger of a confrontation which could escalate into World War III."[89]

The Middle East and North Africa

Although analysis of previous regions has looked primarily at the impact of overall public mood, an understanding of the impact of particular groups also is important to the analysis of United States policy in the Middle East and North Africa.

The general public mood is dominant over particular interests in the determination of American Middle Eastern policy; thus, general mood conditions the influence of Americans strongly supportive of Israel. Because more Americans are interested in foreign policy during extrovert periods than introvert periods, during extrovert phases particular groups are less likely to have an influence since general public concern is so much stronger. Nonetheless, particular groups may have influence during extrovert periods if they agree with the general public mood, as was the case with Americans of East European origin during the last extrovert phase. During introvert phases, particular interest groups may be allowed strong influence because the general public shows a lack of concern or consensus. The result in the Middle East is a moralistic American position that backs Israel at the cost of energy supplies and good relations with allies and at a time of decline in Israel's international support.

The shift between the 1940–1968 extrovert and post-1968 introvert phases has been accompanied by an increase in the influence of the pro-Israel lobby. This increase can be compared to the growth in influence of ethnic American lobbies after World War I and their continued strength until after the Pearl Harbor attack, when the generalized public mood lessened their influence.[90] It is also important to note that just as these lobbies were stronger in the 1920s and 1930s, 1981 case studies on this subject suggest that the lobbies are again more important in this introvert phase than in the 1940–1968 extrovert phase.[91] Whether or not this is the case,[92] the fact that the subject is again being considered is worth noting.

America has not consistently followed its interest in the Middle East and North Africa, which is to maintain an area open to the United States and its allies. In the past this was a level-two interest as described by Bernard Gordon; yet it is now at an intermediate stage and seems to be moving closer to a level-one interest, such as the Western Hemisphere, Europe and East Asia.[93] During the 1940–1968 extrovert phase, the major link of the Middle East and North Africa to American interest was the need to prevent the spread of communism to Arab countries. Recently, however, emphasis has been placed on the continued availability of oil. Another link between the Middle East and American interests is the danger of escalation of a Middle Eastern conflict to the point of a United States–Soviet confrontation.

America followed its interests during the early years of the 1940–1968 extrovert phase. Americans were sympathetic to the plight of the Jewish people in World War II and their desire for a homeland, and more practically the Jewish vote could not be ignored in the U.S. election of 1948. But most Americans realized that it was in America's interest to continue good relations with Arab countries to prevent the spread of communism. There emerged in the 1950s an even-handed United States diplomatic balance between a pro-Israel and a pro-Arab position. This policy was due in a large part to a balance between a concern about the spread of communism into any Arab country and most Americans' support of Israel. Under this even-handed policy, the United States refused to join in the British-French-Israeli effort against the United Arab Republic in 1956.

A crucial strategic consideration in the area is that the Arabs and Iranians control the vast majority of the land, people, and energy resources. Since the June 1967 war just preceeding the 1968 change in American moods, the United States has become Israel's primary, major power backer in the world. America has done what most of its citizens who express opinions believe morally right, contrary to some professional military and diplomatic advice and at the expense of strained relations with allies and the possibility of a renewed oil embargo.

Efforts by former president Gerald Ford and his secretary of state Henry Kissinger to mediate between the Arabs and the Israelis, while providing substantial aid to both sides, were an attempt to achieve balance in American Middle East policy. The maneuvering room available to the president and his secretary of state was limited by the obvious strength enjoyed by pro-Israel forces in the Congress. The economic effectiveness of the Arab oil weapon (demonstrated since 1973) and recent division within pro-Israel forces has lessened this strength, although not to pre-1968 levels. While the United States is at least informally committed to the nation of Israel in any major conflict in the Middle East, necessary attention to economic matters has meant that the energy problem is increasingly important to governmental policy. Egyptian President Sadat's 1977 visit to Jerusalem forced the United States to resume the mediator role between the Arabs and the Israelis, but with less control over the situation than previously. The Carter administration resumed the mediation role it had temporarily downplayed in favor of a general peace effort. The 1978 United States military plane sales to Egypt and Saudi Arabia, as well as to Israel, and the 1981 sale of Airborne Warning and Control Systems (AWACS) radar planes to Saudi Arabia, illustrate reduced enthusiasm for a strong pro-Israel stance in the face of some division within the ranks of Israel's friends.

The 1978 Camp David agreements represented a potential breakthrough on the road to peace in the Middle East, but in the 1980s the United States must still try to reconcile the Israelis and the Arab nations in the face of increasing problems. The 1981 Israeli attack on and destruction of Iraq's nearly completed nuclear reactor, the assassination in 1981 of Egyptian President Anwar Sadat, a major figure in the peace efforts, and instability and foreign presence in Lebanon all serve to severely complicate United States efforts for peace. While Secretary of State Kissinger and President Carter were both personally active in the Mideast peace efforts, President Reagan has operated mostly through envoys and regular diplomatic channels. Placement of U.S. marines in Lebanon in 1982 as part of an international peacekeeping force illustrates continued American interest in the Middle East. However, strong opposition led to their eventual withdrawal from Lebanon in 1984.

The current introvert phase has allowed pro-Israeli groups to gain power. However, if Israel relies too heavily on this support, it may find that this same introversion keeps the United States from backing its promises in a decisive manner. Should the pro-Israel lobby clash with the general public mood, Israeli supporters would lose, as has happened in the past. American support for Israel is necessary to maintain the power balance in the region so that Israel will not have to rely on its reported nuclear ability. However, in the largest sense, the United States has more to gain from inducing a settlement than from having its policy fluctuate between strong and weak Israeli support. It must be kept in mind that our interest is to maintain the Middle East and North Africa as areas open to the United States and its allies.

South Asia and Sub-Saharan Africa

America's definable foreign policy interest in South Asia is to insure that the area remains open and does not upset the balance of power in East Asia. Likewise, in Sub-Saharan Africa, America's interest is to maintain an open area. Mood has not been as obvious a force in the formulation of policy for either geographic area as in other places because South Asia and Sub-Saharan Africa have not been considered areas of priority in American foreign policy. Nevertheless, public mood has influenced American interaction with both areas.

During the 1919–1940 introvert phase, one of the reasons the United States refused to join European alliances was that it did not want to support the perpetuation of European colonialism in these areas. The United States not only wanted to aviod entanglement in European affairs, but also in South Asian and Sub-Sarahan African affairs. The United States usually supported independence from European Colonial rule first for South Asia and then for Africa as it was granted to major countries in these regions during the 1940–1968 extrovert phase.

South Asia was of the most concern during the 1940–1968 extrovert phase when President Eisenhower's secretary of state John Foster Dulles built a ring of American alliances around the communist world. John F. Kennedy's globalist activity fed interest in Africa as well. The Eisenhower administration supported the formation of the Baghdad Pact (later CENTO) and SEATO. India's opposition to the alliances created ill-will between the United States and India, but the Kennedy administration hoped to cure this by emphasizing humanitarian concerns for the people of South Asia in hopes of stopping the spread of communism. In 1960 the Eisenhower administration would not give direct assistance to the strife-torn Congo (now Zaire) government, but it did support United Nations assistance. The Kennedy administration actively urged United States assistance to various newly independent Sub-Saharan African governments. In 1965 one of several Pakistan-India conflicts arose over Kashmir; the United States, whose extrovert mood was beginning to expire, stopped providing military aid to either side. The predictable result of this action was that India was drawn closer to the Soviets and the Pakistanis closer to the Chinese. During the last decade of the 1940–1968 extrovert phase America was concerned about the spread of communism as black nations became independent from colonial rule in Sub-Saharan Africa. However, toward the end of the decade the Johnson administration was necessarily cool to possible involvement in matters related to the 1967 Congo crisis after there was a strong negative congressional reaction to his decision to send three transport aircraft to the area.[94]

In the current introvert phase the United States has been even less willing to have a politico-military presence in Africa and is therefore more tolerant of Soviet and Cuban involvement than it was during the preeceding extrovert phase. This lessened degree of action is illustrated in South Asia by America's largely verbal stance on the 1971 India-Pakistan war; the United States had tilted toward Pakistan which was split into Pakistan and Bangladesh as a result of the war. In South Asia the current introvert concerns of the United States are peace maintenance, humanitarian support for the people, and improved relations with India. In 1975 the United States was unwilling to become involved in Angola even though the Soviets and Cubans were heavily involved. Although recent United States policy has not prevented large-scale Soviet and Cuban intervention in Somalia, Ethiopia, and Angola, the issue has not been ignored. Resolution of the 1977 and 1978 conflicts in Zaire was left largely to European and African powers.

Related to less United States involvement are the United States views regarding the support deserved by the United Nations, a body in which African nations in particular have a strong voice. In the United States, support for the United Nations generally has declined during the current introvert phase. Foreign economic aid needed by countries in South Asia and Sub-Saharan Africa has remained unpopular.[95] Further, the net flow of official United States development assistance as a percentage of gross national product generally has been declining, especially in relation to other donor nations.[96]

American liberal moods affect policy through a changing emphasis in South Asia and Sub-Saharan Africa. During the 1940–1968 extrovert phase, liberal Americans expected these nations to share concern about the threat of communism—an expectation not always met, as in the case of India. In the current introvert phase, liberal Americans, with varying degrees of emphasis, expect these nations to share the American concern about peace. Thus, in the conflict between white- and black-ruled Africa, the United States emphasizes peace while black nations emphasize justice. In recent years, and especially during the Third World–conscious Carter administration, the United States has increasingly tilted toward black-ruled Africa, though the Reagan administration has slowed down this trend. South Africa is now the only remaining white-ruled nation on the continent, and the United States has emphasized a peaceful settlement of this issue.

The constant United States interest in an open area requires some military preparedness and willingness to take strong actions. However, congressional strength in introvert phases can curtail already established United States programs as well as prohibit new assertive actions. Congressional veto of the Ford administration's efforts to aid noncommunist forces in Angola is one example. Congress has also been assertive with foreign aid programs for South Asia and Sub-Saharan Africa.

The American interest in keeping South Asia and Sub-Saharan Africa open has not been abandoned during the recent rise of introversion. In the short-term, the dependence of the United States and its allies upon Middle Eastern oil necessitates American concern about nearby South Asia and Sub-Saharan Africa. In the long term, the natural resource potential of the area necessitates American concern. The United States presence at Diego Garcia is a desirable safeguard in view of Soviet involvement in African nations such as Angola and Ethiopia. Such United States action also is related to maintenance of freedom of the seas.

An increasingly interdependent world requires enough American action to achieve interests even in low priority geographic areas like South Asia and Sub-Saharan Africa. Declining American willingness to take politico-military actions in the two areas is potentially dangerous.

This anlysis of the Interests Proposition and the Mood/Interest Conflict Proposition as related to American foreign policy toward six geographic regions indicates that the propositions are useful for long-term analysis. The nation's constant interests are definable and at times are pursued properly by United States foreign policy. Geographic regions can be stratified by the importance and the amount of action it takes to pursue American interests in each area. At times American foreign policy emphasizes one geographic area to an excess or to the neglect of American interests in another area. The best way to see the overall workings of the Interests Proposition and Mood/Interest Conflict Proposition is to look at the balance among U.S. policies toward each of the geographic areas at various points in time. The Mood/Interest Conflict Proposition when applied to diplomatic history illustrates the ongoing struggle between America's interests and its fluctuating moods.

4. Mood/Interest Pluralism

The Public Rule Proposition of the mood/interest theory maintains that the public mood is a dominant force in American foreign policy, limiting government action. United States government institutions have evolved in a liberal environment; the liberal's distrust of power is evidenced by a penchant for democratic and limited government with power divided among its various components. The founding fathers, taking such views into account in the Constitution, divided the conduct of foreign policy primarily between the executive and legislative branches by a complex set of checks and balances. This joint conduct of foreign policy became confused in practice and strongly subject to the pervasive liberal public mood.

EXECUTIVE/LEGISLATIVE RELATIONS

The effects of mood fluctuation upon executive/legislative relations in American foreign policy have been particularly important, which is the basis for the Executive/Legislative Proposition of the mood/interest theory. The major mood/interest pattern regarding these two governmental branches are: (1) the relative roles of the Congress and the president in foreign policy formulation are directly related to public moods, and (2) although the president always remains influential, the Congress has its greatest foreign policy strength during introvert moods; the president has his greatest foreign policy strength during extrovert moods. One foreign policy scholar, Michael Roskin, has identified Congresses since the 1870s as either "cooperative" (generally corresponding to the extrovert mood phases of the mood/interest analysis) or "obstructive" (generally corresponding to introvert mood phases).[1] The Executive/Legislative Proposition is well supported historically; exceptions have occurred, but a general pattern is clear.

During an extrovert mood phase, the public is not only willing, but anxious, for the United States to assume a significant role in international affairs, whether it be "Manifest Destiny" or "Guarding the Free World." The sense of urgency implied by such stirring slogans allows little patience for the ponderous workings of a legislature divided by its numerous and diverse membership. Thus, foreign policy tends to be delegated to the chief executive, who commands a large bureaucracy and can move without the time-consuming consensus-building necessary for congressional action. The president has more freedom to act and can do so with a dramatic flair, appealing to the adventurous imagination of an extrovert public. In order to satisfy the public demand for quick action, the Congress, with a large legislative workload, is often forced to let some foreign policy powers slide over to the White House where the decision need only be made by one person. Because of public pressure, the Congress tends to approve presidential action in extrovert phases and may even encourage more extreme action. Congress prodded cautious presidents prior to the War of 1812 and the Spanish-American War during the first and third extrovert phases. During the last extrovert phase, Congress encouraged a cautious President Eisenhower to raise defense spending, and the McCarthy hearings stimulated an increasingly anticommunist position in American foreign policy.

Generally speaking, however, the executive needs little prodding during extrovert phases. Examples of strong executive leadership are apparent in each of the extrovert phases throughout American foreign policy history. During the 1798–1824 extrovert phase, President Jefferson commenced an undeclared war with the Barbary state of Tripoli (1801) and President Monroe issued the Monroe Doctrine (1823), without prior congressional approval. In 1846, at the start of the next extrovert phase, President Polk sent American troops into disputed territory near the Mexican border on his own initiative, thus precipitating hostilities with Mexico. War was subsequently declared by the Congress.[2] Later in that extrovert phase, the Civil War was conducted principally by President Lincoln, who assumed broad war powers from an obliging Congress.[3]

In the extrovert year of 1900 President McKinley, without congressional approval, sent 2,500 American troops to China to join an international force in quelling the Boxer Rebellion. McKinley's successor, Theodore Roosevelt, ordered troops ashore in Panama without congressional approval, issued the "Roosevelt Corollary" of the Monroe Doctrine in his 1904 annual message, and sent the American fleet around the world to impress other powers after a hesitant Congress agreed to the idea. President Wilson, belatedly backed by the Congress, initiated armed action in Mexico later during the same extrovert phase.[4] The leadership roles of Wilson in World War I, Franklin Roosevelt in World War II, Truman in the Korean war, and Kennedy during the conflict in Vietnam dominated Congresses which were usually acquiescent. President Johnson, while possibly not intending to take such a leadership role when he first entered office, felt compelled by circumstances and an increasingly extrovert mood to lead the country in its fight against communism in Southeast Asia. The 1968 shift to introversion was accompanied by an increase in the foreign policy assertiveness of the Congress, felt by President Johnson and especially President Nixon. During extrovert phases, the dominant role of the chief executive in foreign policy is rarely decisively challenged on politico-military matters.[5]

During the most recent extrovert phase there was an increase in executive agreements (bypassing the Congress). Most military interventions since World

War II have been largely executive acts, subsequently funded by the Congress to insure the safety of United States troops. However, along with the shift of attention to the president goes an increase in accountability. Should a majority party president deviate too far from the public mood, the minority party has a chance to win the presidency, as in the cases of Dwight Eisenhower succeeding Harry Truman in 1953 and Richard Nixon succeeding Lyndon Johnson in 1969.

During an introvert phase, on the other hand, congressional power in foreign policy usually increases. The Congress is well equipped to support the types of policies advocated by the public mood. Being slow to act and encumbered by complex procedures, the Congress can easily refuse to support presidential initiatives in foreign policy. The Congress can also assert its right to be consulted because the public is not impatient for action. Congressional workload is less of a limitation during introvert phases simply because it does not require the same degree of preparation to downplay presidential requests for authority, reject treaties, or to queston appropriations for overseas politico-military activities as is required to enact decisive new programs.

The result of the congressional role during introvert phases is the restriction of foreign policy activity. More assertive congressional actions regarding major United States armed actions overseas can be seen during introvert phases than during extrovert phases.[6] The attitude of the Senate toward treaties is a somewhat more complicated subject because of the several different types of treaties as well as the complex dynamics of Senate-White House interaction.[7] In general, the Senate has been most assertive regarding politico-military matters during introvert phases.

The introvert assertiveness of the legislative branch is apparent in past American introvert phases. Under the Articles of Confederation during the first part of the 1776–1798 introvert phase, legislative bodies were so strong that a policy consensus was nearly impossible to achieve. In the 1824–1844 introvert phase, President Jackson carefully referred to the Congress foreign policy questions that involved the possibility of war, considering declaration of war and "all the provisions for sustaining its perils" to be a congressional prerogative.[8] The Congress proved perfectly willing to accept this responsibility, as evidenced by the Senate's unanimous rejection of President Jackson's 1834 request to take tough measures against France, which had delayed in making restitution for American property destroyed during the Napoleonic wars.[9]

During the third introvert phase, presidents, wary of congressional power after Andrew Johnson's impeachment, trod carefully in their foreign policy dealings. The Senate, Arthur Schlesinger, Jr., notes, "freely exercised its power to rewrite, amend, and reject treaties negotiated by the President. Indeed, it ratified no important treaty between 1871 and 1898."[10] Later, in reacting to President Wilson's internationalism, the Congress of the fourth introvert phase assumed a strong role in formulating foreign policy, so strong that "at times it almost seemed that two foreign offices vied with each other at either end of

Pennsylvania Avenue." Indeed, Senator William E. Borah of Idaho, chairman of the Senate Foreign Relations Committee for nearly ten years, conducted some of his own international diplomacy.[11] Isolationist senators, despite the conflicting opinions of presidents and pressure groups, ardently and successfully opposed United States participation in the World Court.[12] The Nye Hearings of the mid-1930s reminded those in authority of the investigative powers of the Congress and set a strong introvert tone which cautioned against any obvious expressions of extroversion. In the late 1930s, the Congress enacted the Neutrality Acts, helping to insure that President Roosevelt would not compromise the introvert public mood at that time.

Although congressional assertiveness has not been strictly confined to introvert phases, careful study reveals definite trends which might be expected to continue in the current introvert phase. An increase in congressional power relevant to the president's strength in foreign affairs is one of the clearest indicators of an introvert mood. Although the extent of congressional power may be debated, the relative foreign policy roles of Congress and the president have obviously been altered in the decade and a half since the end of the last extrovert period. Such change has led to a significant amount of new literature on the subject.[13]

Randall B. Ripley identifies four models of congressional involvement in policy making.[14] Although Ripley argues that all four models are in operation in different policy areas at all times, these models are useful for classifying recent literature regarding foreign policy formulation. The first model, which some analysts argue has been and will remain the basis of foreign policy, is *executive dominance*.[15] Analysts supporting this view say that the executive is the primary source of foreign policy power, and apparent trends other than this are either tempoary or nonexistent, although fluctuations might occur. A second model which several contemporary analyses indicate is the growing trend in foreign policy is *congressional dominance*, which argues that Congress is the major policy initiator.[16] Some argue that such presidential weakness is unwise.[17] The remaining two models are *joint program development*, where Congress and the executive work together on policy, and *stalemate*, where the two branches work against each other thereby producing no policy. These last two models can be combined to form a *co-determination* model,[18] which holds that Congress and the executive share policy-making authority.

Although siding with one or another of these models when analyzing foreign policy in recent years is not easy, one consideration is clear: the amount of literature produced on the subject indicates that legislative-executive relationships have changed. Indeed, some recent empirical studies demonstrate how the role of Congress has changed.[19] However, the mood/interest proposition that 1968 marked the beginning of a new introvert mood indicates these changes are part of the pattern of foreign policy history for the last two hundred years. If the pattern continues, Congress can be expected to continue to have at least the current level of influence in foreign policy matters until there is a mood change.

As mentioned above, it may be difficult to determine the extent of congressional foreign policy power but events, such as the late 1970s Angola situation, show that Congress is indeed able to set some foreign policy. When the executive branch attempted to conduct a secret war in Angola by supporting one faction in a civil war, Congress, seemingly reflecting an introvert mood, exposed the situation and forced a halt. As Neil Livingstone and Manfred Von Nordheim note, "Any future covert action undertaken by the executive branch will have to be relatively small and unimportant or Congress will uncover it and expose it to public scrutiny."[20] President Reagan found this out regarding operations in Nicaragua in 1983 and 1984. Obviously, the Congress does have influence.[21]

Similarly, Congress has taken the initiative to limit presidential military action through the passage of the 1973 War Powers Act, which provides a formal mechanism to help the Congress say "no" to executive military initiatives abroad.[22] Indeed, a 1978 study noted that President Carter operated under more than seventy congressional foreign policy constraints, and advocated repealing only three.[23] Likewise, a 1981 study notes what is termed a "Congressional Spring," a sigificant growth in the exercise of congressional control of foreign policy from 1968 to 1978. The study also argues that Congress's new assertiveness is not likely to be reduced.[24] In the past eight years public support for this congressional role has remained high. Public opinion polls in 1974, 1978, and 1982 found that public support for a more important role by Congress in foreign policy ranged from 43 percent to 48 percent. A stronger role for Congress ranked second of the twelve institutions offered as choices to have more influence in 1974 and 1982, and was third—one percentage point behind the president—in 1978. The choice continually given the most support for a stronger role was public opinion.[25] In terms of the mood/interest analysis, the movement to congressional power started with the introvert mood in 1968, and the new relationship probably will remain until the start of extroversion.

A look at President Reagan's actual, as opposed to contemplated, involvement in El Salvador and Central America shows that congressional control has not decreased. Perhaps executive acceptance of much of the current congressional role reflects a hope to prevent additional restrictions. On the other hand, President Reagan has very meticulously taken into account how Congress operates, especially in terms of its foreign policy powers. Thus, Reagan may have achieved some more leeway in these matters at the expense of giving Congress more of what it wants in the first place.[26] In any case, congressional assertiveness reflects the return to introversion, and may in turn help stimulate extreme introversion if the Congress acts as it has during previous introvert phases.[27]

It should be noted, however, that some of Congress's gain in power over foreign policy matters has been compensated by court rulings in favor of the president. Of several examples concerning President Carter, two that stand out are the challenge by a business of Carter's actions in settling the Iranian hostage crisis in 1981 and Senator Barry Goldwater's challenge of Carter's termination of the Mutual Defense Treaty with Taiwan in 1978; in both cases, the courts upheld presidential authority.[28] Similarly, the Curtiss-Wright case, decided by the Supreme Court in 1936, four years before the end of the fourth introvert phase, yielded increased authority for the president. Although the actual decision had to do with approving Congress's right to delegate certain foreign policy powers to the president, the rationale behind the decision was more significant. In essence, the argument was that the head of government has certain inherent powers necessary for dealing with the current nation-state system, and that these powers and needs of the nation-state system antedate the restrictions imposed on the president by the Constitution.[29] A fourth example of court rulings that benefit the president is the 1983 Supreme Court's decision that struck down the legislative veto. The exact scope of this decision is still unclear, but it could involve such important legislative curbs on presidential power as the 1973 War Powers Resolution provision that allows Congress to direct the president to remove troops engaged in foreign hostilities without congressional authoriza-tion.[30] Here it can be seen that sometimes, when foreign policy formulation leans heavily toward legislative control, the court process in the American system can work toward striking a balance.

Stalemate is a likely condition when and if two disagreeing governmental branches each have significant power in a democracy and refuse to compromise. Even compromise often leads to little substantive change. The mood/interest curve shows a rise and plateau effect when combined with rising interests. Part of the plateau effect could be due to stalemate or small changes during introvert phases when policy is made by both the president and the Congress.

Liberal distrust of governmental institutions has created a balance which encourages both the legislative and executive branches to follow the public mood. In extrovert phases, the legislature usually goes along with a fast-acting executive who is responding to public mood. In introvert phases, the slow-acting legislature usually sets a tone in accord with the public mood, and most executives find it prudent to accommodate that tone. The high probability of competition for public favor, if one branch deviates from public mood, probably precludes a joint legislative/executive attempt to harness the public mood. Is such an attempt feasible within the executive branch alone?

PRESIDENTIAL LEADERSHIP STYLES

In 1975 Samuel Huntington wrote, "to the extent that the United States has been governed on a national basis, it has been governed by the president."[31] The president indicates the direction of United States foreign policy, but is in turn guided by the public mood. Having gained office in part by virtue of his closeness to that mood, the president, necessarily knowledgeable in the machinations of politics, aims to please the electorate.[32] If he fails in this endeavor by being unable to respond to changes in public mood or by initiating policy drastically out of line with the prevailing mood, he will be replaced. There has never been a shortage of potential candidates for president, and the public usually has the opportunity to choose one who is attuned to its liberal mood.

An effective president must be good at interpreting contradictory signals from short-term public opinion. For example, in a nationwide March 1978 poll, NBC News asked about the likelihood that the United States would become involved in a war in the next three years. Over half of the respondents replied that war was likely. A month earlier, the Gallup poll reported that only 9 percent rated foreign policy as the nation's most important problem.[33] Recent public opinion studies show that the importance of foreign affairs jumped for a time in 1980, but that it soon dropped again.[34] The president is thus forced to decide how much emphasis to place on foreign policy in order to head off what the majority of people see as an impending threat of war, as opposed to economic problems which have been the nation's most important concern in recent years. Presidential perceptions of overall mood can be a crucial ingredient in such presidential choices on difficult issues. Thus, in an indirect manner, presidents are prone to follow mood when making foreign policy decisions.

Almost anything that the president does in a decisive manner will increase his public support, at least temporarily, but will this support be sustained upon further consideration of the president's action by the public? Again, the underlying public mood will have much to say in the ultimate determination of whether the president's decisiveness was really wise.

A matter that became increasingly important during the post–World War II growth of the foreign policy bureaucracy was presidential management style. The interaction of a president's style and the public mood indicates that mood plays a dominant role, although style variations can have an impact on policy. Major style considerations include decision-making mechanisms and types of informational advice received by the president. Comparisons of the styles of the Kennedy and Johnson administrations as opposed to the Eisenhower and Nixon administrations provide a clear contrast in styles of managing the large foreign policy bureaucracy that has characterized the United States since World War II.

One view of presidential styles widely accepted by American political scientists is that of Richard Neustadt, who argues that a president should encourage informal competition among his advisors to insure that all pertinent information gets through to him.[35] This argument is similar to the capitalistic faith that unencumbered economic competition will best serve the public, and is a strong argument wherever meaningful competition is assured. Domestic policy is one area of assured competition; Americans have a continual interest in domestic affairs and major domestic interest groups are skilled at making known their desires. However, such is not the case with foreign policy. Both presidents John Kennedy and Lyndon Johnson followed much of Neustadt's organizational advice while involving the United States in Vietnam. There are inevitably many different ideas about techniques for handling foreign policy crises, and an activist group of foreign policy advisors selected during a period of extroversion is likely to present a variety of short-range advice reflecting the public mood. Presidents Kennedy and Johnson received such a variety of short-range advice, more on tactics than on overall strategy, from their decision-making systems of competitive advisors.

It would be beneficial for the president to receive a diversity of long-range advice, in addition to short-range advice, some of which might question the wisdom of the current mood. Advice given by groups active in long-range planning, such as the professional military, and groups having regular contact with long-term foreign trends, such as the intelligence community and the State Department, is complex but should be heard regularly as well. These groups can offer a variety of reasoned alternatives which are formulated independently of American public mood.

During the height of the recent extrovert phase, the type of advice most needed was that emphasizing caution, particularly as it related to Vietnam. During the 1963 controversy over the efficacy of the South Vietnamese regime of President Diem, General Paul Harkins repeatedly posed the question of what would follow a Diem overthrow.[36] Without an authoritative answer to this question, the overthrow was permitted, and the United States was drawn deeper into the conflict. Two years later, CIA Director John McCone cautioned against becoming involved in an indecisive land war from which we "will have extreme difficulty in extracting ourselves."[37] This warning was ignored. During the same year, Under Secretary of State George Ball expressed grave reservations about U.S. policy toward Vietnam.[38] Failure to heed such cautions might have been inevitable in view of the prevailing extrovert mood, but these examples nevertheless show the potential value of long-term advice offered independently of the public mood by bureaucratic agencies like the professional military, State Department, and the intelligence community. Admittedly, other bureaucratic advice was less than cautious, and all that can be asserted here is its value in some instances. An introvert illustration of the value of some bureaucratic agency advice is provided by Samuel Huntington, who says that in the late 1930s the military was more realistic than the public.[39]

Followers of Neustadt would perhaps raise the objection that President Kennedy and especially President Johnson did not tolerate individuals who dissented from dominant administration thinking and that this intolerance was a mistake. Practically, it is unrealistic to expect a president to keep those who disagree with his policies as members of his inner circle, or even to retain people who anger his supporters. However, a president could realistically decide to listen to his bureaucracy on a regular basis even when they are not all in accord. Finally, over-dependence on a set of advisors to the exclusion of the bureaucracy is not politically expedient since implementation of major policies requires bureaucratic cooperation.

If agencies that must execute policy are brought into the decision-making process, then they at least are aware of current policy. An activist style can unfortunately make it difficult for those implementing policy to determine it, because of the premium placed on flexibility in foreign policy by top officials. Without clearly defined objectives, policy can too easily become structured by immediate events which may have disastrous consequences, as in the United States conduct of the Vietnam war.

The regularized and formalized decision-making structures used by the Eisenhower and Nixon administrations were valuable because they brought a variety of long-range viewpoints into the system. The National Security Council system introduced ideas from the professional military, the State Department, and the intelligence community. During the Vietnam war, advice offered by these sources which suggested extremely risky actions was usually rejected by the Eisenhower, Kennedy, and Johnson administrations, although some risky actions were taken. Cautious advice was more often heeded by Eisenhower's apparatus than by Kennedy's or Johnson's. In 1954, for example, the Joint Chiefs of Staff called Indochina "devoid of decisive military objectives,"[40] and Eisenhower did not grant the French request for aid. However, Eisenhower's preference for agreed-upon solutions did tend to prevent the bringing of options to his attention.

President Richard Nixon took office just after the change of the foreign policy mood from extrovert to introvert. He preferred a regularized structure like that of President Dwight Eisenhower, but required his National Security Council to proffer alternatives from which he could choose. Nixon's modification of the Eisenhower system worked quite well although eventually the Nixon system became dependent upon one person—national security advisor, and later secretary of state, Henry Kissinger. Kissinger's conservative realism at least provided some balance to the liberalism of the public mood. Whereas Eisenhower was served well by cautious advice which could temper the growing public extroversion of his time, Nixon was best served by consideration of realistic alternatives which satisfied the new introvert mood of his time. The extent to which Eisenhower or Nixon benefitted from their particular structure, as opposed to their position in relation to public mood is debatable, but each of their systems at least provided regular consideration of extra-mood viewpoints.

An important variable in presidential advisory systems, as analyzed by I. M. Destler, is "how much particular Presidents have favored formality and regularity in the flow of analysis and advice to them." Destler ranks Eisenhower as making the most use of regularized channels, and Kennedy as making the least, with Johnson tending more toward Kennedy. Another variable which Destler deems important is "how widely Presidents have wished to cast their nets for advice." Kennedy is ranked highest and Nixon lowest in this consideration.[41] The important factor here is that Kennedy, while looking for a wide range of advice, took it only within the context of the liberal public mood, minimizing regular and more conservative input.[42] Eisenhower, on the other hand, gave greater weight to these extra-mood opinions and Nixon, while consulting fewer advisors, had in those few advisors some viewpoints independent of the public mood, in part because of Kissinger's conservatism.[43]

The Carter administration preferred a style closer to that used by Kennedy and Johnson. Lawrence Korb notes this change in studying the number of Presidential Review Memoranda (PRM) issued to the National Security Council by President Carter during his first year in office. President Carter issued only thirty-two PRMs during his first year in office, while Henry Kissinger, as the assistant to the president for National Security Affairs, issued eighty-five similar requests during the first year. Korb wrote, "The President thus appears to be moving away from the NSC process to the informal arrangements which characterized the Kennedy-Johnson years."[44] While Carter indeed spoke of reducing the NSC's dominant position, in the end he gave assistant for National Security Affairs Zbigniew Brzezinski an even greater role than Kissinger had, making him the first in that position to have cabinet rank.[45] Yet, it can be argued that this still accords with Carter's activist style, in that Brzezinski was not an extra-mood force; as with most of Carter's NSC, he did not deviate from Carter's policy or public mood. This distinguishes Brzezinski from Kissinger in that the latter's balance-of-power approach often dictated actions and methods deviating from the dominant mood.

President Reagan, on the other hand, did significantly reduce the role of the national security assistant, especially as far as public exposure is concerned, as a result of the general feeling that the assistant's power had gotten out of hand in recent years.[46] Reagan's general style in foreign policy seems rather to be that of a delegator, more so than any president since Eisenhower. Like a typical consolidator president, Regan prefers a variety of input to provide foreign policy options from which he can choose. A system with varied inputs can inherently include conflict. Such conflict has been apparent at times in the Reagan administration, but it should be viewed as a natural outgrowth of a system that allows for different sources of input.[47] Although his system is not as structured as Eisenhower's, it is clear that a delegator like Reagan cannot follow an activist style.[48]

Some changes in the Reagan foreign policy administration shed light on the system toward which Reagan is working. In early 1982, National Security Assistant Richard Allen resigned. He was replaced by William Clark who, though he was formerly Reagan's deputy secretary of state, did not have a professional background in foreign policy. Then, in the summer of 1982, Secretary of State Alexander Haig resigned and was replaced by George Shultz. In both of these changes, the question of foreign policy authority was involved to some degree, and the change was from a strong personality to more of a "team player" type.[49] In late 1983 Clark replaced Interior Secretary James Watt, and Robert McFarlane took Clark's position as the national security assistant. The Reagan National Security Council apparatus has a great deal of power while retaining a low public profile.[50] Consequently, Secretary of State Shultz is viewed more as a mediator and implementer while the president and his aides set the broad outlines of U.S. foreign policy.[51] This evidences the fact that Reagan is pursuing an authority balance in his foreign policy system, leading to a variety of input sources.[52] One such source can be seen with Reagan's tendency to appoint national commissions to offer alternatives when his foreign policy decisions are too unpopular with Congress or the people. For example, he appointed commissions to study the MX missile issue and American involvement in Central America.

Alexander George's study of presidential decision-making suggests the desirability of collegial decision-making and some structured multiple advocacy. These possibilities represent ideals which would take considerable presidential effort to realize, as George himself notes. Nevertheless, George's work represents an important contribution that takes advantage of much presidential experience. Such research might provide an opportunty for merging the advantages of the activist and consolidator style in the context of mood, but it would require a degree of presidential fine tuning of which little has been realized.[53]

A president is naturally unlikely to appoint diversity to his inner circle, but should perhaps aim to introduce diversity into the decision-making system through regularized procedures. The independent advice of the military, State Department, and the intelligence community is at least given regular consideration in consolidator decision-making systems. The overbearing influence of public mood can be countered to some extent when such consideration is given. Bureaucratic perspectives alone, however, cannot balance the liberalism of a president responding to public mood. All that they might do is temper it. The relationship of bureaucratic and other important American institutions to public mood must be analyzed to explain why.

THE FOREIGN POLICY BUREAUCRACY

The foreign policy bureaucracy can be a means of public influence on American foreign policy. In one sense, many American bureaucrats, who themselves can reflect public mood, are involved in foreign policy decision-making. A president who deviates from public mood can expect indirect difficulties from some bureaucrats who might, for example, communicate to a receptive Congress and press. The possibility of such communication can restrain actions by the president.

In another sense, the foreign policy bureaucracy includes those groups most likely to surface ideas not necessarily subject to the prevailing public mood: those professional bureaucrats who are ahead of or behind the public mood, government personnel who have frequent contact with foreign governments, and the professional, naturally conservative, military. These are precisely the groups that would have influence in a presidential advisory structure featuring regularized channels. This type of presidential advisory system is supported as a possible means of minimizing problems presented by public mood.

Although the United States foreign policy bureaucracy, including the State Department, the military, and the intelligence community, has a great deal of potential for decisive participation in foreign policy decision-making, it is less powerful than is commonly asserted. Because the president and his advisors make the ultimate decisions regarding major issues,[54] attempts to attribute major policy decisions to bureaucratic-political organizations are misleading.[55] However, the bureaucracy can be quite powerful in policy-making when there is not an immediate public concern.[56] This is not contrary to the argument that the public determines foreign policy since the public, in essence, abdicates its authority and policy-making power at such times. The concept of the president as ultimate authority is also wholly in accord with a mood-oriented theory which argues that the public controls American foreign policy because the president is elected by the public, whereas the continuing bureaucracy is not.

The question of the proper bureaucratic role in foreign policy is complicated by the build-up of the United States foreign affairs bureaucracy since World War II.[57] This bloated structure makes it difficult to induce creativity and often relegates the bureaucracy to opinions which can be agreed upon by several persons with minimum difficulty. Such opinions lessen its potential both in gaining presidential attention on major issues where alternatives are needed and in realizing imaginative solutions to small problems. The structure does, however, usually minimize grave errors and works against hastily formulated policies. These several considerations are in harmony with arguments regarding presidential style because an agreed-upon solution still has the potential to bring up important considerations apart from public mood, and such a solution works against hasty change.

The Department of State is the logical bureaucratic agency to check United States foreign policy moods, but it is inhibited by a number of considerations.[58] For instance, Foreign Service officers are predominantly reform liberals.[59] This is a disadvantage in terms of a balanced liberal perspective on policy options, but increased business liberal representation alone could not check the influence of public moods. Another consideration which limits the State Department's ability to play a stronger foreign policy role is the tendency of Foreign Service officers to view themselves more as grand policy makers than as technical administrators. That perspective, only partially valid at best, creates some dissonance with other elements of the foreign policy decision-making apparatus, especially the president and his experts; it has already been suggested that major policy decisions most often are made in the White House rather than by the State Department, with a direct concern for public mood in any case. When the grand policy maker image of the State Department conflicts with that of the mood-oriented president, the latter naturally wins.

Modern foreign policy complexities and State Department reluctance to assume managerial responsibilities combined to necessitate post–World War II formation of a number of governmental agencies with foreign policy-related responsibilities, independent or quasi-independent of the State Department. These agencies naturally have their own interests, and foreign policy decisions can represent compromises between agency interests. As a result, the State Department is the subject of considerable intermural bitterness which limits its role in policy-making. Under a strong secretary, the State Department can assume its most important position; however, secretaries are given strength by virtue of their relationship with the president, who usually is very close to the public mood.

Bert Rockman notes the recent competition between the State Department and National Security Council over foreign policy. He states that even with the Reagan administration's diminished overt role for the president's national security assistant, it is recognized that foreign policy power has been steadily drifting away from the Department of State and toward the National Security Council since the Kennedy administration. The president and his team of advisors have become bolder in the type of foreign policy that they advocate while the Department of State has become more restrained.[60] This conclusion indicates that the State Department is even more cautious than the president; however, it also might indicate that in a few instances the department is less likely to support change, which generally has been moving in an introvert direction.

A most important role of the State Department and its Foreign Service officers is that of a force which can work to see that due account is taken of world events and the thinking of foreign governments in the formulation of American foreign policy. The strength of American liberalism can prevent consideration of such aspects without a vocal State Department. In the end, American policy rightly will be based on the will of its people, but the insights that can be gained from the regular contact between the State Department and foreign governments are an important policy influence.

The military, a significant potential force within the foreign policy bureaucracy, tends to be conservative by nature and consistently offers a variety of foreign policy alternatives to decision makers independent of the public mood. The dominant liberal society, however, considers such conservative thinking alien and seeks to either assimilate or isolate it.[61] At various times there have been attempts on the part of liberal society to civilianize the military, resulting from a fear of independent armed forces, lack of understanding of the military role, and more recently, perceived dangers of a "military-industrial complex." Such civilianizing compromises the military's natural conservatism and reduces its ability to provide alternative viewpoints. The military tends to be most conservative when it is isolated, as it usually is during introvert phases.[62]

This analysis suggests that even if the military were allowed a role in foreign policy making, the resulting conservative policy would not long be compatible with a liberal society. Soon the military would be either assimilated in the liberal mainstream (more likely in an extrovert phase) or again isolated (more likely in an introvert phase) by the liberal society. With the reinstitution of the traditional pattern of a volunteer standing army, the military faces isolation once more from the mainstream of American society, and it seems likely that its conservative contribution to the range of viable foreign policy options will be downplayed as in earlier times in American history.

A third possible source of advice in the foreign policy bureaucracy independent of the public mood is the intelligence community, primarily the CIA. However, intelligence community activities are generally directed by the president, who, of course, is responsive to shifting public moods. This is clearly illustrated by application of the mood/interest analysis. Growth and expansion of the powers of the intelligence community coincided with the extrovert cold war events from 1947 to the late 1960s, which suggests that the growing extrovert mood of the American public helped in the development of the intelligence community and muted strong criticism of its necessity and usefulness. As the extrovert anticommunist mood grew, the intelligence community grew. Paramilitary operations, not directly related to the information-gathering mandate of intelligence, were accepted perhaps because they were in accord with the public mood, excessively extrovert from 1962 to 1968. At this point, many questionable activities of the CIA were uncovered; however, due to the growing extroversion of the time, the public was not interested in enacting control measures.[63] When the public mood changed around 1968, however, there was increasing public dissatisfaction with the activities of the intelligence community. Perhaps much of this criticism stems from public application of introvert values to actions taken by the intelligence community during an extrovert phase. In any case, President Gerald Ford in 1976 initiated more action by executive order to reform and reorganize the intelligence community than had any other president in the previous twenty-nine years. Jimmy Carter followed in 1977 by ordering the most sweeping reorganization in thirty years.[64] In early 1978 the reorganization was approved by the president. Control in the form of new supervision and tougher regulations was consolidated under CIA Director Stansfield Turner.[65] This was in accord with an increased introvert desire to curb abuses. The Reagan administration has sought some adjustments to these controls, but the intelligence community remains under tight control, as demonstrated by the congressional furor over the CIA role in the mining of Nicaraguan ports in 1984.[66]

Intelligence agencies continue to operate in the context of a suspicious public mood. The intelligence community, like the State Department and the military, has the potential to offer a variety of independent foreign policy alternatives, but it too is subject to the prevailing public mood. A policy overly influenced by a necessarily secretive intelligence community would be unlikely to be long-sustained by a free and dominantly liberal society. The most that can be expected from the intelligence community, therefore, is objective information on foreign countries. Other actions expected of the community vary according to public mood.

It must be emphasized that the foreign policy bureaucracy is staffed by members of the public. This human aspect means that the bureaucracy promotes public desires at the same time that it introduces other considerations into policy making. Members of the State Department, military, and intelligence community bureaucracies are strongest when they reflect public mood and weakest when they are apart from it. While the president controls their actions, they can expose presidential deviations from mood to public scrutiny.

Thus, the three segments of the foreign policy bureaucracy theoretically capable of offering policy alternatives to check the extremes of mood are constrained in doing so. To begin with, each of the three segments of the bureaucracy must operate in the context of the public mood. There are important situations in each segment: the State Department could use more diversity within the liberal tradition and major organizational reforms; the military is apt to become either assimilated or isolated by the dominant liberal society; and the intelligence community's role varies with public mood. Increasing the size of the bureaucracy is no solution for mitigating the effects of mood fluctuation because the State Department, the military, and the intelligence community already have sufficient personnel. The possibilities of a major reorganization effort likewise are limited. A president cannot easily find the time or the resources to trim and redirect the activities of a large and dispersed bureaucracy which is willing to fight to maintain its size and status; his time is too divided by the duties of his office and the complexities of American politics, as illustrated by President Carter's experiences with reorganization. The most that can be expected is that the State Department will see that the thinking of foreign governments is considered, the military will surface some conservative viewpoints, and the intelligence community will provide reliable information.

In terms of the current introversion, the present bureaucratic situation might be healthy insofar as the inertia of the foreign policy bureaucracy works to slow shifting American policies—a phenomenon which can be helpful when the public mood is favorable to policies outside the zone of United States interests. Perhaps this will temper the probable public desire to have policies that are more introvert than is in the American interest. The prospects, however, are that the public mood will continue to win over the bureaucracy, as it did when the desire of a substantial part of the foreign policy bureaucracy to continue fighting the cold war was moderated after the recent public mood shift to introversion. The realizable role of the United States foreign policy bureaucracy is to execute policy within set guidelines and offer needed alternatives for consideration by the president. This role is limited, but within the framework of the mood/interest analysis can be of considerable importance.

THE MILITARY AND BUSINESS

One of the most often identified national security relationships is that between the military and business. There are many views of this situation, some of which speak of active conspiracies. A more sophisticated version might be as follows: The military desires the most recent, up-to-date weapons systems available. Large businesses and industries, through contacts with the military and government officials, obtain contracts at high profit rates to build such weapons or equipment. Many foreign policy agencies support this military-industrial complex for purposes such as aiding allies, gaining foreign policy leverage, and improving balance of payments. All of this can be said to contribute to the world's conflicts and draw the U.S. into unwise military involvements. Such collusion is often cited as one way the public is prevented from asserting itself. All of this could be unrepresentative of public mood. In reality, the situation is far more complex.

Before World War II a basic conflict existed between American business and the professional military. American liberals of both types were distrustful of the traditionally conservative military. The United States operated with a small standing military supplemented by a large militia, or reserve force. Large professional military establishments were viewed in the same critical light as the European penchant for war. The American business liberal was a producer of goods and services in the modern tradition, while the professional military was identified with the ancient tradition as a destructive force.[67]

Many reform liberals, however, and a number of business liberals as well, believed there was decisive collusion between business which profited from war and the military. The Senate Nye Committee investigations of the mid-1930s helped popularize a belief that tied munitions makers to American involvement in World War I. This belief, which gained widespread support, stated that "Merchants of Death" had sold more to the British side than to the German side and that American intervention on the British side was prompted by the necessity to protect loans granted by Americans for British war purchases. The broad public acceptance of such notions helped to consolidate the American introvert mood in the latter half of the 1930s, when Congress passed a series of neutrality acts designed to prevent the possible recurrence of such events. After the start of the 1940–1968 extrovert phase, the munitions makers theory was discredited and the blame was more properly assigned to the German launching of unrestricted submarine warfare just prior to American entry into World War I.[68]

Since World War II, the need for a more permanent United States military preparedness has been acknowledged by more observers. In order to maintain adequate standing military manpower, the draft existed from 1948 to 1973, five years into the current introvert phase. Weaponry became more sophisticated and of even greater strategic importance, necessitating a large armaments industry. President Eisenhower's "Farewell Address" warned against the potential dangers involved with these changed circumstances, which were said to have created a military-industrial complex whose influence needed to be monitored.

The dangers of the military-industrial complex cannot be ignored, even though President Eisenhower issued his warning at a time of increasing extroversion, making it more appropriate then than now. Today's introversion serves as a significant check on the influence of military-business groupings, just as the munitions makers were checked by the introverts of the 1930s.[69] The military-industrial complex which exists today, although more sophisticated than previous military-business relationships, must compete with other highly sophisticated complexes.[70] Additionally, while some segments of the business community benefit from military contracts, a larger and more significant part of the community has to help pay for this benefit in the form of taxes.

Another indicator of the actual relationship between business and the military can be observed in some of the theories regarding the military-industrial complex advanced during the 1960s, noting which ones have best indicated events during subsequent years. Such an exercise indicates that pluralist theorists who emphasize that business and the military can have separate ideas and interests were much more indicative of future trends than theorists emphasizing military-business collusion.[71]

Various tendencies of the past few decades question general theories of business-military collusion. During most of the 1940–1968 extrovert phase the Republican party, the party which is linked most to the business liberal community, generally advocated a lower level of military effort than did the Democratic party.[72] In fact, congressional Democrats often urged the business liberal Eisenhower administration to spend more money on defense. At the height of the last extrovert phase, reform liberal Democrats supported a large and active military establishment. As another example, Republican presidents Eisenhower and Nixon had a defense strategy oriented to a one and one-half war situation; the strategy of Democratic presidents Kennedy and Johnson, on the other hand, was oriented to a two and one-half war situation, employing more conventional weapons and thus generating more business for the conventional armaments industry. To be sure, business liberals sometimes have been more supportive of the military than reform liberals, as is the case with President Reagan today, but this is not a general pattern. Recent documentation of the many sides of the business liberal can be found in a 1975 study by Bruce M. Russett and Elizabeth C. Hanson.[73] These considerations question the analyst who is quick to link business and the military in decisive collusion.

Some recent studies have also noted something of a relationship between the military and business, but their findings do not point to a conspiratorial, profit-making partnership. One study concludes that the so-called military-industrial complex is "a rather amorphous, loosely structured entity" which "grew out of the needs of foreign policy, and not vice versa."[74] Other studies note how established relationships between business and the military have resulted in various problems.[75] Still, none of these studies documents the decisive impact of a self-motivated, self-interested military-industrial complex.

Business-military ties might be helpful during an introvert phase insofar as they could temper introversion; the greatest danger would be during an extrovert phase, when the potential for a dangerous "reform liberal-military" complex is at least as great as that of a dangerous "business liberal-military" complex. Business liberals are constantly on guard against excessive costs, but reform liberals have fewer economic qualms when they perceive the military as advancing their goals. Further, since they too as liberals are hostile to the military function, reform liberals are unlikely to understand it and will either defer to the military on too many issues or attempt to civilianize it. Either alternative can undermine military professionalism.[76]

The business liberal, also distrustful of the military, has been no more likely than the reform liberal to defer to the military or civilianize it during extrovert phases. A number of neo-Hamiltonians, like Theodore Roosevelt, engaged in some civilianization of the military at the turn of the century, indicating that such a propensity is possible. However, actions when business liberal President Eisenhower was in office for eight peacetime years around the middle of the 1940–1968 extrovert phase and when business liberal President McKinley was in the White House during the Spanish-American War indicate that business liberals are no more prone to overly defer to, or civilianize, the military than are reform liberals.[77] Business liberals did not control the White House during the most active parts of the last four American wars (World War I, World War II, the Korean war, and the Vietnam war) and were suspicious of the Kennedy-Johnson civilianization of the military during the height of the most recent extrovert phase, while many reform liberals supported it.

These observations simply do not indicate an overwhelming difference between business and reform liberal attitudes toward the military. Neither is there any indication that business liberals are more prone to support military action; in fact, unrestrained by matters of cost, reform liberals may take up the military banner with less hesitation. Conversely, business liberals might be a little less prone to abandon the defense industry during times of introversion. Both forms of liberalism have an inherent aversion to the use of military persuasion, but are willing to employ it if ideologically justifiable. The mood/interest theory thus questions the concept of a "military-industrial complex" determining politico-military action and allocates the responsibility to the shifting public mood.

THE AMERICAN PRESS

The news media in the United States are an important force in insuring that the liberal public mood determines the direction of American foreign policy. Generally, reporters are not professional foreign policy analysts. Rather than reaching their positions on the basis of their foreign policy expertise, they have usually worked their way up through the journalistic ranks. Thus journalists, more so than government professionals, usually are typical of public mood. Walter Cronkite noted that most newsmen "come to feel very little allegiance to the established order. I think they're inclined to side with humanity rather than with authority and institutions."[78] This aversion to authority and identification with humanity is reflective of the public liberalism. The press feels a loyalty to the public that necessitates prompt reporting of presidential or congressional deviations from public mood.

A free press can select what to report and how to report it. The merest mention of the possibility of implementing extrovert action during an introvert phase, for example, can instantaneously become a major public concern by means of a provocative, front-page headline.[79] This media advantage is especially important in television news programs, in which time is very limited. What the newsperson decides to include in a sixty-second segment may have significant impact on public perceptions of an event. Further, because the public does not choose the news to which it is exposed as in the print media, television tends to encourage opinions where there were formerly none;[80] thus mood could become even more difficult to change as more people have firm opinions. Television news programs, dependent upon good ratings for their very survival, must necessarily be reflective of public mood and eager to report any governmental deviations from the mood.

One method the press, especially the print media, uses to help maintain public control over foreign policy direction is leaks of guarded official information. Leaks were quite common during the recent shift to introversion; some bureaucrats in touch with the public mood and reporters together expressed dissent in such form to bring the nation's leaders back in accord with the public mood. The Pentagon Papers had a significant effect on American attitudes toward the Vietnam war; domestically, press revelations in the Watergate scandal contributed to President Nixon's downfall.

The power of the American press is usually exercised responsibly. However, in a democracy dominated by liberal public mood, responsibility can be interpreted to involve firm advocacy of the will of the people regardless of consequence. "Yellow Journalism" intensified the 1891–1919 extrovert phase through its advocacy of war with Spain. In the mid-1930s press coverage of the Senate Nye Committee reports helped to make the munitions makers theory of the causes of World War I standard with the American public. During the intensifying years of the 1940–1968 extrovert phase, sensational newspaper reports of Senator Joseph McCarthy's anticommunist accusations helped to draw President Eisenhower and the business liberals firmly into extroversion, thus prodding the entire country into firm anticommunism.

Throughout American history the press, rather than restraining excesses of public mood, has generally spurred them on; on the other hand, the press at times has realized early the dangers of excess and fueled the public's mood shift, as in the final years of the most recent extrovert phase when the press began reporting skeptically on the Vietnam war. The American system of a free press, operated by people reflective of the public mood, is unlikely to be changed in the near future. Although it cannot be depended upon to counter early the recurring extremes of American liberalism, it can be entrusted to insure that leaders follow shifting public mood.[81]

CONGRESSIONAL ACTIONS AND PROPOSED CONSTITUTIONAL AMENDMENTS

Whenever attention is strongly drawn to a foreign policy matter, the public can become quite assertive. It will seek to control its leaders when it perceives that they have varied too much from the public mood, but with varying amounts of effort depending on the time and circumstances within the mood.

An amendment to the United States Constitution is the ultimate means of assuring government adherence to the public mood. At times in recent American history, amendments have been proposed to arrest governmental deviation; the most significant are the Ludlow Amendment of the late 1930s and the Bricker Amendment of the early 1950s. Although neither one was adopted, national leaders cannot ignore the supporting rationale and public assertiveness; they also must bear in mind that such an amendment could yet be passed. This threat helps ensure continued presidential and congressional responsiveness to the shifting mood of the American public.

During the 1919–1940 introvert phase, people reacted against American participation in World War I, and it was widely believed that a small number of munitions makers and their backers had caused the president to ask for, and Congress to agree to, a declaration of war. Prevention of future wars would require restrictions on the actions of both the president and the Congress. As one consequence, the Ludlow Amendment to the United States Constitution was proposed, declaring that the United States could not go to war without an affirmative vote of the people, except in case of attack by outside powers on the Western Hemisphere or an attack on United States territory. This concept had widespread public support[82] and almost received a majority vote of the House of Representatives to discharge it from the House Rules Committee.[83] In spite of strong public support, however, by 1938 when the House vote was taken enough governmental measures had been passed and assurances of good faith made to console the public in the defeat of this measure. If the vote had been taken before the public had been at least somewhat placated, the amendment might have passed. Certainly the experience kept the Roosevelt administration cautious in foreign policy. In retrospect, the passage of such a measure could have hastened rather than prevented American involvement in World War II. Knowledge that the United States would not respond to provocation except by a direct vote of the people would have provided additional encouragement to the German and Japanese adventurism which caused American involvement in the war.

After World War II, a number of business liberals and states rights southerners became alarmed over the use of the treaty power and executive agreements. Executive agreements, which are similar to treaties but do not require ratification by the Senate, were particularly questioned, and the increased power of the president became suspect. With some intense support, the Bricker Amendment to the Constitution, which was to go through several versions, was proposed in 1951. Emphasis was on control of the activities of the executive, in contrast to the Ludlow Amendment's emphasis on control of a particular power of both executive and legislative leaders. The Bricker Amendment aimed at subjecting treaties and executive agreements to increased constitutional and legislative scrutiny, and its practical effect would have been to make it extremely difficult for the president to conduct American foreign policy. The country was divided over such a measure in an extrovert phase. Reform liberals and the executive branch led the opposition to the amendment. The executive branch, however, was particularly careful not to deviate from public mood, a consideration which might explain a good deal of the Eisenhower administration's public reluctance to tackle Senator Joseph McCarthy or sign the 1954 Geneva Accords on Indochina. In the end, the attempt to have a version of the amendment referred to the states was defeated in the Senate by a narrow margin.[84] If the amendment had been successfully referred, it is probable the states would have ratified it since it also increased their power. The need for action against communism, the opposition to the amendment by business liberal President Eisenhower, and the ever-clearer dictates of the growing extrovert mood helped dissuade the public from pursuing the measure. Support for the amendment faded as the 1940–1968 extrovert phase took greater hold.

Proposed constitutional amendments, whether ultimately passed or not, are a very powerful method of curbing governmental deviation from public mood. Less severe means, such as congressional acts and resolutions, can also be useful for such a purpose. The 1969 National Commitments Resolution and the 1973 War Powers Act are examples of the public mood asserting itself through congressional restraints on the president.

The Vietnam war, like World War I, provoked a reaction away from extroversion but, unlike World War I, the Vietnam war had not been declared by Congress. This distinction is important because the public directed its efforts in the late 1960s and early 1970s largely toward controlling the executive, even though indications are that before public support eroded the Congress would not have hesitated to declare war had it been asked. In fact, the Gulf of Tonkin Resolution and subsequent voting of appropriations can be viewed as congressional support for the war.

As public enthusiasm for the Vietnam venture waned, however, so did congressional support. The Senate in 1969 by a vote of 70 to 16 adopted the National Commitments Resolution[85] to press for congressional involvement in major foreign policy decisions. Four years later, with substantial public support, the War Powers Act was passed to insure that the Congress would participate in deliberations on future wars. Major support for such legislation came from the reform liberal community, a major source of opposition to the earlier Bricker Amendment; this community had become concerned, however, with preventing another limited war situation. Some reform liberals went so far as to worry that the legislation delineated too many presidential powers. Some business liberals, more apt to support remnants of the 1940–1968 extroversion, were less enthusiastic about the legislation. Nevertheless, the solidifying introvert mood and the Nixon administration's continued assertion of executive prerogatives in foreign policy gave the War Powers bill enough support to pass both houses of Congress over a presidential veto and become law in 1973. The act, as intended, helped to keep secretary of state Henry Kissinger in line with the public's increasing introversion. If the War Powers Act had not achieved this result, a constitutional amendment could have been proposed. At the very least, these measures demonstrate that the public will assert itself against its leaders when it perceives its will has been or is being violated.

PRESIDENTS AND MOODS: WHO RULES, AND HOW?

American presidents are of political necessity most often creatures of the public mood in foreign policy.[86] Usually elected in part as a result of their closeness to public mood, presidents throughout American history have felt its impact through checks and balances, which keep them engrossed in problems of the day. Although presidents have little time to worry about subsequent historical analysis of their performance, such analysis may hinge in part upon the public mood prevailing during their tenure in office. Thus, public mood has contributed to disaster for some presidents and great accomplishment for others.

One crucial period for presidents is the time of a foreign policy mood shift from extroversion to introversion, or vice versa. Throughout American history, presidents have faced similar dilemmas at such times. They have found that the mood which existed when they assumed power and on which they had based their policies disappeared during their term in office. Does a president then change policies in order to conform to public perceptions or cling to those policies once believed sound? Presidents who have chosen the latter course have paid for it with a loss of public support.

Such situations are particularly difficult when a president has been successfully promoting extrovert policies and discovers that his support is weakening. The most recent examples are presidents Woodrow Wilson and Lyndon Johnson. Both presidents led the United States into war with strong public support for their policies. In the process of "selling" the public, they heightened unrealistic expectations. Woodrow Wilson led the American public to believe that the United States could fight one war and thus make the world safe for democracy. Lyndon Johnson thought that the United States could "win the hearts and minds" of the Vietnamese people as it showed them how to fight communism. Both goals were formulated during the height of extrovert phases; neither was fully realizable. Both of these reform liberal presidents saw an important portion of their reform liberal support crumble as a result of their foreign policy actions. Both presidents remained true to their extrovert causes at considerable cost as previous supporters abandoned them and as opponents seized political opportunities. The problem, thus, was not one of presidents changing policy, but rather one of the American public changing its liberal mind. In both cases the American public mood prevailed. The United States never formally joined the League of Nations and the United States, in frustration, abandoned South Vietnam.

The inconsistencies in United States policy as a result of these two instances are pronounced. President Woodrow Wilson was a world leader in drafting the covenant of the League of Nations, and yet his own country was the only major power never to join. President Lyndon Johnson led the United States into a larger military commitment in South Vietnam in order to keep the country noncommunist, but less than a decade later the United States was not even willing to maintain the equipment levels of the South Vietnamese armed forces, and the country steadily succumbed to communists.

At the start of an earlier introvert phase, President John Quincy Adams was not particularly successful with foreign policy. This is puzzling, because Adams had previously been a successful secretary of state and diplomat. The problem is clarified by noting that Adams served as secretary of state and diplomat during an extrovert phase, and this service could have posed difficulties in pleasing the introvert public during his presidency.

At the start of the 1871–1891 introvert phase, a disappointed President Ulysses S. Grant saw the Senate table his strong efforts to annex the Dominican Republic in 1871, although it had supported the purchase of Alaska in 1867. Viewed in terms of the mood curve, the above inconsistencies in foreign policy are actually very American and very regular. Generally speaking, one could say that strong-willed presidents, reluctant to lose their extrovert glory, are least able to adapt a new-found introversion and create the most long-range repercussions, as with Wilson and Johnson. Weaker presidents, such as Grant, have trouble adapting also, but eventually do so.

Presidents also seem to have difficulty adjusting to a shift from introversion to extroversion. The one exception is President Franklin Roosevelt, who had inclinations toward an extrovert policy but was restrained by his emphasis on getting the United States out of the Great Depression of the 1930s. Although he followed well the public shift to extroversion in 1940, previous presidents at similar times had difficulties. The presidential election after the 1798 beginning of the first extrovert phase (1800) saw the defeat of incumbent president John Adams. Corresponding to the 1844 change in mood, the presidential election that year saw a change in political parties, with James Polk coming into the White House on an expansionist Democratic platform. Following the third shift to extroversion, incumbent president Benjamin Harrison, who might have been too far ahead of public mood, was defeated in 1892 and the White House changed parties, as it had in 1888 and did again in 1896. Most American presidents at times of mood change experienced great difficulty, and, in most cases, the incumbent or his party lost the ensuing presidential election.[87]

Presidents who did not assume office until after a mood phase had solidified seem to have succcssfully adjusted personal convictions in order to follow the public mood. Although Andrew Jackson had aggressively pursued Indians beyond United States borders into Florida during the first extrovert phase and even risked war by hanging British instigators, he followed introvert foreign policies after his election to the presidency in the introvert year of 1828. Democratic President Grover Cleveland, who was elected for the second time in 1892, was not generally considered an extrovert; yet he took a strong stand in the extrovert year of 1895 against Great Britain during the Venezuelan Boundary Crisis. In 1954 Senator Lyndon Johnson was one force preventing unwise U.S. involvement in Indochina, but a decade later he led an increasingly extrovert public into greater participation in the Vietnam War, pursuing extrovert policies even after public enthusiasm had begun to wane. Throughout the middle years of the last extrovert phase, Richard Nixon was an ardent anticommunist; nevertheless, assuming the presidency at the beginning of an introvert phase, he opened the way for improved relations with communist China. The most politically expedient course a president can follow is adherence to the liberal public mood.

Credibility gaps are often mentioned in analyses of American presidents and their foreign policies. Presidents are said to be less than candid with the public, making adverse public reaction most understandable. However, these credibility gaps can be related to changing public moods. President Franklin Roosevelt was criticized for making unnecessary concessions to the communists during World War II. Since public mood did not move back into the United States interest zone until 1947, two years after Roosevelt's death, part of his reasoning undoubtedly was related to making allowances for the introvert sentiment remaining in the United States during the war. President Dwight Eisenhower, whose passive foreign policies were at variance with some of his firm anticommunist rhetoric, did not have a credibility gap, perhaps because his rhetoric was ahead of the public mood, which grew more anticommunist during his term in office. President Lyndon Johnson had a foreign policy credibility gap during his final years in the presidency which was identified and exploited. His rhetoric trailed behind the less anticommunist American public mood toward the end of his term in office. Perceptions of foreign policy credibility gaps can be as much related to whether a president's thinking is ahead or behind the liberal public mood as they are to whether a president is actually credible.

Occasionally a president will make a rare decision which seems to go against public opinion. Historian Ernest R. May has written: "Looking back through American history, one can almost count on one's fingers the number of occasions when American statesmen made major decisions that they thought contrary to the public will."[88] Presidential policy decisions which lie outside of the foreign policy parameters, even when the president knows public views on an issue, cannot automatically be seen as a refutation of the Public Rule Proposition. The public ultimately desires change, and what is favorable to public opinion in the short-term can be unfavorable when viewed in a long-term context. Polls constantly change, but the president was elected by the people and is likely to have a general idea of public desires. In conflicts between opinion and policy needs, the president acts as a reasonable interpreter of what the public wants in the long-run.

An example of this type of decision making is provided by the Panama Canal treaties. When the Carter administration had to make the decision whether or not to back the treaties in the spring of 1977, public opinion polls showed that Americans were overwhelmingly opposed to turning ownership and control of the Panama Canal over to the Republic of Panama.[89] The Carter administration knew that the possibility of conflict with other nations existed if the issue was not settled and was cognizant of the diminishing desirability of

U.S. ownership of the canal; thus, the administration had to choose between the short-term desires of the public and its long-term goals. The Carter administration backed ratification of the compromise treaties in seeming defiance of public opinion but in ultimate accord with the public mood. One might argue that the Carter administration sold the public on a policy, but it would be more appropriate to say that the administration made a long-range interpretation of public desires regarding all aspects of the situation. Most of the discretion exercised by the Carter administration on this matter concerned timing of the treaties, rather than substance.

Another type of situation which might have a relationship to foreign policy cycles is a major domestic scandal at the national level. The administrations of Ulysses Grant, Warren Harding, and Richard Nixon, each during the early years of an introvert phase, faced a domestic scandal of major proportions. One can speculate that these types of scandals relate to a public demand that those coordinating policy exhibit and follow high standards of official conduct, an expectation which can suffer neglect during extrovert phases when attention is focused on foreign affairs.

Presidents who are given the opportunity by an extrovert mood to assume a role of aggressive leadership fare better in later historical analyses than do their introvert counterparts. A president in the top third (or top twelve) of those in the posterity rankings in table 18 served at the start of six of the eight major American wars since 1789. The presidents presiding over the major annexations which composed the Continental United States (Washington—unification of the thirteen colonies; Jefferson—the Louisiana Purchase; and Polk—Texas, Mexican Cession, and Oregon) were all ranked in the top third. This posterity relationship is also apparent with those presidents who served during the first stage of an introvert period. Richard Nixon, Ulysses Grant, and Warren Harding received the lowest three posterity ranks.

The degree of license given presidents in the pursuit of foreign policy, their success or failure in that field, their ability or that of their party to retain the highest office, the extent to which they must compromise personal conviction in order to function, public estimates of their candor, historical analyses of their performance—all hinge in part upon the constant fluctuation of American foreign policy moods manifested in liberalism.

5. American Introversion

The year 1968 can be documented as the end of the last extrovert phase. Is America in a period of introversion that will end in an extreme which fails to protect American politico-military interests, as happened in the late 1930s? Probably so, if the United States remains as curiously predictable as it has in the past. In a nuclear age this is particularly dangerous. Not much time is left in this introvert phase for an extreme, but an extreme is possible and may happen suddenly and with little warning. It may be recognized as an extreme only in retrospect.

To adequately assess the current American mood it is necessary to view mood in a composite manner, as the product of various experiences rather than a single experience. The mood/interest theory therefore stresses the difference between long-term mood and short-term opinion. A mood at a given time is a composite of many different indicators, any one of which occasionally might deviate from the composite mood. Scientific public opinion polls, although useful in composite to indicate thinking at specific points in time, were not taken during the first three-fourths of U.S. history. Therefore, the most appropriate comparison with the past is of American foreign policy, as determined by the liberal public during the previous periods of American introversion.

TRADITIONAL AMERICAN INTROVERSION

The historical operation of American introversion provides important clues regarding the development of the current introvert mood. American liberal introvert phases have been characterized by a similarity in the nature of diplomatic events. Such phases usually show little aggressiveness, feature no annexed territory, and focus upon preventive settlements and the maintenance of existing relationships. Also, introvert phases have often been characterized by more restrictive immigration legislation than have extrovert phases.

In introvert periods American presidents have been peacetime presidents,[1] generally concerned with limiting the development or expansion of American politico-military concerns beyond the borders of the United States. Having lived through a period of extroversion, each has been aware of the problems that developed from the extremes at the conclusion of the phase. In order to prevent similar difficulties, they have looked to George Washington's advice: "The great rule of conduct for us, in regard to foreign nations, is, in extending our commercial relations, to have with them as little political connection as possible. So far as we have already formed engagements, let them be fulfilled with perfect good faith. Here let us stop."[2]

Presidents who have served near the time of a mood change from extroversion to introversion have faced intense problems. Woodrow Wilson and Lyndon Johnson lost support when their views did not adjust according to public mood and saw their extrovert worlds crumble. Each of the last three introvert phases (1871–1891, 1919–1940, and 1968 to the present) included a major domestic scandal during its early years. One can speculate that public attention, quite concerned during extrovert periods with foreign policy actions, is redirected during introvert periods toward the personal conduct of its leaders. Similar undesirable behavior might have been present in other leaders at other times but received less attention because of the emphasis on foreign policy characteristic of extrovert moods.

Treaties have been a major tool of foreign policy throughout United States history, although they are increasingly being supplanted by executive agreements. The character of major treaties and agreements differs according to the type of mood orientation. Conclusive treaties or agreements, such as annexations, are more likely in extrovert phases and preventive treaties or agreements are more likely in introvert phases. Such preventive documents include Jay's Treaty in 1794 with England, the 1831 Claims Convention with France, the Pan-American Conference of 1889 with its agreement to establish the Pan-American Union, the Kellogg-Briand Pact of 1928, and the Strategic Arms Limitation Talks (SALT) of the 1970s.

The frequency of U.S. use of armed forces abroad has been another indicator of introversion; during introvert phases, Americans are less prone to resort to force in international dealings. Admittedly, the existence of nuclear weaponry since 1945 minimized the number of American military ventures abroad during the last extrovert phase. American presidents, fortunately, have not been willing to risk nuclear war in order to redress an insult to the flag or to punish hostile indigenous inhabitants, actions that were taken without fear of serious repercussions during the first one hundred fifty years of United States history. Analysis of uses of armed forces abroad during the three introvert and three extrovert phases between 1798 and 1939, however, yields a definite pattern: the three extrovert phases featured an average of 1.44 uses of military force overseas per year; the three introvert phases had less than half that number—.69 uses per year.[3]

Major armed intervention abroad has not been a prominent United States policy during introvert phases, although it has resulted occasionally as a carry-over from policies initiated during extrovert phases. American reactions to unfavorable or threatening international events, particularly during the two most recent introvert phases, often have been characterized instead by verbal condemnations or statements of dissatisfaction. These responses include the Hoover-Stimson Doctrine (1932), the "Quarantine Speech" (1937), and current condemnations such as those of North Korea for the *Pueblo* seizure (1968), the Soviet Union and Cuba for intervention in Angola and Ethiopia, and Soviet Union for the invasion of Afghanistan. Most major U.S. armed interventions abroad have taken place during extrovert phases.

Another familiar response to conflicts in introvert phases is neutrality. Neutrality has also been present in extrovert phases, but has not usually been as well defined and final. Each extrovert phase has included a war which the United States had tried to avoid during the previous introvert phase. In 1793 the United States proclaimed neutrality in the Anglo-French conflict, but during the following extrovert phase fought an undeclared naval war with France and the War of 1812 with Great Britain. During the second introvert phase the United States government was neutral in the Mexico-Texas conflict, even to the point of seizing Texan vessels attempting to sever the Mexican lifeline in the Gulf of Mexico.[4] Yet, during the initial years of the following extrovert phase, the Texas situation culminated in the Mexican War. The United States avoided war with Spain following the 1873 seizure of a ship illegally registered in the United States and the execution of her partially American crew during a Cuban insurrection, but fought the Spanish-American War after the sinking of the battleship *Maine* in Havana Harbor in 1898. American attempts to remain neutral through the Neutrality Acts of the late 1930s did not keep the United States out of World War II. All major American wars have begun during extrovert phases, although they were perhaps kindled during introvert phases.

Another characteristic of introversion has been an emphasis on arms control and disarmament. Most successful advances in this area have tended to occur toward the beginning of introvert phases, when demands of the public correspond more closely to realistic opportunities. As the United States progresses further into an introvert mood, public demands become more and more unrealistic. Toward the end of an introvert phase, public mood can become so unrealistic that American governmental institutions are limited to only unilateral action, since other countries will not concur in the policies called for by extreme American introversion.

The United States was a major participant in and signatory of the Washington Conference agreements in 1921–1922, was active in the crafting of the 1928 Kellogg-Briand Pact which outlawed offensive warfare, and signed the London Naval Conference agreement of 1930. However, once the strong introversion of the 1930s took hold, the United States acted most often in a unilateral manner. The Neutrality Acts of 1935–1937 included regulations regarding American provision of arms to belligerent groups in the hope that this would at least avert American involvement in any war.

During the last decade of the 1940–1968 extrovert phase, a few arms control agreements, such as the Antarctic and Limited Test Ban Treaties, were concluded; such action continued as the extrovert mood yielded to the current mood of introversion. A 1967 treaty signed by the United States prohibited nuclear weapons in outer space. During the present introvert phase the United States has undertaken ambitious efforts; these include the Nuclear Non-Proliferation Treaty, a new biological warfare agreement, Strategic Arms Limitations Talks and other agreements with the Soviet Union, exploration of the possibility of mutual and balanced force reductions in Europe, and the 1975 United States ratification of the 1925 Geneva Protocol on gas and bacteriological warfare. It is worth noting that the SALT I agreement was settled early in the current introvert phase (1972) with relative ease. The SALT II treaty, however, struggled through the middle stages of the current mood and was never formally ratified. Similarly, part of the American public has recently begun calling for a United States–Soviet freeze of all nuclear weapons testing, production, and deployment; however, whether or not the proposal will be negotiated remains to be seen.

During extrovert phases American interest in arms control and disarmament generally lessens. During these times, American interest in such measures usually is limited to those applying primarily to other nations or those measures of obvious benefit to the United States. For example, the 1817 Rush-Bagot agreement restricting United States and British naval forces on the Great Lakes was beneficial to U.S. security. The United States was particularly active in helping other nations solve disputes during the middle and latter part of the 1891–1919 extrovert phase, even though having no direct stake in some of the settlements. In 1946, the year after the United States dropped the atomic bomb on two Japanese cities, it sponsored the Baruch Plan which called for the establishment of a United Nations agency to control nuclear energy activities. On the one hand, adoption of this plan would have weakened the United States since it had demobilized conventionally and depended on its atomic position to balance Soviet power on the Eurasian mainland. On the other hand, the plan would have served the United States interest insofar as it required that any atomic weapons-controlling authority be satisfactory to the United States before American sacrifices would have to be made, and would have kept atomic weapons out of the hands of others. The 1940–1968 extrovert phase was not solidified until 1947, and by then the United States had lost some interest in the plan; thus it does not constitute an exception to the generalization about less arms control and disarmament interest in extrovert phases than in introvert phases.

American attitudes toward international law and organization appear inconsistent. The United States, like most nations, tends to support and oppose international law and organization as it suits national interests and convenience.[5] However, the United States differs from most other nations in that its inconsistencies often stem from the foreign policy moods manifested in liberalism.

Throughout most of its history, the United States has been a strong advocate of international law. Americans have believed that the rule of law can solve international problems, particularly those of the often warring nations of Europe. However, when international law is applied to the United States, the usual tendency is to make absolutely certain that the rulings do not impede U.S. contributions to world peace or overall interests, as perceived in the light of American foreign policy moods. The United States Senate, with its treaty ratification power, is in a strong position to assert the nation's right to determine when to submit to international judgment, since treaties are a primary source of international law. The Senate has been most protective of American sovereignty during introvert phases, but in extrovert phases assertive policies conducted by the executive branch are frequent. Becoming increasingly active in the world balance of power in more recent times, the United States has tended to view international law in a more pragmatic manner.

As international organizations have grown in importance, they have increasingly been the object of the inconsistent attitudes of American moods. President Woodrow Wilson was the world leader in the formation of the League of Nations, but was unable to lead his own country to join. The United States was cooperative while Wilson helped to draft the proposed covenant of the league, but with the mood change to introversion during 1919, the Senate rejected the covenant. America cooperated with the League of Nations in the 1920s, but its support faded during the 1930s when the introvert mood became stronger.[6]

During the first years of the 1940–1968 extrovert phase, special care was taken in the drafting of the United Nations charter to insure that it would be acceptable to the United States Senate following World War II. This, coupled with the growing American mood of extroversion, made the United Nations attractive to the Senate and a majority of Americans. Once the United Nations was in existence, the United States was able to exercise leadership so as to be on the winning side of most votes. However, as extroversion progressed to an extreme during the 1960s, America lost support in the international organization as other countries found it difficult to agree with increasing American assertiveness. This was particularly evident among Third World nations, many of which had not entered the United Nations until the early 1960s and then came into contact with a strongly extroverted United States. As a result, Americans became frustrated by the seeming uncooperativeness of the United Nations.

The American mood changed from extroversion to introversion during 1968. Since that time the Third World has grown stronger and more assertive in the United Nations and American frustrations have increased. Current American policy works within the United Nations with reservations, not unlike the informal American cooperation with the League of Nations in the 1920s. A 1981 public opinion poll shows that while 77 percent of the American public supports continued United States membership in the United Nations, less than 50 percent feel the United Nations has been effective in most areas of involvement.[7] In recent years the United States has been slow to recognize world opinion of Israel. American willingness to defend Israel's rights in the United Nations is not unlike the unilateral Hoover-Stimson Doctrine which simply refused to accept the results of Japanese aggression in the early 1930s. The American view of Japanese aggression and the ostracization of Israel could well be correct; the American willingness to undertake a unilateral approach to such problems rather than to emphasize work within the frustrating structure of international organizations is far more characteristic of an introvert mood than an extrovert mood.

The Neutrality Acts of the late 1930s were an extreme manifestation of American introversion. They soon were demonstrated to be an unrealistic answer to dealing with the world events which culminated in World War II, revealing the costs of such a policy: the neglect of the United States' interests in Europe and East Asia.

THE CURRENT INTROVERT PHASE

A considerable body of evidence suggests that the current introvert phase has been firmly implanted and generally growing in intensity. An early indication of the mood shift to introversion occurred with the decidedly introvert reaction to the July 1967 crisis in the Congo (now Zaire).[8] The early 1968 Tet offensive in Vietnam was the prelude to a political year which evidenced a marked lack of support for President Johnson and his extrovert Vietnam policies. From May 1967 to August 1968 there was a dramatic shift from a majority of Republicans, Democrats, and Independents supporting the war to a majority of each opposing it.[9] Business liberal Richard M. Nixon was elected at least partially and significantly on his pledge to end the war in Vietnam. A study conducted from September 1968 through September 1969 identified a post-Vietnam, nonintervention syndrome on the part of those groups directing American foreign policy.[10] In his 1970 book, *The Hidden Crisis in American Politics,* Samuel Lubell states that a "desire to impose some manageable limit upon our role in policing the peace was shared quite generally by . . . both critics and supporters of the Vietnam War."[11] A book entitled *No Clear and Present Danger,* which appeared in print in 1972, was written by Bruce Russett in 1971 as a skeptical view of American entry into World War II. Its dedication reads: "For Mark and Daniel, No foreign wars for them."[12] Such views usually surface in introvert phases just as views critical of "isolationists" most often surface in extrovert phases.

By 1973 the American direct military commitment in Vietnam was brought to an end. As the defense establishment was significantly reduced in size, the draft ended. The Congress passed the War Powers Act in 1973 restricting the power of the president to engage in prolonged politico-military activities. Leslie Gelb concluded in that year that "increased emphasis on domestic priorities and wariness about foreign military involvements seem to be a trend, not a fad."[13] Bruce Russett has identified "a marked shift away from acceptance of the political 'responsibilities of world power' " which "appears likely to be prevalent for a long period." Russett also projects the Klingberg data on the percentage of State of the Union addresses devoted to foreign affairs,[14] indicating that we have indeed embarked upon another introvert phase. Klingberg updates his analysis by analyzing international as opposed to domestic content of annual presidential messages from 1967–1983, inclusive. He found that of all messages during these years only President Carter's 1980 message devoted more time to international than domestic issues. The next highest international percentage in those years was 45 percent in President Johnson's 1967 message.[15] Steven Hildreth, in a 1981 report, writes that introversion is likely to remain strong through the 1980s.[16] In addition, both official development assistance (ODA) to other countries as a percentage of gross national product and Department of Defense (DOD) outlays as a percentage of total United States government federal outlays have declined since the latter years of the 1940–1968 extrovert phase.[17]

Recent works note a lack of consensus in American foreign policy.[18] A lack of consensus makes extroversion difficult and introversion likely, because if an agreement on policy cannot be reached it is most likely that the ensuing conflict will allow for little to be done in the international arena. George H. Quester, in *American Foreign Policy: The Lost Consensus,* cites the late 1960s as a time when American foreign policy took a turn inward and states "the American public in the 1980s remains confused, and deeply divided, about the goals it wishes to serve in the world."[19] This continuing lack of consensus in American foreign policy can be viewed as normal introversion within the framework of the mood/interest theory.

Another strong indicator of the current introvert mood is the prominent foreign policy role of the Congress, a clue to public mood which has proved reliable historically. As suggested by the Executive/Legislative Proposition of the mood/interest theory, in the last decade and a half Congress has made better use of its ability to limit executive politico-military activities than prior to 1968. Should the introvert mood continue, the Congress can be expected to continue its policy effectiveness.

An example of introvert congressional assertiveness, and itself indicative of the progress of this introvert phase, is former Secretary of State Henry Kissinger's difficulties toward the end of his term in office. Although his balance-of-power approach to foreign policy brought America back from its liberal excess of extroversion, further public movement toward introversion caused Kissinger's conservative policies to lose support.[20] He and President Gerald Ford, when 1976 found the United States fully in its current introvert orientation, were prevented by the Congress from quietly supporting one

Angolan faction in the face of large-scale Soviet and Cuban intervention in favor of another faction. In contrast, when the Congolese "Force Publique" revolted and Belgian troops intervened in July of 1960, the United States played an active, nonmilitary role in the crisis.[21] The Eisenhower administration in the extrovert year of 1960 had to resist public and congressional pressure for a more militant, anticommunist role.

A like voice can be heard from both former presidents Ford and Carter on the issue of constraints imposed upon them by the Congress. Carter showed concern, warning, "There's a trend in Congress that is building up that puts too much constraint on a president to deal with rapidly changing circumstances." This statement points in the same direction as Ford's comment that "Congress has encroached much too far on the prerogatives of the executive . . . to conduct foreign policy."[22] Despite these complaints, public support around 1976 seemed to be in favor of a more dominant role for the Congress in the making of foreign policy.[23] A later nation-wide study showed that in 1978, 43 percent of the public felt Congress should play a more important role in foreign policy, compared to 44 percent for the president.[24] In 1982, 44 percent of those polled in a national survey believed that Congress should play a more important role in foreign policy, compared to 39 percent for the president.[25] Overall, such surveys indicate that the public is generally satisfied with a balance that includes an important role for Congress.

President Carter and the Congress each demonstrated important introvert traits in their approach to United States defense policy. Carter halted development of the B-1 bomber and deferred development of the neutron bomb. He proposed to withdraw United States ground troops from South Korea, but had to delay because of congressional resistance and reluctance to pass military aid bills for South Korea. The Congress asserted itself on the issue of arms sales, which made it difficult for the president to push through such sales as military aircraft to Middle Eastern nations. Congress also forced modification of some sales, such as airborne warning and control systems to Iran. It took a major effort by the Carter administration to push the Panama Canal treaties through, and the Senate never ratified the SALT II treaty.[26] Complex legislative-executive relations most often give the edge to introvert policies, since new programs need some agreement before they can be enacted.

President Reagan's approach to foreign policy has involved stronger rhetoric, but his foreign policy actions generally have not been more extrovert than other recent presidents.[27] Although Reagan's more extrovert rhetoric indicates that perhaps he is beginning to recognize the need for better protection of American interests, it is obvious that the introvert public and the Congress are staying his hand to a large degree.[28] Some of the foreign policy actions that Reagan did get through Congress were accomplished with his ability to work through the complexity of legislative-executive relations and his ability to tailor his proposals to satisfy an introvert Congress.

The current introvert mood working through Congress and through the public to limit presidential action is reflected in the recent United States involvement in El Salvador. President Reagan's attempt to provide extensive aid to center-right regimes in the El Salvador conflict was met with strong public disapproval and soon downplayed.[29] Even the issue of Cuban and Soviet expansionism could not elicit public support; as one author noted, "Floating El Salvador as a red menace to our security has had all the success of an iron balloon."[30] Reagan has found it even more difficult to aid the forces fighting against the Nicaraguan government. Indeed, congressional assertiveness led President Reagan to appoint a commission headed by former Secretary of State Henry Kissinger to try to formulate an acceptable policy for Central America. Obviously, Reagan's strong talk cannot overcome the introvert mood dominating the American public. In fact, Reagan himself may have some introvert orientations from his upbringing in the Midwest.[31]

The mood/interest theory contends that short-term indicators, such as public opinion polls, are not alone reliable clues to the direction of foreign policy mood; however, importance is generally attached to polls.

Defense spending is one issue on which public opinion is often in transition. The seemingly paradoxical "belligerent isolationists" of past history are witness to the fact that public support for defense spending need not correlate with foreign policy mood. From 1937 to 1939, years of extreme introversion, only 5 to 20 percent of the American public favored reducing military spending.[32] The percentage favoring reduction even in the cold war years fluctuated from nearly zero to over 30.[33] The current introvert phase began with a definite increase in public demand for less defense spending;[34] in fact, Bruce Russett and Miroslav Nincic noted in a 1976 article that surveys conducted since December 1968 regularly discovered that 40 to 50 percent of the populace wanted defense spending reduced.[35] By 1976–1977 opinion polls indicated, with some fluctuation, that the public was gradually drifting away from a philosophy of reduction to one of maintaining levels of military strength. The Gallup organization from 1969 to mid-1977 determined that those who thought that too much was being spent on defense fluctuated from 52 percent in 1969 to 23 percent in 1977,[36] and Potomac Associates surveys discovered that those who wanted defense spending reduced or ended altogether gradually decreased from 42 percent in 1972 to 24 percent in 1976.[37] This does not seem surprising in view of the fact that defense spending declined from a wartime level of 9.3 percent of GNP in fiscal year 1968 to 5.2 percent of GNP in fiscal year 1977.[38]

Similarly, Louis Harris and Associates surveys place those desiring decreased defense spending at 30 percent in December 1976, dropping to 19 percent in July 1978, and falling further to 9 percent in November 1978; those supporting increased defense spending went from 28 percent to 38 percent and finally to 52 percent on the same dates. It is worth noting that according to the same surveys these changes in attitude toward defense spending correspond closely with changes in public perceptions of American strength. As support for increased defense spending rose, percentages of the public who felt that the United States military defense was weaker than that of the Russians rose from 30 percent in December 1976 to 34 percent in July 1978 and to 43 percent in November 1978. Likewise, the drop in support for decreased spending corresponds to a drop in the public feeling that the United States defense system was stronger than that of the Russians: from 23 percent to 20 percent to 15 percent on the same dates.[39] Since 1978 public support for increased defense spending has continued to rise, to as much as 50 percent or more in 1980 and early 1981,[40] though one study notes a sharp decline by late 1981.[41]

Public opinion on defense spending may have leveled off at a position of maintenance. One poll shows that in 1982, 24 percent of those surveyed thought that too much was being spent on defense while 21 percent felt that too little was being spent. However, a much larger percentage, 52, felt that the amount being spent on defense was about right.[42] This leveling off of those who wish to spend more on defense may be due to the Reagan administration's emphasis on military spending. The public may believe, because of Reagan's strong rhetoric and his actual increase in the defense budget, that enough has been done to bolster American forces. This belief is reflected by a 1983 study that shows that the percentage of Americans who feel the United States is about as strong/ almost as strong as the Russians has risen from 40 percent in January 1980 to 51 percent in March 1983.[43]

Figure 7 shows percentages of Americans supporting increased defense spending from 1935 to 1982, on the basis of a recent study combining public opinion polls.[44] What is implied by these fluctuations in public opinion? It is certainly not the direction in which the public foreign policy mood is moving. Regular fluctuations within a mood prevent the direct correlation of public opinion on defense spending to foreign policy mood. It alone, therefore, is not a reliable indicator.

Another area of interest is the willingness of the American public to use military force abroad, particularly to help friends. A *Time*-Louis Harris poll printed in May 1969 showed that, of twenty-two possibilities outside of the United States itself, only in the cases of Canada and Mexico were a majority of Americans willing to use American military force to repel an invasion by outside communist military forces.[45] Recent data, however, indicates an increased willingness to defend United States allies: a 1976 survey found that 56 percent of the American public favored defending its major European allies in case of attack by the Soviet Union, and studies in February and July 1981 note that 51 percent and 53 percent, respectively, would support deployment of U.S. troops if the Soviet Union or communist China invaded Western Europe. Although only 45 percent in 1976 favored defending Japan under similar circumstances, that figure climbed to 74 percent by 1980. Also in 1980, 64

Figure 7.   Support for Increased Defense Spending, 1935-1982

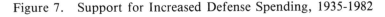

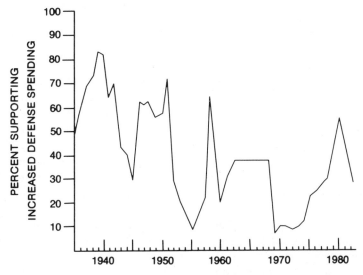

Source: Farid Abolfathi, "Threats, Public Opinion, and Military Spending in the United States, 1930-1990," in *Threats, Weapons, and Foreign Policy* (Sage International Yearbook of Foreign Policy Studies, vol. 5), eds. Pat McGowan and Charles W. Kegley, Jr. (Beverly Hills: Sage Publications, 1980), pp. 98-99. For a 1980 and 1982 update, see William Schneider, "Conservatism, Not Interventionism: Trends in Foreign Policy in the 1980s, in *Eagle Defiant: United States Foreign Policy in the 1980s,* ed. Kenneth A. Oye, Robert J. Lieber, and Donald Rothchild (Boston: Little, Brown, and Co., 1983), p. 36.

percent were willing to send troops to protect the Persian Gulf, an area which previously was not of such importance to the United States.[46] In a 1982 poll 65 percent of those surveyed favored sending U.S. troops if the Soviet Union invaded Western Europe and 51 percent if the Soviets invaded Japan. Of the other eight possibilities offered, including the Persian Gulf, less than 40 percent of those polled favored sending U.S. Troops.[47]

Comparison with similar studies in the years immediately preceding World War II indicates that support of allies alone, like defense spending, is not an adequate indicator of foreign policy mood. From November 1938 to July 1940, American willingness to defend Brazil and Mexico skyrocketed (from 27 to 55 percent and from 43 to 76 percent, respectively), and willingness to protect Canada jumped 15 percentage points. In April 1975 public willingness to come to Brazil's defense reached a low of 15 percent, while Mexico and Canada retained the highest but not very impressive percentages of 42 and 57, respectively.[48] It is apparent that American willingness to defend allies can vary according to public perceptions of actual threat and is not alone an indicator of public foreign policy mood. Further, it must be remembered that introvert phases do not preclude meeting present commitments as much as they do acquisition of new commitments, and in the current introvert mood the public has not shown a willingness to support new commitments.[49]

Another important indicator is analysis of what the public perceives as the most important problem facing America. Analysis of the years from 1941 to 1967, inclusive, shows that an international problem was rated most important for twenty of the twenty-seven years; whereas from 1969 to 1983, inclusive, a domestic problem was rated most important for eleven of the fifteen years.[50] A 1976 survey of the relative importance of thirty-one problem areas discovered that the first international affairs item was ranked as eleven after ten domestic problems.[51] Likewise, a 1982 analysis of surveys between 1974 and 1982 shows that public concern for United States relations with other countries and the possibility of getting into another war consistently ranked between sixth and twelfth in a list of twelve items containing ten domestic concerns.[52] The details of this analysis are presented in table 27 (page 190). A 1983 poll found that only 16 percent of those surveyed thought that foreign affairs/national defense was the most important problem facing the country today, while 84 percent thought that economic needs/issues were the most important problem.[53]

While the most important issue area alone cannot indicate mood, it would seem to be one of the more important factors. For example, in reference to the 1940 mood change, from March 1939 to October 1941 the percentage of the American public indicating they would vote against American entry into war against Germany and Italy registered a small decrease from 83 percent to 79 percent.[54] In sharp contrast, the percentage regarding a foreign policy issue as the most important problem facing the American people jumped from 14 percent in January 1939 to 81 percent in November 1941. However, the limitations of this dramatic indicator are pointed out by a later survey. In October 1945 the percentage of the American people naming foreign problems as most important was down to 7,[55] while at the same time the United States was beginning to assume a role as a world superpower. Also, the importance of foreign affairs in the public opinion jumped drastically in 1980 in response to the Soviet invasion of Afghanistan and the Iranian hostage crisis, but fell back to previous low levels almost immediately,[56] as Americans had not yet exited from the introvert phase. Events in Grenada and Lebanon, as well as concerns about possible nuclear war, moved foreign policy issues up on the list of public concerns in late 1983.[57] Only time will tell whether such movement indicates a long-term trend.

Zbigniew Brzezinski, who would later become President Carter's national security advisor, wrote in the summer of 1976 about a number of politico-military and a few economic matters on which the public was less international than it had been previously. His most optimistic words concern a constant public support for international human rights efforts and a heightened public concern over new global problems such as energy, inflation, and food.[58] In terms of the mood/interest analysis, which contends that economic and humanitarian concerns are not subject to the same variation as politico-military concerns, his optimism is overstated in the context of overall foreign policy.

None of these indicators alone can accurately and consistently point toward overall politico-military foreign policy mood. The most useful polling data may be that gathered in composite, such as some Potomac Associates efforts, which identify a significant growth in isolationist sentiment from 1964 to 1974.[59] Indications are that the internationalist to isolationist movement leveled off during 1974–1976,[60] and has reversed (moved back toward internationalism) between 1976 and 1980.[61] Three factors, however, should be noted regarding this reversal and the mood/interest theory: first, the introvert/extrovert dichotomy used in the mood/interest theory, unlike the isolationist/internationalist dichotomy, concerns foreign policy actions relative to United States interests at a particular time in history rather than to some sort of absolute definition; second, an introvert mood, whereby politico-military interests are not adequately pursued, does not require a pure isolationist consensus but rather can consist of a lack of an extrovert consensus; and third, the mood/interest theory does contend that elements of extroversion begin seeping into the public mood toward the end of an introvert phase, and vice versa, without changing the political effects of the dominant mood.

The above material just touches upon the opinion data available. Its purpose is not to be comprehensive, but rather to indicate that it is difficult to prove or disprove a foreign policy mood based on such data. Indeed, even indicators other than opinion polls may differ from overall mood. Historically, temporary ups and downs during a phase are not uncommon, as Frank Klingberg's 1952 analysis indicates. Irregular fluctuations of some individual indicators charted in his historical analysis of foreign policy mood phases are apparent.[62] Ultimately one must avoid concentrating on relatively short spans of time and endeavor to look at the long-term picture.

Perhaps reliable clues regarding current American introversion can be gained from determining whether similarities exist between situations toward the latter end of previous introvert phases and the present situation, for if the present introvert phase started in 1968, past patterns would dictate that it is now more than two-thirds over.

Halfway through the first introvert phase, operating as a loose confederation with little diplomatic prestige, the United States was understandably hesitant to be assertive in world affairs. The French Revolution, beginning in 1789, mustered a great deal of sympathy from the fledgling nation, but military aid was not offered to assist the revolutionaries.

The 1824–1844 introvert phase saw the United States siding vocally with the more liberal democratic regimes of Europe. Sentiments were aroused on behalf of the Greek rebels fighting against Turkish rule. And in 1830 President Jackson and members of his Cabinet did not hesitate to appear at rallies supporting the July revolution in France.[63] No military action was taken, however, to support such foreign democratic causes. Similarly, the Carter administration started out questioning repressive governments and sympathizing with dissidents. However, its enthusiasm diminished and little thought was ever given to the possibility of military intervention even in the name of humanitarianism. President Carter's reluctance to use military force was highlighted by his statement that "we do not want to send our military forces into Africa to meet the challenge of Soviet and Cuban intrusion."[64] Still there was a limit to American introversion during the 1824–1844 introvert phase, as there is now. President Jackson pressed claims owed by France in the face of war talk and a reluctant Senate prior to final resolution in 1836. President Carter vocalized his concerns over Soviet-Cuban moves in Africa, allowed United States military planes to transport foreign troops to help Zaire, and supported increased United States aid to help African countries defend themselves. Along the same lines, President Reagan worked to provide military support to center-right regimes in the El Salvadoran civil conflict, but that support was limited by an introvert mood.

Another step in the historical analysis of the middle and late stages of introvert phases brings us to the early 1880s, a decade into the 1871–1891 introvert phase. The United States at this time showed little enthusiasm for the worldwide colonialism perpetrated by the European powers. Naval modernization, however, was belatedly begun in the early 1880s after the United States realized that several South American republics had stronger navies.[65] A parallel can be drawn to recent increases in public approval of defense spending; such concern in 1881 did not herald the beginning of a period of extroversion and, likewise, need not to do so now. Humanitarian concern in the 1871–1891 phase was especially apparent in 1882 when, after Senate approval, President Arthur officially proclaimed that the United States would adhere to the international Red Cross covenant.[66]

Ten years after the start of the 1919–1940 introvert phase, Herbert Hoover was president and the American public, still discouraged over World War I, showed little interest in the affairs of Europe and Asia. Although conceding that the United States had not done its part in the past to insure world peace and to encourage international cooperation in humanitarian, cultural, and crime-preventive associations, Hoover insisted upon keeping his nation apart from future politico-military rivalries in Europe.[67]

At similar points in the progression of different introvert phases, Presidents Hoover and Carter have a number of similarities. Sons of farmers, both men were educated as engineers and became successful businessmen. Hoover was the first president elected from west of the Mississippi River, Carter the first from the Deep South since Zachary Taylor. Each man succeeded a "white knight" president who, in turn, had succeeded a president ruined by a scandal in his administration. Both Hoover and Carter, skilled administrators and strong in religious belief, demonstrated strength on humanitarian issues: Hoover served as chairman of the American Relief Commission following World War I and of the Famine Emergency Commission after World War II; Carter's stance on human dignity and human rights is well known. The Hoover administration significantly increased the acreage of national forests and parks; Carter likewise was strong on environmental issues. The Hoover-Stimson Doctrine of 1932 proclaimed that the United States would not recognize the results of Japanese aggression in the Far East. President Carter exhibited a similar tendency to formulate policy by unilateral declaration in his first few months in office; although this tendency later diminished, he never abandoned it. Indeed, his 1980 reactions to the Soviet invasion of Afghanistan could be viewed as an updated Hoover-Stimson Doctrine insofar as the Carter response made use of the nonmilitary capabilities of the United States while hinting at military reaction if the situation expanded. International economic problems consumed much of the energy of both leaders, although Hoover confronted more severe problems. Both Hoover and Carter emphasized international disarmament; Hoover's 1932 proposal to the General Disarmament Conference suggested that "the arms of the world should be reduced by nearly one-third,"[68] and Carter voiced similar strong aspirations in the nuclear age, stating in his inaugural address that "we will move this year a step toward our ultimate goal—the elimination of all nuclear weapons from this Earth."[69] Both Hoover and Carter, generally reluctant to compromise their idealism, demonstrated in foreign policy a somewhat less than realistic grasp of the complexities of international politics.

Finally, each introvert phase has ended in excess—during these periods the United States clearly has not done enough to protect its national interests. Toward the end of the first introvert phase, President Washington issued his neutrality proclamation with regard to the conflict between England and France. The position of a neutral desiring trade with both sides was difficult to maintain. Although some long-standing differences with the British were settled by the Jay Treaty, the compromise barely passed the Senate in early 1795. From 1795 to 1797, the United States also agreed to tribute treaties with three Barbary states. The nation had betrayed its interests in freedom of the seas in too many instances.

In 1836 Texas achieved independence after a bitter struggle with Mexico. Although the undeclared neutrality of the United States was laxly enforced on land, the mood of the United States was introvert and annexation was not forthcoming. Britain indicated willingness to protect Texan independence and Mexico threatened war should the United States annex the new nation. Tensions with the British over the involvement of individual Americans in Canadian insurrections grew, yet the United States government continued its endeavors to enforce strict neutrality. The United States also experienced boundary problems with Britain, particularly in the areas of Maine and the Oregon Territory. A settlement regarding the Maine boundary was reached in 1842, but it met with great popular dissatisfaction. Clearly, American foreign policy actions in the latter part of the 1824–1844 introvert phase were overly restrained.

During the 1871–1891 introvert phase, the United States had a relatively consistent disinterest in world affairs, even though European powers were increasing their influence throughout the world. American military strength, especially naval, was downplayed in favor of internal industrial and commercial growth. United States foreign policy interests were neglected most toward the end of the phase, since European imperial assertiveness was continually growing without an appropriate American counterbalance.

The Neutrality Acts of the late 1930s, demanded by strong introvert sentiment, were an extreme of introversion that proved to be most damaging. These acts, which prevented the United States from protecting its interests in both Europe and Asia, were an irrational solution to the politico-military maneuverings of the world powers at the time—maneuverings that in due course would ignite into World War II.

Evidence of current dissatisfaction with the international situation can be seen in the United States' willingness to withdraw from organizations like the International Labor Organization, the International Nuclear Regulatory Agency, and the United Nations Educational, Scientific, and Cultural Organization. Another manifestation of introversion is the Reagan administration's refusal to accept the Law of the Seas Treaty as negotiated by previous administrations. The strength of the nuclear freeze movement can be viewed as the product of the frustrations of many Americans with the nuclear arms race, an unfortunate power reality. Such measures are compatible with mid- to late-stage introversion.

Although extremes occur toward the end of each introvert phase, it is important to realize that in the long-term view of the mood/interest theory, circumstances leading to those extremes could be set in the middle third of the introvert phase. According to the theory, the middle of an introvert period is when public mood and realistic short-term interests most closely coincide. The least amount of foreign policy activity occurs in the middle third, illustrating this fact. Thus, introvert policies meet with less immediate international reaction than at previous times. As the introvert mood grows, foreign policy patterns continue to develop in the direction set in the middle stage, and the United States is carried into extreme introversion. Expectations of other countries formulated during second stages may need to be corrected by a rise in action during the last third of a phase despite the increasingly introvert mood. The United States is comfortable with doing less in the international arena during second stages and the rest of the world comes to take this lack of action for granted, insufficiently considering American interests during the third stage. Thus, the United States is forced to increase its actions to cope with a weak image initiated by the little action taken in the second stage. Since the world misunderstands American mood fluctuation, the beginning of extroversion can be the time of greatest danger. Throughout introvert phases, the world becomes accustomed to the United States' lack of concern about its interests and takes advantage of the situation. When the American mood changes, the United States may use military force against those unsuspecting countries who are taking advantage of it.

One contention of the mood/interest theory is that such excesses at the end of a phase do not necessarily go totally unnoticed; undoubtedly someone recognizes the growing threat, but the momentum of the dominant mood at the time overwhelms such recognition. If the United States is now moving into the latter stages of an introvert phase, as the mood/interest theory suggests, it might be hearing the beginnings of a reaction to the extreme introversion. It appears that this is indeed the case. For example, the recent movement for a nuclear freeze has been gaining nationwide support, but those arguing the dangers of such a policy have at least commanded some attention. Also, some have noted that since the mid-1960s the Soviet Union has gained a dangerous superiority in military capabilities over the United States, to the point that even Reagan's proposed increases are insufficient to meet the threat.[70] Indeed, it could be argued that the difference between President Reagan's foreign policy rhetoric and action evidences this fact: being closer to the foreign policy scene, Reagan and his advisors recognize to some extent the need to protect our interests, but the dominant introvert mood in the public and Congress prevents such action.

Similarly, warnings against the current direction of American foreign policy are appearing in other places. In a recent address, analyst Midge Decter argued:

> The fact of the matter is that in a world more and more of whose real estate is coming to stand in the shadow of the Soviet empire . . . the United States has only *two* choices of policy. . . . (a) we have the option to do everything in our power to undermine the economic, political, and military strength of our enemy . . . or (b) we have the option of accommodating ourselves to the ever-increasing spread of the enemy's power, a power which at this moment threatens to castrate our friends and allies and, after them, us.[71]

Perhaps such strong statements, and the fact that they go largely unnoticed, are indicative of the extent of current introversion. Unfortunately, if America is in an extremely introvert mood, the likelihood that such a condition will be recognized in time is small. Also, a recent study noted that "political science elites" have a tendency to side together in significant proportions on many issues.[72] If this is the case, and if these elites are responsible for a large share of the interpretation of the current situation, this could be another obstacle to recognition of current introversion.

By thus comparing current introversion with that in the same stage of development in past introvert phases, no indication is found that the current mood phase has dissipated. The danger of a strong introversion similar to that of the 1919–1940 period is significant. This is not to say that today's introversion is akin to that disastrous period immediately preceding Pearl Harbor, but rather that it is generally similar to the introversion of the mid 1930s. Early introversion helped temper the extreme extroversion of the late years of the 1891-1919 extrovert phase;[73] extreme introversion was not to come until 1935.[74] Extreme introversion in the current phase, in accordance with the historical analysis of the mood/interest theory, could very well be the United States' mood during the next several years.

In the current introvert phase, the intense concern about politico-military power which is so typical of extrovert phases has been reduced. Although talk of the importance of maintaining strength is still prevalent, talk of the possible use of American military power has greatly declined. The current introversion has been fostered by business liberals who want to advance peace by making trade concessions to the Soviet Union and by reform liberals who want to advance peace by using economic power to liberalize the Soviet attitude toward human rights. These diverse methods make the current degree of liberal convergence on introversion not quite as strong as the degree of convergence in the late 1930s, when business liberals wanted to insure peace by denying our economic power to warring nations and reform liberals wanted to insure peace by leaving other nations alone. America today probably has not reached such extreme introversion, but it could in the near future. Major indications are that the current introvert phase is clearly established, generally progressing in intensity and, so far, following the basic pattern of liberal mood alternation evidenced historically in American foreign policy.

ARGUMENTS AGAINST THE RETURN OF EXTREME INTROVERSION

Care must be taken to avoid confusion caused by the use of strong words. For example, use of the word *isolationist* is confusing simply because introvert Americans have not wanted to be isolated as much as they have wanted introvert responses to politico-military problems. Use of *isolationist* makes the danger of extreme introversion all too easy to dismiss. *Globalism* as well could be approached in a simplified manner in order to dismiss a possible return of extreme extroversion. In order to avoid such confusion, the mood/interest theory has minimized use of the globalist/isolationist terminology. The theory does not argue that there has ever been a strictly defined, pure isolationist period, but that there have been times when the United States has not done enough to protect its politico-military interests and that such a shortcoming could happen again.

American foreign policy analysts often argue that it is impossible to return to the isolationist posture of the 1930s. This argument, however, does not repudiate the application of the mood/interest theory to modern American foreign policy: the extremes of the current phase may not duplicate those of the last period of introversion, but they need not do so in order to be historically consistent; all that is required is that the United States fail to do enough to maintain its foreign policy interests.

In fact, such a shortcoming could just as easily happen now as in past introvert phases, since protection of the United States interests now requires a more active politico-military role. In every introvert phase extremes have occurred in part because the United States has had to do more than in the preceding introvert phase to protect its interests. For instance, the American interest in the prevention of one-nation dominance in Europe in the late 1930s realistically required that the United States unite with Great Britain and France to oppose German designs. Currently, the same interest requires more—that the United States not only cooperate in the defense of Europe, but that it assume the leadership role. Likewise, management or curtailment of the increasing proliferation of nuclear weapons throughout the world requires leadership by major powers.[75]

In a similar manner, Herbert Spiro notes changes in the relationship between the public and foreign policy since the cold war era. The writer notes that considerations such as Henry Kissinger's performance in foreign policy matters and the increasing complexity of foreign affairs have led to greater expectations, greater interest, and greater knowledge of foreign policy activities by the public. These changes will significantly affect the development of any new foreign policy consensus.[76] In terms of the mood/interest theory, this analysis supports the contention that the current introvert phase is somewhat different from past introvert phases, and the greater demands and interest in foreign policy contribute to the likelihood that support for extrovert policies will not consolidate into a consensus for several years.

These considerations are not, however, intended to suggest that patterns evident in previous introvert periods should be disregarded. Rather, the mood/interest theory contends that introvert moods are typified by certain general characteristics, the sum of which leads to neglect of real American politico-military interests, even though exact circumstances may be different in different introvert phases. Thus, by extrapolating general characteristics from previous introvert phases, one can compare them to those of the current introversion.

With this in mind, some of the recent literature covered in Chapter 1 could be looked at in terms of the present introvert phase. A majority of the recent writing on the American public's attitude regarding foreign policy concludes that America is currently internationalist, not isolationist. However, as mentioned above, the internationalist/isolationist (or globalist/isolationist) dichotomy can be misleading. If we look to the isolationists of the 1930s and filter out general characteristics, we can see many parallels with the so-called internationalists of current times.

Manfred Jonas defined five categories of 1930s isolationists,[77] and there are similarities to elements in the current introvert phase. Jonas's foreign-oriented isolationists, who were sympathetic to the Axis powers or the Soviet Union, are comparable to today's American Communist party. Belligerent isolationists who vigorously supported defense of American rights and interests, reliance on international law, and nineteenth-century unilateral policies are similar to those elements of the public today which support outdated cold war–era policy. Isolationists that Jonas called timid were willing to surrender some traditional American rights to minimize direct contact and entanglement. Comparable feelings are voiced today by those who are willing to sacrifice some interests in the name of compromises, i.e., arms control agreements. Jonas's radical isolationists wanted to avoid war to facilitate establishment of new social order in America (the New Deal vs. military spending). A similar sentiment today is expressed by the reform liberal emphasis on social programs rather than military spending. Conservative isolationists were afraid that war would destroy the old order and institutions which needed to be preserved (war effort vs. free enterprise and business interests). The same basic position is taken by business liberals today.

Jonas's categories have many similarities with three recent studies, all of which conclude that America is predominantly internationalist. Maggiotto and Wittkopf, Holsti, and Mandelbam and Schneider[78] all note the loss of consensus in American foreign policy and divide the different elements into factions that they label as one or another brand of internationalism. However, these branches of internationalism have common characteristics with those elements Jonas labeled isolationist. The Maggiotto and Wittkopf label of internationalists is the only label that does not include an element that can be related to one of the Jonas categories. The point is—regardless of the labels—that there are very few pure isolationists or pure internationalists. This lack of purity results in a division of the public into factions that current analysts prefer to call predominantly internationalist. However, almost all of the elements include some isolationist sentiments. In the American system of government, a lack of consensus, such as the one that currently exists, can lead to a deadlock that effectively becomes an introvert policy. Thus, the degree of convergence on introversion does not have to be as great as the degree of convergence on extroversion.

In essence, during the late 1930s introverts saw a choice between peace and war, and chose peace. Dissenting extroverts saw a choice between democracy and dictatorship, and chose democracy.[79] Both peace and democracy are liberal choices. It is reasonable to assert that today's introvert Americans see a choice between peace and war, while extrovert Americans see a choice between

American democracy and Soviet dictatorship. As in the late 1930s, the argument centers on which choice is the more relevant one.

Although the speech was written almost two hundred years ago, George Washington's Farewell Address contains some surprisingly relevant ideas which apply to the past decade and a half in American foreign policy. Washington supported the fulfillment of existing commitments and the expansion of commercial relations, yet asked that no new political commitments be made. The United States has continued to support such commitments as NATO and pursues expanded commercial relations with other countries, but since 1968 has not committed itself to new politico-military obligations except those necessary to meet previous commitments. Washington advises the United States to have no permanent enemies; similarly, efforts have been made in the past decade to breach the gaps separating the United States from such rivals as the Soviet Union and the People's Republic of China. Humanitarian concerns are expressed by Washington and such concerns remain important. Thus, comparison of similarities in the introvert advice of George Washington and the foreign policy of the United States since 1968 supports a continuation of past patterns. [80]

Few people are eager to accept the suggestion that the public might carry American foreign policy into another period of extreme introversion. Many arguments have been raised and differences noted in order to demonstrate why such a revision is not likely. The most common of these are examined below and answered by application of the mood/interest analysis.

One difference between the introverts of the 1930s and those of today is that the latter often are most upset by politico-military policies of the United States and the Soviet Union, whereas the former were most upset by policies of European nations. This might indicate that the United States is not duplicating the path of the 1930s. However, it is more accurate to view American introvert criticisms in the light of America's liberal view of power. Before 1940 the international center of power was Europe, and liberal concerns about such power were directed there during times of introversion. Today the United States and the Soviet Union are the international centers of power and, consistent with liberalism, today's introverts direct their criticisms at both powers. Differing objects of criticism simply do not indicate that the United States will avoid extreme introversion in the future.

The critique of the American power center of world politics today might be said to make Americans less nationalistic than when they opposed the European power center of the 1930s. However, both introvert phases are supported by arguments evidencing varying degrees of nationalism. Nationalist elements in both phases have included the idea that America must take care of itself before other countries and have a military capability focused on its own defense. Nonnationalistic arguments can be seen both in the 1920s argument that the League of Nations unwisely preserved the status quo of European rule over the world, preventing self-determination for many people, and the 1970s argument that developing nations should be able to determine their destiny without American military oversight. In fact, there seems to be a good degree of continuity over time between introvert rationales; for example, John Cooper, Jr., showed "how the isolationists of the 'Great War' established all the rationales that would be used by their successors down to Pearl Harbor."[81]

The pressures resulting from the advent of the nuclear age lead to an argument against the return of extreme introversion: it is too risky for the United States to withdraw from the central role in a world with self-destructive capabilities. Before 1945 the United States could exist in isolation and feel only limited effects of international disputes. The nation was protected by geography, having weak neighbors to the north and south and expansive oceans to the east and west. In a power-political sense, the shield of the British navy for most of American history provided sufficient indirect protection of our shores to allow periodic entrances and exits from world politics. Since 1945 the situation has changed, making the United States one of the two most powerful nations in the world. Nuclear weapons and other advances in military technology make it exceedingly difficult to limit the consequences of a future war. The argument continues that the American public cannot avoid foreseeing the dire results of introversion and will therefore refrain from it. The mood/interest theory, however, maintains that even though the United States' role as a world leader and the danger of nuclear weapons no longer allow it to alter its foreign policy without worldwide repercussions, the ability to do so remains. The freedom of political movement that the United States enjoyed earlier, thanks to geography and the British navy, has continued because of nuclear superpower status. What nation would challenge a United States determined to withdraw from the world center stage? Superpower status does not preclude the ability to revert to extreme introversion—it might even enhance that ability.

The contention that the world has become increasingly dependent on the United States in so many areas that its role is indispensable is based more on dogma than on history, and is reminiscent of some people's view of nineteenth-century Britain. No nation is indispensable. If one nation steps out of the limelight, other world powers will become more assertive and move closer to center stage. George Modelski's theory of long cycles in world politics argues that this has happened regularly throughout recent history, with one nation holding a position of world dominance for a little more than one hundred years.[82] Communist powers are known for their ability to move into vacuums. An intensifying of American introversion could also provoke more assertive behavior in such countries as West Germany and Japan, or provide more incentive for the formation of a powerful United States of Europe. In any event, the "indispensable America" argument seems unwarranted.

A similar argument advanced is that the United States is now part of an economically interdependent world and cannot retrench. However, the mood/ interest theory contends that American liberal moods operate differently from tariff fluctuations, business cycles, and most other economic indicators. Regardless of mood, economic interests have been fairly consistently pursued throughout American history, though they gain emphasis during introvert phases. There is no persuasive evidence that economic prosperity depends upon politico-military position in the world, as demonstrated by the present-day health of the West German and Japanese economies. Liberal America views politico-military and economic interests as being separate from each other; in fact, American politico-military introversion coupled with active American commercialism in an economically interdependent world is believed to be possible.[83]

On a related topic, Jon Alexander and Tom Darby offer the idea that the spread of American technology has developed into a type of American imperialism. The study notes that the last extrovert phase was followed by a period of detente and a technological race. It was America's technological superiority, the authors argue, that brought China into a "tacit alliance" with the United States, and "henceforward, Americans came to understand that they could more easily spread their empire through technology than through terror."[84] The mood/ interest theory, however, would construe modern technological exchanges as a form of economic activity, not exactly as imperialistic advances. Thus, ties with China would fall into the characteristic pattern of an introvert mood. Also, continuing shifts in Sino-American relations show that the technological bridges are none too secure.

It can be asserted that Americans have altered their ideology to the extent that it might be called a form of socialism. If this were the case, it would be plausible to argue that Americans are no longer subject to the liberal extremism in foreign policy evidenced in the past. However, the "socialism" in the "welfare state" begun in the 1930s is and has been a domestic phenomenon with no outward manifestations in foreign affairs behavior. Further, it lacks some major characteristics of the socialism manifested in other countries.[85] This weak "socialism" is a poor candidate to subdue the transcendent liberalism that has thrived for at least two hundred years and whose major values seem to remain among the vast majority of Americans. The argument that socialism has replaced liberalism as the dominant ideology is not relevant to American behavior on the international scene.

Some might view the isolationists of the 1930s as simple-minded people who did not understand the real nature of the world. This would be a matter of historical bias and easily refuted. Isolationists of the 1930s were a complex and far from homogeneous group. As noted earlier, Manfred Jonas lists five major types of isolationists in his study of the latter half of the decade: foreign-oriented, belligerent, timid, radical, and conservative.[86] Gabriel Almond lists the following five type of isolationists in his 1950 study: communist elements, noncommunist Wallacites, reactionary-nationalists, pacifists, and the extreme internationalists.[87] A variety of both reform and business liberals was represented among these groups, and all embraced the isolationist cause for diverse and often sophisticated reasons.

Senator William Borah (R-Idaho), who served several years as chairman of the Senate Foreign Relations Committee, certainly is one of the best known isolationists of the interwar period and typifies the complexity of American introvert thought. He was a reform liberal senator who voted for American participation in World War I, voted against the 1917 Espionage Act, called for a clear statement of war aims, supported amnesty for World War I political prisoners, and opposed the Treaty of Versailles in part because he was concerned that it was a vengeful peace that guaranteed European dominance over the colonial world. On other issues, Borah offered a resolution for establishment of relations with the Soviet government in 1922 (he believed that 140 million people could not be outlawed if peace were to be maintained in Europe), opposed United States membership in the World Court, denounced American intervention in Nicaragua and extraterritorial rights in China, supported the Kellogg-Briand Pact to outlaw offensive war, and regularly implied that European disputes prior to World War II were just more European power politics. Many intellectuals considered him the conscience of national politics because of his willingness to take an independent stance on important issues. Borah has been roundly criticized for his statement that Britain was behind Hitler after the German invasion of Czechoslovakia, but he was motivated in part by the belief that a secretly plotting Britain would allow Hitler a free reign in central Europe as long as it could insure the safety of its empire. He also recognized Hitler's potential in Europe and expressed the hope that the German chancellor would modify his character enough to take a place in history alongside Charlemagne.[88]

A belief that Borah was "simple-minded" ignores the complexity and sophistication of his record on American foreign affairs. Another isolationist leader, Senator Arthur Vandenberg (R-Michigan), also exhibited a complex official record on foreign policy.[89] Vandenberg, Borah, and other Americans of the time made typically American liberal errors in judgment. The fact that these introverts of the 1930s were not simple-minded argues the possibility that intelligent, reasoning people in our time might enter upon another era of extreme introversion in which American interests are not adequately maintained.

One argument that could be raised against a return of extreme introversion in mood/interest terms is that, whereas in past introvert phases the United States has been a growing power and has used introversion as a respite from dynamic expansion, requirements for United States actions are no longer growing. This may be so, but instead of negating a return of introvert excesses, this argument simply reduces the danger inherent in those extremes. If the amount of action required to protect American interests is leveling off or decreasing, some introversion may keep the nation from taking overly aggressive foreign policy action. Thus, some introversion in a time of steady or diminishing requirements for action could be beneficial for United States interests. However, successful introversion could add enough fuel to the introvert fire that the United States might not do enough to meet its interests. Thus, counting on declining requirements for action to check introversion is a dangerous gamble that could easily backfire. Indeed, this author sees a continuing rise in the actions required to meet United States interests in an increasingly complex world.

That events have caused the United States to mature is one final argument. One can claim that although the United States acted in accordance with fluctuating moods in the past, it has now matured, learned its lessons from the past, and is not destined to repeat past mistakes. This is wholly in keeping with the optimism which is so much a part of the American liberal heritage. Just as extrovert rationales such as William McKinley's religiously inspired 1899 support of the Philippine acquisition[90] and introvert rationales such as the 1930s isolationism appear peculiar and outdated to us today, so might Lyndon Johnson's desire to win the hearts and minds of the Vietnamese people and the current preference for introversion appear equally dated in the future. This analysis suggests that it is more accurate to state that arguments in behalf of both introversion and extroversion have themselves become more complicated and mature. The nation could be experiencing a new and more sophisticated type of introvert rationale that will lead to another extreme of introversion which Americans do not yet recognize as fitting the traditional pattern of fluctuating liberal moods in foreign policy.

Interestingly, a number of foreign policy writers, such as Bruce Russett and Zbigniew Brzezinski, acknowledge a changed public mood even though an optimism generally surfaces that the depth of this change is limited.[91] However, at present the introvert mood is past the two-thirds point in terms of the past mood phases identified in Klingberg's analysis. The optimism of Americans is all too characteristic of liberalism and needs to be balanced by a degree of pessimism in order to produce a reliable analysis.

Why would it be impossible for America to go through another period of introversion culminating in extremes outside of its national interest? America still has a dominant liberalism. The mass public still sets the parameters for foreign policy and the leadership of the country is in no position to deny mass desires. Presidential decision-making is a complex matter that does not indicate a reversal of moods, particularly since presidents are usually elected as a product of mood. Congressional assertiveness, a normal feature of introvert phases, projects rather than arrests public mood. Bureaucracy does not offer a realistic prospect of preventing extreme moods. The move to introversion has generally continued as in the past and there seems to be no reason why it does not have the potential to go to an extreme; all the while, American international behavior could remain curiously predictable.

It must be concluded, however, that the mood/interest analysis cannot predict the future. Any of its tenets may eventually be discarded: world events could make continuing shifts impossible; American liberalism could be abandoned for a new ideology; the time spans of the phases could narrow to ten years, or six years, or one year. However, the essential argument of the mood/interest theory remains valid: the forces pointing toward a return to extreme introversion are greater than is commonly recognized and a faith that this will not happen is not fully justified. The long-standing pattern of recurring extremes needs to be broken if American interests are to be realistically pursued in the future.

6. Conclusion

This book presents and defends the mood/interest concept as a valid interpretation of American foreign policy. The Introduction identified the six propositions of the mood/interest theory and argued that such long-range analyses are vital to a balanced foreign policy perspective. Chapter 1 defined American liberalism and demonstrated how it has been reflected in alternating American foreign policy moods for more than two hundred years. The second chapter showed how independent methodologies also support the mood/interest theory. Other influences on foreign policy were also described, but liberalism was discovered to be the crucial influence.

Chapter 3 defined the politico-military interests of the United States, described their incompatibility with basic American liberalism, and showed how their successful pursuit has been periodically negated by liberal public moods. The chapter noted economic and humanitarian interests and how their compatibility with American liberalism has, for the most part, spared them from the regular fluctuations in mood characteristic of the pursuit of politico-military interests. American wars, the most notable expression of the pursuit of politico-military interests, were seen to relate to the mood/interest framework. A geographic application of the Interests Proposition and Mood/Interest Conflict Proposition demonstrated that the theory can be applied to specific areas of U.S. concern.

Chapter 4 described various tools that the public possesses to insure that its mood is implemented in foreign policy, such as the president, the Congress, the bureaucracy, the press, and proposed constitutional amendments. If one of these forces fails to respond to public mood, it can be brought into line by the other forces. The electorate selects leaders exemplifying its moody liberalism. Current American introversion was then explored in Chapter 5, which began with an examination of the characteristics of past introvert phases. A subsequent historical comparison concluded that the United States is currently in a middle to late stage comparable to past introvert phases. Arguments that the phase will not intensify to a dangerous extreme were refuted, leaving strong indications that the United States in this decade may again fail to adequately protect its politico-military interests.

THE LONG VIEW

The mood/interest theory indicates that policy makers cannot ignore internal indicators, especially public mood, in the formulation of foreign policy. Constantly changing short-term opinion should not be allowed to eclipse long-term moods, which can be better appreciated when viewed as a continuation of historical trends.

Policy makers can also benefit from an understanding of the all-embracing nature of American liberalism. The public is not likely to change its liberal ideology; its expectations are not easily satisfied, and once the public rolls toward a liberal objective, it is not likely to stop until it has overrun realistic goals and is in the extremes of a foreign policy mood. Successful policy makers must satisfy liberal idealism, and thus retain their policy-making position, while still pursuing realistic foreign policy goals. Such a task is difficult at best.

The mood/interest theory suggests that the current congressional foreign policy assertiveness is to be expected during an introvert phase and, if history is a guide, congressional assertiveness will contribute to future extreme introversion. A balanced view of the strengths and weaknesses of the Congress, the presidency, and other foreign policy-making institutions is best obtained through a long-range analysis such as the mood/interest theory. Executive excesses during the Vietnam era should be contrasted with legislative excesses during the late 1930s to promote valid conclusions on the balance of legislative and executive powers. Policy extremes like those taken by the executive during the height of extroversion and conversely, the legislature during the height of introversion, might be avoided by improved public understanding of moods.

The constancy of American economic and humanitarian concerns is, on the whole, commendable; the real challenge facing the American public is to view politico-military interests with a similar consistency. Motivations behind the United States contribution to world peace differ greatly from those of other countries whose international relationships are stabilized by considerations such as weakness necessitating accommodation of more powerful neighbors, geographic location which restricts policy flexibility, authoritarian rulers who impose their will in a consistent manner, and diverse ideologies which necessitate compromise and limit foreign policy extremes. Thus, many countries less liberal than the United States have more consistent foreign policies.[1]

In order to make a greater contribution to international peace and stability, America needs a more consistent foreign policy. Each major shift of American foreign policy necessitates a new set of relationships with governments less subject to liberal mood shifts and therefore rarely sympathetic to American foreign policy dilemmas. These public mood and foreign policy shifts involve dangers of instability which could lead to war; yet the American liberal public mood continues to fluctuate. Policy makers aware of the dangers of these fluctuations can work at encouraging maintenance of politico-military interests at realistic levels.

Admittedly, a nuclear war, a drastic change in American ideology, or some other unexpected consideration could permanently interrupt the undulating moodiness of the American public. There are no strong indications of such an approaching disruption, however. The only apparent solution is to harness the public mood or at least modify it so that its extremes are still within the bounds of the reality-interest zone.

Policy makers need to recognize this problem. Someone has to worry about what to do in the next ten years, the next twenty years, and the next fifty years. Someone aware of the dangers of long-range tendencies, such as those posited in the mood/interest theory, should begin work now on preventive action lest American policy makers be forever doomed to putting out small fires whose smoke obscures the wider blaze. The mood/interest theory does not pretend to be the answer to tomorrow's problems; but policy makers who ignore the portent of long-range considerations will continually help create tomorrow's problems.

RESEARCH PRIORITIES

From a research perspective, if the mood/interest concept is valid and long-range moods are important, this work is merely a start in the right direction. It has been suggestive of the potential value of researching foreign policy moods in a specific manner rather than the more common practice of accounting for them in a general sense. In the process of preparing this work, the author has considered research possibilities related to each of the six propositions.

In the Public Rule Proposition, the relative influence of the elite as opposed to mass is difficult to discern. The argument of the proposition is that the mass is more important than commonly acknowledged. Once this is accepted, the research question becomes one of the mechanics of elite-mass interaction. Assertions made here could be examined with an eye toward clarifying the nature of limits set by the mass and the realm of choice available to foreign policy leaders. Research on activities of competing potential elites also would help describe the operation of moods.

The Liberal Moods Proposition noted that moods were manifested in American liberalism. At times, the author has speculated that moods were caused by American liberalism. However, more research is needed for a cause to be stated with certainty. A first step would devise empirical tests which would point to the more promising hypotheses. This is, of course, easier said than done; indeed, Chapter 1 noted important differences between opinion and mood with the latter being less tangible.

The Interests Proposition says that the U.S. has definable interests. Is there any way to apply interests in specific terms to specific current cases? What is the possibility that the degree of U.S. action necessary to realize interests might level off or decline in view of our current world position? If this does happen, what are the implications for mood? Economic interests generally are secondary to politico-military interests, but there are some interesting relationships between the mood/interest analysis and long cycles by N. D. Kondratieff that need to be further researched.

The Mood/Interest Conflict Proposition hypothesized that there was a fundamental conflict between liberal moods and interests as defined by power politics. If so, is there a viable way to lessen this conflict? If mood and interest do not fit as the hypothesis has speculated, what are other viable explanations? This work assumed that the U.S. must compete in the world of power politics. Some would question such an assumption, but still might view mood as an important concept. Is there a way to make a specific interpretation of mood without relation to interest?

One field which has seen a lot of recent research is executive-legislative relations in foreign policy. If the Executive/Legislative Proposition is valid, it needs to be specifically related to this body of research. An increasing number of writers are also working on long-range cycles. This work has identified a number of these persons and their ideas, but a systematic search followed by some empirical testing could be a helpful line of inquiry. In a related sense, since Frank L. Klingberg's U.S. foreign policy moods research proved to be crucial in the development of the mood/interest theory, a detailed analysis of some of his other works could be productive.[2]

The application of the mood/interest theory in Chapter 1 subdivided phases into three subphases. Klingberg divides phases into liberty and union segments. The mood/interest analysis itself indicates that there are certain years where mood is outside the interest zone, but that these probably vary by individual situations. Research into possible ways to construct and document subphases could advance knowledge in what the mood/interest analysis indicates is an important area.

Important research possibilities exist for the Extreme Introversion Proposition. The empirical verification done in Chapter 2 indicated that there can be a lead time between the period when the United States might be quite unlikely to act and the time when it actually is not doing enough to protect its interests. How does lead time work? Does it mean that we are locked into extreme introversion around the mid-introvert stage? Do extrovert moods work in the same manner? In general, lead time makes prevention of extremes even more difficult.

SPECULATIONS: THE COMING DECADE

The challenge of the next decade will be to realize that the United States might now be almost locked into a path toward extreme introversion, due to the directions established in the past decade and a half, and that this path must be discouraged. One measure which could help prevent extreme introversion would be to minimize unrealizable rhetoric. Extreme introversion can feed on unrealized expectations. Some policy makers might be able to combine a strong introvert rhetoric with realist policies in order to realize the best of both worlds. Historically, however, the public soon expects the rhetoric to be enacted into policy. Frustration with American actions in the world could result whether or not rhetoric becomes policy. If it becomes policy, policy becomes more unrealistic and likely to experience problems. If it does not become policy, America can be seen as betraying its ideals. In essence, policy makers should enunciate realistic policy objectives that recognize American interests of the next decade as well as those of the next few years. Introvert rhetoric that satisfies the public today could endanger United States interests in the coming decade. At least some policy makers should view policies in terms of the overall introvert-extrovert cycle involving approximately fifty years.

The next ten years will probably find the United States under great public pressure to avoid military measures which could result in another Vietnam-type situation. Whenever feasible, the United States will tend toward a solution not involving decisive United States military action or even semimilitary intelligence operations. Most often this pressure could be expected to produce a nonviolent solution to problems. A series of nonmilitary responses by the United States should not be mistaken for a normal pattern. If the United States realizes that it is failing to meet interests, it could become more inclined toward strong military response after repeated frustrations, thus heralding a return to extroversion.

In fact, since mood change is a multiyear process even though the overall change occurs in a single year, the beginnings of the next extrovert phase could surface soon. In one sense, these beginnings will set the stage for a future extreme. However, in the most immediate sense, mood change is a valuable force which prevents an even greater extreme in the previous direction.

Speculation on expectations of American policy by other governments based upon previous cycles offer both opportunities and dangers. In the realm of opportunities, internal forces checking excessive American politico-military actions are likely to be strong over the next decade. This should produce opportunities for the reduction of tension. Economic and humanitarian concerns of American policy probably will remain, and Congress will continue to be assertive. As the decade progresses, American policy is likely to become less realistic and more unilateral, particularly in a politico-military sense.

Conclusions regarding the next ten years also can be drawn in terms of worldwide and geographic interests. The following section will emphasize dangers of extreme introversion. This does not mean that the author advocates extreme extroversion, which would be equally dangerous. However, this danger is known by a public which has experienced Vietnam. Creative solutions within the American interest zone are needed, as defined by world events rather than American moods.

The American interest in the prevention of a nuclear exchange will probably be increasingly difficult to maintain if nuclear proliferation continues over the course of the coming decade. Perhaps nuclear weapons will make each possessor part of a cautious balance of terror. However, proliferation could also require an increased United States role if military super-powers must provide restraint. Even if problems of proliferation are solved, relations between the United States and its fellow military superpower, the U.S.S.R., will remain of crucial importance. In particular, the United States will have to maintain an appropriate strategic balance with the Soviet Union and must be aware that changing mood could precipitate Soviet miscalculation. Recent calls for a freeze on production and deployment of nuclear weapons are obviously indicative of the magnitude of the current introversion. While such goals are indeed valuable, Americans need to recognize that, at a time of strong introversion, moves toward reduction in American strategic capability could be detrimental.

Maintenance of freedom of the seas will require a strong role for the American navy. This is important not only for American access to the rest of the world, but also for major United States allies whose dependence on freedom of the seas is often greater than that of the United States. The United States faces a challenge in maintaining naval strength and competence at a level equal to the demands of the coming decade.

One of the most difficult challenges facing the United States in the next decade will be retention of a realistic set of geographic priorities. The American position is complicated by a number of considerations in addition to the basic mood/interest conflict. First, Americans do not have a fine sense of geography since they have been privileged, being protected from other major powers by the Atlantic to the east and the Pacific to the west. Second, ethnic groups traditionally have had a stronger voice during introvert phases in the absence of a general interest in foreign policy than they have had in extrovert phases, when this general interest is quite high. Thus, the United States can adopt a tough stance regarding Eastern Europe, Cyprus, and Israel in response to various ethnic pressures. At the time, however, general NATO strength, vital to a military posture in each of these three areas, may be barely maintained in the face of increasing Soviet capabilities. Third, the priority of Europe over Asia in American policy could result in another underestimation of an Asian security threat should a changing balance of power require an increased American role in the region, or economic relations with Japan deteriorate. Finally, the United States has not placed as high a priority on Latin America in relation to other less developed countries as a geographically-oriented interest strategy would indicate is wise. Any one or combination of the above considerations could cause serious difficulty for the United States in the next ten years.

If the lessons of American diplomatic history prove reliable for the future, the United States can expect a return to extroversion within the next decade, perhaps as early as the late 1980s. Looking back to the beginnings of past extrovert phases, it is obvious that such changes are characteristically significant events. The beginnings of the first two extrovert phases (1798–1824 and 1844–1871) were marked by enormous land acquisitions, both doubling the former land area of the nation and including the Mexican-American War in the annexation of Texas. The first few years of the third and fourth extrovert periods as well were occupied by the Spanish-American War, indicating a move toward overseas possessions, and World War II, indicating a move toward major world power. Thus, one can speculate that another switch from extreme introversion to extroversion is likely to be equally significant, and the author will leave it to the imagination of the reader to determine what this change might involve. At least it is safe to say that in a nuclear age, Americans can hardly afford to wait and see if the mood/interest pattern proves reliable. If Americans refuse to accept this possibility of a mood/interest conflict and don't try to avoid it, one can only hope that some of the violent energy of mood shifts will be channeled into constructive use. Indeed, because half of the coming decade could feature the beginning of an extrovert phase, it is important to consider the workings of early extrovert phases in detail. Knowledge of past patterns should be used to avoid moves which could undermine international peace.

What can harness the fluctuation of American liberal public moods? The importance of governmental leaders and institutions in this regard has already been noted. The ambiguous stances of national-level politicians indicate that leaders are still attempting to cater to the mass public in order to win or retain public office and therefore cannot be the reforming influence. Indeed, since major policy makers in a democracy are subject to the direction of elected politicians, the policy maker is not in a good position to formulate a long-term solution. Recognition of the problems is probably the limit of the policy makers' contribution. If a change is going to come, the public must be made aware of and accept the need for consistency in American foreign policy. Who, then, is in a viable position to undertake this formidable task?

The educational community, especially higher education, could provide needed leadership if some of its preferences are changed. Foreign policy teaching has tended to correspond to public mood fluctuations, though generally preceding them slightly, and often reacts to a particular phase just before it has run its course. Most often, an academician reacting to a phase falsely assumes that his or her students understand the events which sparked it, an assumption which usually complicates matters. About the time students complete their education, they are well equipped to support the current foreign policy mood, which eventually is carried to an extreme in terms of foreign policy interests. Educators then attempt to correct this mood excess in the next generation of students; again, mistakenly, without a meaningful explanation of events which had originally sparked that mood phase. Thus, the educational community, which has some potential elites among its members, influences the public which chooses the exact elite in control. This at least has the potential to stimulate positive change.

Another significant shortcoming, especially in higher education, is that courses in political science tend to concentrate on contemporary events. While there is value in this, a distorted picture results if it is not tempered by a balanced historical perspective. Such concentration on the present, as viewed in terms of the immediate past and periods similar to the immediate past, has reinforced the mood fluctuations that are apparent in American foreign policy history.

The broad historical approach is not always the easiest nor the most interesting to students. One can be tempted to cover current concerns and state that background can be acquired by interested students who choose to take advanced courses. Such statements do little for most students who take only introductory courses. By concentrating on the present while failing to take a broad, historical perspective, an educator loses the advantage of historical comparison and contrast and the additional benefit of long-term relevance.

Educational community effectiveness is limited by the elitist view of American foreign policy taken by many scholars. Contending that an elite determines foreign policy and the mass public, therefore, has little power, these elitist educators erringly believe that educating average people cannot lead to meaningful change, thereby limiting their own influence.

A greater public awareness of the foreign policy problems caused by extreme moods would probably make the public more conscious of and less prone to extreme shifts in mood. Such an increase in awareness can only be accomplished over a long period of time, particularly since it takes approximately fifty years for a complete introvert-extrovert cycle. The educational community has the tools, the flexibility, the freedom from inhibitions, and the talent to take on the task of alerting the American liberal public to this problem. At a minimum, educators should explain the reasons for past policy overreactions and work at presenting a balanced, historical picture, emphasizing the influence and dangers of long-term moods.

The problem exists. Scholars continue to discover the wisdom of a less active world role for the United States and communicate their discovery to students who have not been exposed to the opposite arguments, just as a few decades ago intellectual leaders were advancing the need for active involvement in world affairs to students who had little exposure to the need for restraint. Modern weapons of mass destruction cannot be combined with the past degree of American foreign policy shifts. Thus, for the future we must decide: will we meet our problem head-on or will we continue to be singularly predictable? Perhaps this is the ultimate question raised by the mood/interest theory.

Tables

Table 1. Wars and Annexations of Territory in Introvert and Extrovert Phases, 1776–1967

	Cycle							
	1st 1776–1823		2nd 1824–1870		3rd 1871–1918		4th 1919–1967	
Mood	Wars	Annexations	Wars	Annexations	Wars	Annexations	Wars	Annexations
Int.	1	0	0	0	0	0	0	0
Ext.	1	3	1	5	2	8	3	1

Source: U.S. Bureau of the Census, *Historical Statistics of the United States—Colonial Times to 1970,* Bicentennial Edition, House Doc. 93–78 (Washington, D.C.: G.P.O., 1975), Part I, p. 428 and Part II, p. 1140.

Note: Wars included are: War of Independence, War of 1812, Mexican-American War, Spanish-American War, World Wars I and II, Korean war, and Vietnam war. The Civil War was excluded because it was not an international war.

Table 2. Uses of Force Abroad in Introvert and Extrovert Phases, 1798–1967

	Cycle						Average
Mood	1st 1776–1823	2nd 1824–1870	3rd 1871–1918	4th 1919–1967	Total	Average	Per Year
Int.	Data not in study	15	12	15	42	14.0	0.69
Ext.	23	38	56	21	138	34.5	1.27

Sources: Information in this table comes from Foreign Affairs Division, Legislative Reference Service, Library of Congress for Subcommittee on National Security Policy and Scientific Developments of the House Committee on Foreign Affairs, *Background Information on the Use of U.S. Armed Forces in Foreign Countries* (Washington, D.C.: G.P.O., 1970), Appendix II, pp. 50–57; and J. David Singer and Melvin Small, *The Wages of War: 1816–1965: A Statistical Handbook* (New York: John Wiley & Sons, Inc., 1972), pp. 17–39 and 59–75.

Note: Criteria for counting uses of force abroad are listed on p. 191.

Table 3. Introvert and Extrovert Uses of Force Abroad, by Mood Stage

Mood Phase	Stage			Total
	1st	2nd	3rd	
	Introvert Phases			
	1824–30	1831–36	1837–43	
2nd (1824–43)	4	5	6	15
	1871–77	1878–83	1884–90	
3rd (1871–90)	5	1	6	12
	1919–25	1926–32	1933–39	
4th (1919–39)	11	3	1	15
Total (introvert)	20	9	13	42
	Extrovert Phases			
	1798–1806	1807–14	1815–23	
1st (1798–1823)	4	9	10	23
	1844–52	1853–61	1862–70	
2nd (1844–70)	7	19	12	38
	1891–99	1900–08	1909–18	
3rd (1891–1918)	17	17	22	56
	1940–48	1949–57	1958–67	
4th (1940–67)	9	4	8	21
Total (extrovert)	37	49	52	138

Sources: Information in this table comes from the Committee on Foreign Affairs, Appendix II, pp. 50–57; and Singer and Small, *Wages of War*, pp. 17–39 and 59–75. See page 191 for counting criteria.

Table 4. Uses of Force Abroad by Mood Cycle and Stage, 1798–1967

Mood Cycle	Introvert Stages			Extrovert Stages			Cycle Total
	1st	2nd	3rd	1st	2nd	3rd	
				1798–1806	1807–14	1815–23	
1st (1776–1823)	Not in study			4	9	10	23
	1824–30	1831–36	1837–43	1844–52	1853–61	1862–70	
2nd (1824–70)	4	5	6	7	19	12	53
	1871–77	1878–83	1884–90	1891–99	1900–08	1909–18	
3rd (1871–1918)	5	1	6	17	17	22	68
	1919–25	1926–32	1933–39	1940–48	1949–57	1958–67	
4th (1919–67)	11	3	1	9	4	8	36
Stage Total[a]	20	9	13	37	49	52	180
				(33)	(40)	(42)	(157)

Source: Adapted from table 3.
[a] Figures in parentheses are totals without the first extrovert phase.

Table 5. Introvert and Extrovert Second-Stage Dates and McClelland High Power/Low Power Years

Mood Curve Second Stages	McClelland High Power/Low Power Years[a]	Fit or No Fit
1783–89	1785 Low	Fit
1807–14	1805 High	No Fit
1831–36	1835 Low	Partial Fit
1853–61	1855 Low	Fit
1878–83	1875, 1885 Low	Fit
1900–08	1905 Low	Fit
1926–32	1925 Low	Fit
1949–57	1945, 1955 Low	Fit

Sources: The McClelland years of high and low power are adapted from David McClelland, "Love and Power: The Psychological Signals of War," *Psychology Today* 8 (January 1975), chart, p. 46. See table 3 for stage dates.

[a] When affiliation is high in relation to power, McClelland defines these years as low power.

Table 6. Swing Decades for Mood Curve and McClelland High Power/Low Power Years

Mood Curve Swing Decade[a]	McClelland High Power/Low Power Years	Fit or No Fit
1793–1803	1795 High	Fit
1819–29	1825 High	Fit
1839–49	1845 High	Fit
1866–76	1875 Low	No fit
1886–96	1895 High	Fit
1914–24	No data	No data
1935–45	1935 High	Fit
1963–73	1965 High	Fit

Source: Adapted from McClelland, "The Psychological Signals of War," chart, p. 46.

[a] Within five years of a transition year.

Table 7. Motive and Power Divergence Scores (PDS) for Second-Stage-Only (SSO) and Non-SSO Presidents (Polk–Reagan)

Mood Phase	President and Years in Office[a]	Motive Scores[b]				Ave. PDS for Phase Presidents		
		Achievement	Power	Affiliation	PDS	All	SSO	Non-SSO
2nd	Polk 1845–48	28.4	55.3	16.3	39.0	23.94	8.15	34.47
Ext.	Taylor 1849–50[c]	36.4	45.5	18.2	27.3			
1844–70	**Pierce 1853–56**	**32.9**	**44.3**	**22.8**	**21.5**			
	Buchanan 1857–60	**47.4**	**23.7**	**28.9**	**–5.2**			
	Lincoln 1861–65[c]	22.3	57.4	20.3	37.1			
3rd	Grant 1869–76	28.5	43.0	28.5	14.5	–0.15	–13.9	4.43
Int.	**Hayes 1877–80**	**30.5**	**27.8**	**41.7**	**–13.9**			
1871–90	Cleveland 1885–88	27.8	33.4	38.8	–5.4			
	B. Harrison 1889–92	29.2	37.5	33.3	4.2			
3rd	Cleveland 1893–96	26.8	62.5	10.7	51.8	31.48	37.5	29.98
Extrovert	McKinley 1897–1901[c]	53.2	18.2	28.6	–10.4			
1891–1918	**T. Roosevelt 1901–08**	**37.5**	**50**	**12.5**	**37.5**			
	Taft 1909–12	25.1	54.9	20.1	34.8			
	Wilson 1913–20	31.3	56.2	12.5	43.7			
4th	Harding 1921–23[c]	25.8	41.9	32.2	9.7	22.35	11.1	26.1
Introvert	Coolidge 1923–28	26.9	50	23.1	26.9			
1919–39	**Hoover 1929–32**	**44.4**	**33.3**	**22.2**	**11.1**			
	F. Roosevelt[d] 1933–45[c]	41.7	50	8.3	41.7			
4th	F. Roosevelt[d] 1933–45[c]	41.7	50	8.3	41.7	21.3	–3.5	27.5
Extrovert	Truman 1945–52	27.0	48.6	24.3	24.3			
1940–67	**Eisenhower 1953–60**	**25.0**	**35.7**	**39.2**	**–3.5**			
	Kennedy 1961–63[c]	33.4	40.7	25.9	14.8			
	L. Johnson 1963–68	45.8	41.7	12.5	29.2			
5th	Nixon 1969–74[c]	45.0	27.5	27.5	0	2.73	–3	5.6
Introvert	**Carter 1977–80**	**36.4**	**30.3**	**33.3**	**–3**			
1968–	Reagan 1981–	45.8	32.7	21.5	11.2			
	Average of all presidents					17.56	6.36	21.91
	Average of extrovert presidents					25.57	12.58	30.3
	Average of introvert presidents					8.82	–1.93	12.85

Sources: Statistics in table 7 are adapted from David G. Winter and Abigail J. Stewart, "Content Analysis as a Technique for Assessing Political Leaders," in *A Psychological Examination of Political Leaders,* ed. Margaret G. Hermann (New York: The Free Press, 1977), table 2.3, p. 53. Scores from Polk through McKinley and Carter and Reagan are derived from our own coders, who follow the Winter Manual in Appendix I of David G. Winter, *The Power Motive* (New York: The Free Press, 1973), pp. 247–66.

[a] Elected presidents with one or more years in office. Second-stage-only presidents are listed in boldface type. For stage classification criteria, see page 191.

[b] Achievement, power, and affiliation scores, the three components of the total motive score, may not add up to 100 because of rounding.

[c] These presidents died or resigned while in office, and their successors took over in mid-year.

[d] F. Roosevelt is included in both the fourth introvert phase and the fourth extrovert phase according to the rules of classification. Therefore, his score is used once when finding the average of all presidents and once in each average when finding the average of introvert and extrovert presidents.

Table 8.   Ratio of Affiliation Motive to Total Motive Score (Polk–Reagan)

Phase and President	Affiliation Ratio	Average Ratio for Phase [a]
2nd Extrovert		1:4.69
Polk	1:6.13	
Taylor	1:5.49	
Pierce	1:4.39	
Buchanan	1:3.46	
Lincoln	1:4.93	
3rd Introvert		1:2.81
Grant	1:3.51	
Hayes	1:2.40	
Cleveland	1:2.58	
B. Harrison	1:3.00	
3rd Extrovert		1:5.92
Cleveland	1:9.35	
McKinley	1:3.50	
T. Roosevelt	1:8	
Taft	1:4.98	
Wilson	1:8	
4th Introvert		1:4.66
Harding	1:3.11	
Coolidge	1:4.33	
Hoover	1:4.50	
F. Roosevelt[b]	1:12.05	
4th Extrovert		1:4.54
F. Roosevelt[b]	1:12.05	
Truman	1:4.12	
Eisenhower	1:2.55	
Kennedy	1:3.86	
L. Johnson	1:8	
5th Introvert		1:3.65
Nixon	1:3.64	
Carter	1:3.00	
Reagan	1:4.65	

Source: Ratios were found by dividing 100, the total motive score, by the affiliation score (from table 7) for each president. The average ratio for each phase was derived by dividing the sum of the total motive scores by the sum of the affiliation scores.

[a] To nearest hundredth.

[b] F. Roosevelt was president for twelve years during the fourth introvert and extrovert periods. It might be expected that Roosevelt's third inaugural in 1941 would have an even lower ratio than his first one in 1933, since the 1941 mood was extrovert. We checked and found the third inaugural devoid of affiliative imagery. However, in accord with Winter's view that only first inaugurals show the motives, we used the 1933 score in both the 1919–40 introvert and 1940–68 extrovert phases.

Table 9. Presidential Power Divergence Score (PDS) and McClelland High Power/
Low Power Years (Polk–L. Johnson)

Mood Stage of Presidency	President and Years in Office	PDS and Inaugural	McClelland High Power/ Low Power Years	Correlation/No Correlation[a]
Ext. 1st	Polk 1845–48	39.0 (1845)	1845 High	Correlation
Ext. 2nd	Buchanan 1857–60[b]	− 5.2 (1857)	1855 Low	Correlation
Int. 1st	Grant 1869–76[b]	14.5 (1869)	1865 Low	Correlation
Int. 2nd	Hayes 1877–80[b]	− 13.9 (1877)	1875 Low	Correlation
Int. 3rd	Cleveland (1st inaugural) 1885–88	− 5.4 (1885)	1885 Low	Correlation
Ext. 1st	McKinley 1897–1901[b]	− 10.4 (1897)	1895 High	No Correlation
Ext. 2nd	T. Roosevelt 1901–08	37.5 (1905)	1905 Low	No Correlation
Ext. 3rd	Wilson 1913–20	43.7 (1913)	1915 No Data	No Data
Int. 1st	Coolidge 1923–28	26.9 (1925)	1925 Low	No Correlation
Int. 3rd	F. Roosevelt 1933–45	41.7 (1933)	1935 High	Correlation
Ext. 1st	Truman 1945–52	24.3 (1949)	1945 Low	No Correlation
Ext. 2nd	Eisenhower 1953–60	− 3.5 (1953)	1955 Low	Correlation
Ext. 3rd	L. Johnson 1963–68	29.2 (1965)	1965 High	Correlation

Sources: Stage information in table 9 is adapted from table 3. Presidential power divergence scores come from table 7. McClelland years are found in McClelland, "The Psychological Signals of War," chart, p. 46.

[a] The average power divergence score (Polk–L. Johnson) is 19.58. For comparison with McClelland's data, we designated power divergence scores below that average as low and those above the average as high.

[b] These presidents' first inaugurals are closest to the McClelland years specified, although they were not in office in those years. This analysis assigned McKinley to the McClelland high power year of 1895, but it is interesting also to note Cleveland's second inaugural of 1893. In this speech Cleveland's power divergence score was 51.8, the highest of any president. This correlation between high power divergence and a high power year supports our hypothesis, because there is a marked difference in the power divergence scores of Cleveland's first and second inaugurals. These two speeches both correlate with McClelland's data, and the change in Cleveland's dominant motive seems attributable to the change in the general public mood.

Table 10.   Presidential Power Divergence Scores and Uses of Force
(Polk–L. Johnson)

President	Power Divergence Score	Uses of Force[a]	Years in Office[b]	Uses of Force per Year in Office
		Ten Highest Power Divergence Presidents		
Cleveland (2nd term)	51.8	7	4	1.75
Wilson	43.7	16	8	2
F. Roosevelt	41.7	9	12	.75
Polk	39.0	2	4	.5
T. Roosevelt	37.5	14	8	1.75
Lincoln	37.1	4	4	1
Taft	34.8	10	4	2.5
L. Johnson[c]	29.2	6	5	1.2
Taylor	27.3	1	2	.5
Coolidge	26.9	8	6	1.33
Average[d]	36.9	—	—	1.35
Total	—	77	57	—
		Ten Lowest Power Divergence Presidents		
Hayes	−13.9	0	4	0
McKinley	−10.4	9	5	1.8
Cleveland (1st term)	−5.4	3	4	.75
Buchanan	−5.2	9	4	2.25
Eisenhower	−3.5	2	8	.25
B. Harrison	4.2	6	4	1.5
Harding	9.7	2	2	1
Hoover	11.1	0	4	0
Grant	14.5	7	8	.875
Kennedy	14.8	2	3	.67
Average[d]	1.59	—	—	.87
Total	—	40	46	—

Sources: Information on power divergence scores is derived from table 7. Information on uses of force comes from the Committee on Foreign Affairs, Appendix II, pp. 50–57.

[a] In years when a president died in office or a new president was inaugurated, a use of force is credited to the president who initiated it; if a major war was in progress, the use of force is attributed to the president who served the greater part of the year.

[b] Rounded to the nearest full year. A president must serve at least one-third of a year in order for that year to be counted as a year in office.

[c] Although earlier tables give the Vietnam war only four force counts, L. Johnson is given five for the war. This is because the earlier tables ended with the conclusion of the fourth extrovert phase (1967), whereas Johnson's term ended in 1968.

[d] Average is found by dividing total uses of force by total years.

Table 11. Power Divergence Scores (PDS) and Uses of Force by Second-Stage-Only Presidents and by First- and Third-Stage Only Extrovert Presidents

Mood Phase	Stage Dates	President and Years in Office[a]	PDS	Years in Office During Stage	Uses of Force During Stage	
					Number	Per Year in Office
				2nd-Stage-Only Presidents[b]		
2nd Ext.	1853–61	Pierce 1853–56	21.5	4 (1853–56)	10	2.5
		Buchanan				
		1857–60	−5.2	4 (1857–60)	9	2.25
3rd Int.	1878–83	Hayes 1877–80	−13.9	3 (1878–80)	0	0
3rd Ext.	1900–08	T. Roosevelt				
		1901–08	37.5	8 (1901–08)	14	1.75
4th Int.	1926–32	Hoover 1929–32	11.1	4 (1929–32)	0	0
4th Ext.	1949–57	Eisenhower				
		1953–60	−3.5	5 (1953–57)	1	.2
Average[c]			7.92	—	—	1.21
Total			—	28	34	—
				1st- and 3rd-Stage-Only Extrovert Presidents[b]		
2nd Ext.	1844–52					
	(1st)	Polk 1845–48	39.0	4 (1845–48)	2	.5
	1862–70					
	(3rd)	Taylor 1849–50	27.3	2 (1849–50)	1	.5
		Lincoln				
		1861–65	37.1	3 (1862–64)[a]	4	1.33
3rd. Ext.	1891–99					
	(1st)	Cleveland (2nd term)				
		1893–96[b]	51.8	4 (1893–96)	7	1.75
		McKinley				
		1897–1901	−10.4	3 (1897–99)	6	2
	1909–18					
	(3rd)	Taft 1909–12	34.8	4 (1909–12)	10	2.5
		Wilson 1913–20	43.7	6 (1913–18)	12	2
4th Ext.	1940–48					
	(1st)	F. Roosevelt[d]				
		1933–45	41.7	5 (1940–44)[a]	8	1.6
	1958–67					
	(3rd)	Kennedy 1961–63	14.8	3 (1961–63)	2	.67
		L. Johnson				
		1963–68	29.2	4 (1964–67)[a]	5	1.25
Average[c]			30.9	—	—	1.5
Total			—	38	57	—

Sources: Stages in extrovert and introvert mood phases are shown in tables 2–4. Presidential power divergence scores are from table 7; for rules of Presidential classification see page 191. Information on uses of force is from Committee on Foreign Affairs, Appendix II, pp. 50–57.

[a] President Lincoln was not counted as serving in 1865 because he died April 15, after serving less

Table 11, continued

than one-third of the year. President Franklin Roosevelt was not counted as serving in 1945 for the same reason. Likewise, President Lyndon Johnson was not counted as serving in 1963 because he did not take office until November of that year.

  b Presidents from the first mood cycle and the second introvert period are omitted because not covered by our power divergence analysis. Presidents from the fifth introvert period (1968–) are omitted because a count of uses of force was not available for this period.

  c Average is found by dividing total uses of force by total years.

  d F. Roosevelt served longer than any other president, and dominated both a third-stage introvert and a first-stage extrovert period. Under these unique circumstances, we thought that assigning him an "only" classification for both stages would be most appropriate for comparative purposes.

Table 12. Power Divergence Scores (PDS) and Uses of Force by Introvert Second-Stage-Only and Extrovert First- and Third-Stage-Only Presidents

President	PDS	Uses of Force Per Year in Office During Stage
	Introvert Second-Stage-Only Presidents	
Hayes	− 13.9	0
Hoover	11.1	0
Average	−1.4	0
	Extrovert First- and Third-Stage-Only Presidents	
Polk	39.0	.5
Taylor	27.3	.5
Lincoln	37.1	1.33
Cleveland (2nd term)	51.8	1.75
McKinley	− 10.4	2
Taft	34.8	2.5
Wilson	43.7	2
F. Roosevelt	41.7	1.6
Kennedy	14.8	.67
L. Johnson	29.2	1.25
Average	30.9	1.5

Source: Data selected from table 11.

Table 13. Classification of Presidents by Barber Categories (Polk–Carter)

	Mood	Party
Active-Positives		
James Polk	Extrovert	Democrat
Abraham Lincoln	Extrovert	Republican
Rutherford B. Hayes	Introvert	Republican
Grover Cleveland	Introvert, Extrovert[a]	Democrat
Theodore Roosevelt	Extrovert	Republican
Franklin Roosevelt	Introvert, Extrovert[a]	Democrat
Harry Truman	Extrovert	Democrat
John F. Kennedy	Extrovert	Democrat
	7/10 (70%) Extrovert	5/8 (62.5%) Democrat
	3/10 (30%) Introvert	3/8 (37.5%) Republican
Active-Negatives		
Zachary Taylor	Extrovert	Whig
James Buchanan	Extrovert	Democrat
Andrew Johnson	Extrovert	Union Democrat
Woodrow Wilson	Extrovert	Democrat
Herbert Hoover	Introvert	Republican
Lyndon Johnson	Extrovert	Democrat
Richard Nixon	Introvert	Republican
Jimmy Carter[c]	Introvert	Democrat
	5/8 (62.5%) Extrovert	5/8 (62.5%) Democrat
	3/8 (37.5%) Introvert	3/8 (37.5%) Republican or Whig[b]
Passive-Positives		
Millard Fillmore	Extrovert	Whig
Franklin Pierce	Extrovert	Democrat
Chester A. Arthur	Introvert	Republican
William McKinley	Extrovert	Republican
William H. Taft	Extrovert	Republican
Warren G. Harding	Introvert	Republican
Gerald R. Ford[c]	Introvert	Republican
	4/7 (57%) Extrovert	6/7 (86%) Republican or Whig[b]
	3/7 (43%) Introvert	1/7 (14%) Democrat
Passive-Negatives		
Ulysses S. Grant	Introvert	Republican
Benjamin Harrison	Introvert[d]	Republican
Calvin Coolidge	Introvert	Republican
Dwight D. Eisenhower	Extrovert	Republican
	3/4 (75%) Introvert	4/4 (100%) Republican
	1/4 (25%) Extrovert	0/4 (0%) Democrat

Sources: Introvert/extrovert classifications are from table 7. Information on presidential character is from James David Barber, *The Presidential Character: Predicting Performance in the White House* (Englewood Cliffs, N.J.: Prentice-Hall, Inc., 1977). Presidents T. Roosevelt–Nixon were rated by Barber; the rest were classified by the authors, using Barber's criteria.

[a] Roosevelt and Cleveland were counted in both an introvert and an extrovert phase according to the three-year rule. See page 191.

[b] Whigs are classified with Republicans because their beliefs were similar.

[c] Ford and Carter took office after Barber's theory was published. Because the theory has been

popular, we believe presidents and their staffs sometimes tried to conform to Barber's preferred active-positive category. We recognize that we differ from Barber on Ford and Carter.

[d] Klingberg lists 1891 as a transition year. In this study we have arbitrarily assigned transition years to the later mood phase for reasons of clarity. This left Harrison with two years in an extrovert phase and two years in an introvert phase. We assigned Harrison to the third introvert phase because according to Klingberg his term falls two years in the third introvert phase, one year in transition, and one year in the third extrovert phase.

Table 14. Presidents' Years in Office and Stage(s) Occupied in Mood Period (Polk–Reagan)

President and Years in Office	Classification by Stage and Mood	Years of Stage
Polk 1845–48	1st Stage Extrovert	1844–52
Taylor 1849–50	1st Stage Extrovert	
Fillmore 1850–52	1st Stage Extrovert	
Pierce 1853–56	2nd Stage Extrovert	1853–61
Buchanan 1857–60	2nd Stage Extrovert	
Lincoln 1861–65	3rd Stage Extrovert	1862–70
A. Johnson 1865–68	3rd Stage Extrovert	
Grant 1869–76	1st Stage Introvert	1871–77
Hayes 1877–80	2nd Stage Introvert	1878–83
Arthur 1881–84	2nd Stage Introvert	
Cleveland 1885–88	3rd Stage Introvert	1884–90
B. Harrison 1889–92	3rd Stage Introvert	
Cleveland 1893–96	1st Stage Extrovert	1891–99
McKinley 1897–1901	1st Stage Extrovert	
T. Roosevelt 1901–8	2nd Stage Extrovert	1900–08
Taft 1909–12	3rd Stage Extrovert	1909–18
Wilson 1913–20	3rd Stage Extrovert	
Harding 1921–23	1st Stage Introvert	1919–25
Coolidge 1923–28	1st Stage Introvert, 2nd Stage Introvert	1926–32
Hoover 1929–32	2nd Stage Introvert	
F. Roosevelt 1933–45	3rd Stage Introvert, 1st Stage Extrovert	1933–39 1940–48
Truman 1945–52	1st Stage Extrovert, 2nd Stage Extrovert	1949–57
Eisenhower 1953–60	2nd Stage Extrovert	
Kennedy 1961–63	3rd Stage Extrovert	1958–67
L. Johnson 1963–68	3rd Stage Extrovert	
Nixon 1969–74	1st Stage Introvert	1968–74
Ford 1974–76	2nd Stage Introvert	
Carter 1977–80	2nd Stage Introvert	1975–81
Reagan 1981–	3rd Stage Introvert	1982–

Sources: Information on stage years in table 14 is derived from table 3. See table 7 for presidents and years in office and page 191 for stage classifications.

[a] Because the fifth introvert phase is still in progress, the end years of stages in this phase are tentatively selected, relying on the average twenty-one-year pattern of introvert phases and assuming seven-year stages.

Table 15. Bridgepoint Presidencies and Barber Categories

President and Years in Office	Barber Category	Bridgepoint Years
J. Adams 1797–1800	AN	1797–99
Monroe 1817–24	PP	1823–25
J. Q. Adams 1825–28	AN	1823–25
Tyler 1841–44	AN	1843–45
Polk 1845–48	AP	1843–45
Grant 1869–76	PN	1870–72
B. Harrison 1889–92	PN	1890–92
Wilson 1913–20	AN	1918–20
F. Roosevelt 1933–45	AP	1939–41
L. Johnson 1963–68	AN	1967–69
Nixon 1969–74	AN	1967–69
	8/11 (73%) Active; 3/11 (27%) Passive	
	8/11 (73%) Negative; 3/11 (27%) Positive	

Sources: Derived from table 13 and mood cycle transition years.

Note: A bridgepoint president is defined as one who is in office within a year of a transition year. For example, to be a bridgepoint president for 1798, one would have to be in office in 1797, 1798, or 1799. Presidents J. Adams through B. Harrison were coded by the authors according to Barber's criteria. Barber categories are abbreviated as follows: A = active, P = passive; N = negative, P = positive.

Table 16. Barber Category and Party Affiliation of Presidents, Divided by Stage (Polk–Carter)

President	Barber Category	Party Affiliation
	1st and 3rd Stage Extrovert	
Polk	AP	Democrat
Taylor	AN	Whig
Fillmore	PP	Whig
Lincoln	AP	Republican
A. Johnson	AN	Union Democrat
Cleveland	AP	Democrat
McKinley	PP	Republican
Taft	PP	Republican
Wilson	AN	Democrat
F. Roosevelt	AP	Democrat
Truman	AP	Democrat
Kennedy	AP	Democrat
L. Johnson	AN	Democrat
	$^{10}/_{13}$ (77%) Active; $^{3}/_{13}$ (23%) Passive	$^{8}/_{13}$ (62%) Democrat
	$^{9}/_{13}$ (69%) Positive; $^{4}/_{13}$ (31%) Negative	$^{5}/_{13}$ (38%) Republican or Whig
	1st and 3rd Stage Introvert	
Grant	PN	Republican
Cleveland	AP	Democrat
B. Harrison	PN	Republican
Harding	PP	Republican
Coolidge	PN	Republican
F. Roosevelt	AP	Democrat
Nixon	AN	Republican
	$^{3}/_{7}$ (43%) Active; $^{4}/_{7}$ (57%) Passive	$^{2}/_{7}$ (29%) Democrat
	$^{3}/_{7}$ (43%) Positive; $^{4}/_{7}$ (57%) Negative	$^{5}/_{7}$ (71%) Republican
	2nd Stage	
Pierce	PP	Democrat
Buchanan	AN	Democrat
Hayes	AP	Republican
Arthur	PP	Republican
T. Roosevelt	AP	Republican
Coolidge	PN	Republican
Hoover	AN	Republican
Truman	AP	Democrat
Eisenhower	PN	Republican
Ford	PP	Republican
Carter	AN	Democrat
	$^{6}/_{11}$ (55%) Active; $^{5}/_{11}$ (45%) Passive	$^{4}/_{11}$ (36%) Democrat
	$^{6}/_{11}$ (55%) Positive; $^{5}/_{11}$ (45%) Negative	$^{7}/_{11}$ (64%) Republican

Sources: Derived from tables 13 and 14.

Table 17. Barber Categories Related to Winter Ratings, Introvert/Extrovert Phases, and Force Indicators (Polk–Carter)

	Active-Positive[a]	Active-Negative	Passive-Positive	Passive-Negative
Winter ratings				
Power divergence score	25.21	14.73	13.9	10.53
Achievement	30.6	40.96	34.25	27.4
Affiliation	22.09	22.16	25.93	31.03
Introvert/extrovert	7/10 (70%) Extrovert	5/8 (62.5%) Extrovert	4/7 (57%) Extrovert	3/4(75%) Introvert
Force indicators (per year in office)				
Uses of force abroad Polk–L. Johnson)	.88	1.41	1.71	.88
Major wars[b] (Polk–Nixon)	.16[c]	.35	.01	.02
Major war casualties (Polk–Nixon)	24,070[c]	19,807	196	983

Sources: Derived from tables 7 and 13. Data for force indicators was obtained from Committee on Foreign Affairs, Appendix II, pp. 50–57; Melvin Small and J. David Singer, *Resort to Arms: International and Civil Wars, 1816–1980* (Beverly Hills: Sage Publications, 1982), pp. 82–95; and *The World Almanac and Book of Facts, 1983* (New York: Newspaper Enterprise Association, Inc., 1982), pp. 337. Those wars defined in Small and Singer as "interstate" were counted as major wars, and casualty counts were obtained from *The World Almanac.*

Note: Some presidents were omitted when data were inapplicable or unavailable.

[a] Cleveland's addresses were both coded and included in the Active-Positive averages.

[b] The length of major wars was calculated in months in order to obtain a more accurate picture of their duration. The Boxer Rebellion was not included in our analysis because of its short duration and because American battle deaths numbered only twenty-one.

[c] The Civil War is not included. If it were, major wars and major war casualties for active-positive presidents would be considerably higher.

Table 18. Presidential Rankings: Schlesinger (1948 and 1963) and Murray and Blessing (1983)

President	Rank	President	Rank	President	Rank
Washington	2	Pierce	32	Wilson	4
J. Adams	10	Buchanan	33	Harding	36
Jefferson	5	Lincoln	1	Coolidge	31
Madison	15	A. Johnson	27	Hoover	22
Monroe	16	Grant	35	F. Roosevelt	3
J. Q. Adams	14	Hayes	17	Truman	8
Jackson	6	Arthur	23	Eisenhower	18
Van Buren	21	B. Harrison	26	Kennedy	12
Tyler	28	Cleveland	13	L. Johnson	9
Polk	11	McKinley	20	Nixon	34
Taylor	29	T. Roosevelt	7	Ford	24
Fillmore	30	Taft	19	Carter	25

Source: These calculations are taken from Bernard J. Vonk and Kimberly L. Japinga, "Popular Moods and Presidential Posterity: The Influence of American Foreign Policy Mood Shifts on 'Presidential Greatness' " (a paper presented to the Political Science Section, Michigan Academy, Eastern Michigan University, Ypsilanti, Michigan, March 25, 1983).

Table 19. Rankings Summary (Polk–Carter)

Barber Category	Ranking by Historians	Power Divergence Score[a]	Party Affiliation		Mood	
Active-Positive	9.0	25.21	Democrat	5	Extrovert	70%
			Republican	3	Introvert	30%
Active-Negative	22.88	14.73	Democrat	5	Extrovert	62.5%
			Republican[b]	3	Introvert	37.5%
Passive-Positive	26.29	13.9	Democrat	1	Extrovert	57%
			Republican[b]	6	Introvert	43%
Passive-Negative	27.5	10.53	Democrat	0	Extrovert	25%
			Republican	4	Introvert	75%

Sources: Derived from tables 13, 17, and 18.
[a] Power divergence scores and other Winter material were calculated for elected presidents only.
[b] Including Whigs.

Table 20. Historians' Ranking, Power Divergence Scores, and Uses of Force, by Mood Stage

Mood Stage	Average Ranking by Historians[a]	Average PDS	Total Years in Office[b]	Uses of Force[b]	
				Total	Average per Year
1st stage introvert	34 (30)	12.78	21	20	.95
2nd stage introvert	23.7 (21.1)	5.28	19	9	.47
3rd stage introvert	14 (15.5)	13.5	21	13	.62
1st stage extrovert	16.3 (14.3)	28.95	36	37	1.03
2nd stage extrovert	19.6 (18.8)	14.92	35	49	1.4
3rd stage extrovert	12 (12.6)	31.92	38	52	1.37
Introvert phases	24.1 (21.2)	8.58	61	42	.69
Extrovert phases	16.2 (15.3)	25.57	109	138	1.27

Sources: Average historians' rankings are derived from table 18. Power divergence scores are from table 7, and uses of force are found in table 3.

[a] Averages, by stage, for presidents from Polk through Carter. Ranks in parentheses are averages by stage from Washington through Carter. Classifications of presidents before Polk are: Washington 3rd stage introvert; J. Adams 1st stage extrovert; Jefferson 1st stage extrovert; Madison 2nd stage extrovert; Monroe 3rd stage extrovert; J.Q. Adams 1st stage introvert; Jackson 2nd stage introvert; Van Buren 3rd stage introvert; Tyler 3rd stage introvert.

[b] 1798–1967.

Table 21. Public Policy Cycles (Elected Presidents, Polk–Carter)

Mood Phase and Stage	President	Ranking by Historians[a]	PDS[a]	Barber Category	Policy Cycle Points	Average Uses of Force per Year[b]
2nd Extrovert						
1st stage	Polk/Taylor	20	33.15	AP/AN	War	.78
2nd stage	Pierce/					
	Buchanan	32.5	8.15	PP/AN	Reform	2.11
3rd stage	Lincoln	1	37.1	AP	Reform/War	1.33
Average		21.2	23.94	80% A		1.41
3rd Introvert						
1st stage	Grant	35	14.5	PN	Scandal	.71
2nd stage	Hayes	17	− 13.9	AP	Reform	.17
3rd stage	Cleveland/				(Propriety)	
	B. Harrison	19.5	− .6	AP/PN	Quiescence	.86
Average		22.8	− .15	50% A		.6
3rd Extrovert						
1st stage	Cleveland/					
	McKinley	16.5	20.7	AP/PP	Reform/War	1.89
2nd stage	T. Roosevelt	7	37.5	AP	War/Reform	1.89
3rd stage	Taft/Wilson	11.5	39.25	PP/AN	War	2.2
Average		12.6	31.48	60% A		2

Table 21, continued

Mood Phase and Stage	President	Ranking by Historians[a]	PDS[a]	Barber Category	Policy Cycle Points	Average Uses of Force per Year[b]
4th Introvert						
1st stage	Harding/ Coolidge	33.5	18.3	PP/PN	Scandal	1.57
2nd stage	Coolidge/ Hoover	26.5	19	PN/AN	Reform (Propriety)	.43
3rd stage	F. Roosevelt	3	41.7	AP	Reform	.14
Average		23	22.35	50% A		.71
4th Extrovert						
1st stage	F. Roosevelt/ Truman	5.5	33	AP/AP	War	1
2nd stage	Truman/ Eisenhower	13	10.4	AP/PN	War/ Quiescence	.44
3rd stage	Kennedy/ L. Johnson	10.5	22	AP/AN	Reform/War	.8
Average		10	21.3	80% A		.75
5th Introvert						
1st stage	Nixon	34	0	AN	Scandal	—
2nd stage	Carter	25	–	AN	Reform (Propriety)	—
Average		29.5	– 1.5	100% A		

Sources: Presidents and mood phase stages are adapted from table 14. Rank numbers are from table 18 and power divergence scores from table 7. Barber categories are taken from table 13 and uses of force from data summarized in table 3.

[a] In both historians' ranking and power divergence score, the phase average is obtained by taking each president's rank or score separately and dividing by the total number of presidents per mood phase.

[b] Average for each stage is determined by the number of uses of force divided by the number of years in the stage regardless of presidents. Average for the entire phase is calculated in the same manner.

Table 22. Summary (Polk–Carter)

Mood Phase	Average Ranking by Historians	Average PDS	Policy Cycle Points	Average Uses of Force per Year
2nd extrovert	21.2	23.94	War Reform War	1.41
3rd introvert	22.8	−.15	Scandal Reform (Propriety) Quiescence	.6
3rd extrovert	12.6	31.48	Reform War Reform War	2
4th introvert	23	22.35	Scandal Reform (Propriety) Reform	.71
4th extrovert	10	21.3	War War Quiescence Reform War	.75
5th introvert	29.5	−1.5	Scandal Reform (Propriety)	—

Source: Data selected from table 21.

Table 23. Senate Votes of Sparsely Populated Great Plains and Western States

Issue	Actual Senate Vote Y–N	Comparable G.P. & W. Vote[a]	Actual G.P. & W. Vote	Dominant Public Mood[b]	Significance for Perceptions of Pragmatism
1930s Isolationist Leaders[c]	12	4	7	Introvert	As extreme position, made slightly less introvert position appear pragmatic.
1949 NATO	82–13	N = 4	N = 8	Extrovert	By contrast, made extrovert NATO votes appear more pragmatic.
1954 Bricker Amendment	60–31	N = 10	N = 5	Extrovert	Support of introvert amendment made extrovert mood appear more pragmatic.
1964 Gulf of Tonkin Resolution	88–2	N = 1	N = 2	Extrovert	Only opposing votes made sharp. extroversion appear more pragmatic.
1969 National Commitments	70–16	N = 5	N = 9	Introvert	By contrast, made introvert votes appear more pragmatic.
1978 Panama Canal Treaties[d]	68–32	N = 10	N = 17	Introvert	By contrast, made introvert votes appear more pragmatic.
1981 Sale of AWACS to Saudi Arabia[e]	52–48	Y = 17	Y = 24	Introvert	Significantly carried extrovert vote; allowed President to act pragmatically outside of dominant mood.

Sources: The Congressional Record, Congressional Quarterly Weekly Report, and Manfred Jonas, *Isolationism in America, 1935–1941* (Ithaca, N.Y.: Cornell University Press, 1966). For specific references, see notes to chapter 2.

[a] This column lists what G.P. & W. votes would have been if they were proportionate to these states' percentage of the total Senate vote. These percentages are: 1930s, 1949, and 1954—31% (30 G.P. & W. votes out of 96); 1964, 1969, 1978, and 1981—32% (32 G.P. & W. votes out of 100).

[b] This column refers to the long-range mood phases as developed in this text, which are not to be confused with temporary public opinions on the particular issues.

[c] This issue did not, of course, have a direct vote, so vote counts cannot be listed. Rather, the numbers are of the isolationist leaders; of twelve such leaders in the Senate, four should have come from G.P. & W. states by proportion, whereas seven actually were from these states.

[d] There were two treaties, but the votes were identical.

[e] The actual resolution was opposed to the sale; 52 votes supported the sale, 48 votes opposed the sale.

Table 24. International War Nation-Months by Mood Phase

Mood Phase[a]	Years	Nation-Months War Under Way[b]	Average Nation-Months per Year
2nd Int. 1824–43	20	11.52	.576
2nd Ext. 1844–70	27	19.18	.710
3rd Int. 1871–90	20	13.44	.672
3rd Ext. 1891–1918	28	21.83	.780
4th Int. 1919–39	21	7.95	.379
4th Ext. 1940–67	28	28.47	1.017

Sources: Mood phases taken from table 3. Information regarding nation-months of war under way taken from Small and Singer, *Resort to Arms,* pp. 151–54.

[a] For the purposes of data comparison, divisions between mood phases were set at the beginning of transition years, rather than trying to pinpoint a specific date. Transition years are counted in each new phase on the assumption that elements of the new mood begin having some effect prior to the full mood shift.

[b] Nation-months of war are adjusted by Small and Singer to account for the number of nations in the international system each year.

Table 25. American Moods and Van Duijn's Divisions of Kondratieff, 1782–1973

	Prosperity[a]	Recession	Depression	Recovery
Introvert	20.48%	21.69%	34.94%	22.89%
Extrovert	76.15	14.68	0	9.17

Source: Jacob J. van Duijn, "Fluctuations in Innovations Over Time," *Futures* (August 1981), p. 268.

Note: For statistical counting reasons, transition years have been included in the new phase for both the mood/interest and van Duijn analyses.

[a] Van Duijn includes two war periods in his analysis. These periods are presented in a manner that suggests they extend prosperity and should therefore be considered part of that category.

Table 26. American Diplomatic Action in Introvert and Extrovert Phases, 1776–1967, by Region

Phase	North America	Latin America	Europe	East Asia	Mid-East and N. Africa	S. Asia and Sub-Saharan Africa	Total by Phase	Average Actions Per Year
1st Int. 1776–97	74	0	51	3	5	0	133	6.05
1st Ext. 1798–1823	61	12	33	1	5	0	112	4.31
2nd. Int. 1824–43	36	11	6	8	0	0	61	3.05
2nd Ext. 1844–70	49	62	1	11	0	0	123	4.56
3rd Int. 1871–90	18	10	2	13	0	0	43	2.15
3rd Ext. 1891–1918	41	86	56	48	2	0	233	8.32
4th Int. 1919–39	23	17	80	35	2	0	157	7.48
4th Ext. 1940–67	40	43	130	109	41	24	387	13.82
Total by Region	342	241	359	228	55	24	1249	

Source: Fred W. Wellborn, *Diplomatic History of the United States* (Totowa, N.J.: Littlefield, Adams, & Co., 1970)

Note: All important events listed by Wellborn are included; multiple year or extended actions were counted only once, in the year of initiation. Generally, events were tabulated in the region of primary impact. Certain events deemed to be of major international importance—world conferences, major treaties, multinational negotiations—are counted in more than one geographic region. U.S. activity in multinational negotiations has increased since 1890. Mexico is included in Latin America. South Asia includes India, Pakistan, Bangladesh, and Sri Lanka. Southeast Asian countries are included under East Asia. Events were initially tabulated by the author's research assistants and independently verified by Tamra Avritt and David Hendershott.

a For statistical counting reasons, the transitional year is always included in the new phase.

Table 27. Public Concern About Foreign Policy, 1974–1982

	Respondents concerned about			
	Our relations with foreign countries		Getting into another war	
Date of Poll	Percent	Rank[a]	Percent	Rank[a]
January 1974	18	8	7	12
January 1975	10	12	11	10
July 1975	11	11	9	12
January 1976	13	10	10	12
January 1977	9	11	8	12
January 1979	15	8	9	12
January 1981	19	7	18	8
January 1982	21	6	16	10

Source: "Environmental Update," in "Opinion Roundup," *Public Opinion* 5 (February/March 1982), p. 33.

[a] Out of 12—the other 10 concerns were domestic.

Note on the Compilation of the Tables

Uses of Force Abroad

Counts of uses of force, which appear in tables 2, 3, 4, 10, 11, 12, 17, 20, 21, and 22 are based on the following criteria:

Actions listed in Committee on Foreign Affairs, *Background Information,* receive one count. Major wars (those classified as "interstate" or "extra-systemic" wars in Singer and Small, *Wages of War*) continuing for more than one year, according to dates given in Committee on Foreign Affairs, are given one additional count for each year beyond the first in which the United States was involved for four months or longer. (Criteria for inclusion and data on major wars are in Singer and Small, pp. 17–39 and 59–75.)

In addition to the interstate and extrasystemic wars covered in Singer and Small, two wars outside the time span of that study were classified as major wars. The War of 1812 (1812–14) was given a force count of three and the Vietnam War (1964–67) a count of four. Also not included in Singer and Small are the undeclared naval war with France (1798–1800) and the two U.S. conflicts with the Barbary pirates (1801–05, 1815); these were counted as single instances because they did not meet the Singer and Small criteria for major wars.

Actions not classified as major wars but listed in Committee on Foreign Affairs as continuing for more than one year receive one count in the year of initiation, unless force is indicated as peaking in a later year, in which case both year of initiation and peak year are counted.

Major wars receiving multiple counts and bridging division years are divided proportionately: years of a war prior to division are included in the earlier phase or stage, and years of a war following a division are included in the later phase or stage.

Actions listed in Committee on Foreign Affairs under a single year entry are counted as single instances (e.g. 1823–Cuba–April 8, April 16, July 11, July 21, and October 23—one count). *But* separate year entries for the same year and same country are counted separately (e.g., 1864–Japan and 1864–Japan—two counts).

Transition years are included in the new phase (e.g., 1940 in the fourth extrovert phase).

Presidential Classification

Stage classifications of presidents, used in tables 7, 9, 11, 12, 14, and 21 are based on the following criteria:

Presidents who spent two full terms or more in office must spend more than three years in the stage to be put in that stage. Presidents spending more than one full term, but less than two full terms must spend more than two years in a stage to be so classified. A president with one term or less is placed in the stage where he spent most of his time in office; a president who served equal time in two stages is included in the stage during which he was elected. A year of elected succession is counted in only one stage, but a year in which a president dies in office or resigns is allowed to overlap. President Garfield, who served less than seven months, is not included in our analysis.

A second-stage-only president is one who is classified exclusively in a second stage. Presidents Coolidge and Truman are classified as second-stage presidents but not as second-stage-only presidents because they are also classified in other stages.

For the fifth introvert phase, which is still in progress, we assume the average twenty-one-year pattern of introvert phases, divided into seven-year stages.

For a complete listing of presidents by stage of mood phase see table 14.

Notes

Introduction

1. Frank L. Klingberg, "The Historical Alternation of Moods in American Foreign Policy," *World Politics* 4 (January 1952): 239-73.

2. For example, George H. Quester cites Klingberg's mood cycle theory as a specific interpretation of the history of American diplomacy, which he then uses as an example in his review of two more general theories. ("The Malaise of American Foreign Policy: Relating Past to Future," *World Politics* 33 [October 1980]: 82-95).

3. Frank L. Klingberg, *Cyclical Trends in American Foreign Policy Moods: The Unfolding of America's World Role* (Lanham, Md.: University Press of America, Inc., 1983).

4. Samuel P. Huntington identified several characteristics of liberalism which influence foreign policy actions in *The Soldier and the State* (New York: Vintage Books, 1957). The relevance of liberalism to U.S. foreign policy thinking is discussed on pp. 90-91 and 143-57.

5. Regional variations in U.S. foreign policy priority are defined and the interaction between various levels is discussed in Bernard K. Gordon, *Toward Disengagement in Asia: A Strategy for American Foreign Policy* (Englewood Cliffs, N.J.: Prentice-Hall, Inc., 1969), pp. 9-30.

6. Frank Klingberg noted in 1979 that the first signs of the new extroversion might appear around "say, 1983." Klingberg identifies an earlier start (1966) of the current introvert phase than does the analysis in the text (1968). If the mood/interest analysis is on the late side in estimating the start of the current introvert phase, then the possible return to extroversion may be earlier than is inferred in the text. Frank L. Klingberg, "Cyclical Trends in American Foreign Policy Moods and Their Policy Implications," in *Challenges to America: United States Foreign Policy in the 1980's,* eds. Charles W. Kegley, Jr., and Patrick J. McGowan (Beverly Hills: Sage Publications, 1979), p. 43.

7. Gene E. Rainey, *Patterns of American Foreign Policy* (Boston: Allyn and Bacon, 1975), pp. 44-57.

8. Harold D. Lasswell endorses the significance of moods, predicting that "when the climate of international action is made the object of more extended investigation by the full armory of methods appropriate to the task, the results will greatly illuminate the pace and goals of world history. For the mood phase of action is the stream bed where all tributary initiatives and messages meet and fuse in a dominant channel." Harold D. Lasswell, "The Climate of International Action," in *International Behavior: A Social-Psychological Analysis,* ed. Herbert C. Kelman (New York: Holt, Rinehart and Winston, 1965), p. 352.

1. Liberalism, Moods, and American Foreign Policy

1. See John Locke, *Two Treatises of Government,* 2nd ed., ed. Peter Laslett (Cambridge: Cambridge University Press, 1967), especially the "Second Treatise of Government," pp. 285-446.

2. Edward Weisband, in his 1973 study, maintains that "Lockean liberalism . . . is as relevant to American society today as it was in Jefferson's time despite the many changes in culture and belief." Edward Weisband, *The Ideology of American Foreign Policy: A Paradigm of Lockean*

Liberalism (Beverly Hills: Sage Publications, 1973), p. 11. At the end of his book, however, Weisband asserts that the United States has recently abandoned but not replaced Lockean liberalism (p. 62). The analysis in this book does not agree with Weisband on the abandonment issue. For a discussion indicating the continuing underlying presence of American liberalism, see Everett C. Ladd, Jr., "Traditional Values Regnant," *Public Opinion* 1 (March/April 1978): 45-49.

3. Louis Hartz, *The Liberal Tradition in America* (New York: Harcourt, Brace & World, Inc., 1955), p. 3.

4. The terms *business liberal* and *reform liberal* are used in Huntington, *Soldier and the State*.

5. Thomas Jefferson, "First Inaugural Address at Washington, D.C., March 4, 1801," *Inaugural Addresses of the Presidents of the United States* (Washington, D.C.: Government Printing Office, 1974), pp. 14-16.

6. Richard Milhous Nixon, "Inaugural Address, January 20, 1969," *Inaugural Addresses*, pp. 276-79.

7. U.S. Congress, Senate, 95th Cong., 1st sess., 20 January 1977, *Congressional Record* 123, no. 11: S1132.

8. "President Reagan's Inaugural Address," *Congressional Quarterly Weekly Report* (24 January 1981), pp. 186-88.

9. W. Wayne Shannon, "Mr. Reagan Goes to Washington: Teaching Exceptional America," *Public Opinion* 4 (December/January, 1982); 13-20. Quotations on pages 15 and 17.

10. Many ideas in this paragraph are developed in Hartz, *Liberal Tradition*, and in Huntington, *Soldier and the State* pp. 146-47. Also, for a further development of Huntington's views on American liberalism, see Samuel P. Huntington, *American Politics: The Promise of Disharmony* (Cambridge, Mass.: Harvard University Press, 1981).

11. Hartz, *Liberal Tradition*, p. 308.

12. Huntington, *Soldier and the State*, pp. 90-91 (quotations), 149-50 and 289-94.

13. Weisband, *Ideology*, p. 9.

14. Wilson indicated this in a 1917 speech, "Peace Without Victory," *Messages and Papers of the Presidents*, 17 (New York: Bureau of National Literature, Inc., 1923): 8203-4.

15. U.S. Congress, Senate, William E. Borah giving "The Case for Non-Entanglement," 66th Cong., 1st sess., 19 November 1919, *Congressional Record* 58, part 9:8783.

16. See Hans J. Morgenthau, "The Mainsprings of Foreign Policy: The National Interest vs. Moral Abstractions," *The American Political Science Review* 44 (December 1950):848-51. See Arthur Schlesinger, Jr., for a discussion of the negative influences of the idealist mood versus the realist mood in the American character, "Foreign Policy and the American Character," *Foreign Affairs* (Fall 1983):1-16. In addition, Robert Dallek acknowledges the nonrational influences of the public on foreign policy. A strong domestic mood is registered in the complexity of this policy *(The American Style of Foreign Policy*, [New York: Alfred A. Knopf, Inc., 1983] pp. xi-xx.

17. Here cited from Justus D. Doenecke, *The Literature of Isolationism* (Colorado Springs: Ralph Myles, Publishers, 1972), p. 33, who refers to Karl Ernest Meyer, "The Politics of Loyalty: From La Follette to McCarthy in Wisconsin: 1918-1952," a doctoral thesis (Princeton University, 1956).

18. See Arthur A. Ekirch, Jr., *The Civilian and the Military: A History of the American Antimilitarist Tradition* (Colorado Springs: Ralph Myles, Publisher, Inc., 1972), p. 149; and Harold and Margaret Sprout, *The Rise of American Naval Power, 1776-1918* (Princeton, N.J.: Princeton University Press, 1946), pp. 267-68.

19. See Huntington, *Soldier and the State*, especially p. 289, for an observation on business liberal opposition to militarism from Woodrow Wilson through Franklin Roosevelt; and Ekirch, *Civilian and the Military*, p. 252, for an account of business liberal Herbert Hoover's opposition to Franklin Roosevelt's prewar policies.

20. See particularly Selig Adler, *The Isolationist Impulse* (New York: The Free Press, 1957),

pp. 400-405, for an account of Senator Robert Taft's leadership of business liberal opposition to such cold war measures as NATO membership.

21. Bruce M. Russett and Elizabeth C. Hanson, *Interest and Ideology* (San Francisco: W. H. Freeman and Company, 1975), especially pp. 244-70.

22. Herbert Hoover, "Our National Policies in this Crisis," *Addresses Upon the American Road, 1950-1955* (Stanford, Cal.: Stanford University Press, 1955), p. 7.

23. Henry Brandon, "A Talk with Walter Lippmann, at 80, About This 'Minor Dark Age,' " *New York Times Magazine* 68 (14 September 1969): 25-27 and 134-40, especially p. 27.

24. Donald Bruce Johnson and Kirk H. Porter, eds., "Whig Platform of 1852," *National Party Platforms, 1840-1972*, 5th ed. (Urbana, Ill.: University of Illinois Press, 1973), p. 20.

25. J. William Fulbright, *The Arrogance of Power* (New York: Random House, 1966), p. 21.

26. Jimmy Carter, "Humane Purposes in Foreign Policy," a speech delivered at the Commencement Exercises of the University of Notre Dame, South Bend, Ind., 22 May 1977 (U.S. Department of State News Release), p. 3.

27. "Republican Platform of 1864," in Johnson and Porter, *Party Platforms*, p. 36.

28. General James F. Rusling, "Interview with President McKinley," *The Christian Advocate* 78 (22 January 1903):137.

29. John F. Kennedy, "Inaugural Address, January 20, 1961," *Inaugural Addresses*, p. 268.

30. Russett and Hanson, *Interest and Ideology*, p. 52.

31. Manfred Jonas lists these five major types of isolationists from the late 1930s: foreign-oriented, belligerent, timid, radical, and conservative. Manfred Jonas, *Isolationism in America, 1935-1941* (Ithaca, N.Y.: Cornell University Press, 1966), pp. 34-35. This list obviously includes groups from both the business liberal and reform liberal traditions.

32. Huntington, *American Politics*, pp. 13-30, 246.

33. For an interesting analysis that generally equates reform liberalism with extroversion and business liberalism with introversion, see Jon Alexander and Tom Darby, "Technology, Ideology, and Marginality: A Perspective on the New World," (a paper prepared at Carleton University: Ottawa, Ontario, Canada, 1983), pp. 1-55.

34. Klingberg, "Historical Alternation," pp. 239-73.

35. There are some possible one-year differences in Klingberg's dating of phases since 1918. In his 1952 *World Politics* article, Klingberg dates 1919 as the end of the third extrovert phase and the beginning of the fourth introvert phase. However, in a 1979 publication, Klingberg cites 1918 as the end of the third extrovert phase and the beginning of the fourth introvert phase. In his 1952 article he lists 1940 as the end of the fourth introvert phase and beginning of the fourth extrovert phase, but he also notes that 1941 may be the correct date. In his latter publication Klingberg cites 1966 or 1967 as the end of the fourth extrovert phase and beginning of the fifth introvert phase. "Cyclical Trends, 1979," p. 38; "Historical Alternations," pp. 240 and 250. The mood/interest analysis uses the dates chosen by Klingberg in his 1952 article and bases a 1968 introvert phase start on research in Ch. 5.

36. Klingberg, "Historical Alternation," pp. 250-60.

37. Ibid., p. 241.

38. Short-term indicators such as Gallup polling data, available since 1935, were gathered for the mood/interest analysis, and the "Most Important Issue Polls" were of particular interest. See George H. Gallup, *The Gallup Poll, Public Opinion, 1935-1971*, vols. 1, 2, and 3 (New York: Random House, 1972); and George Gallup, ed., *Public Opinion: 1972-1977*, vols. 1 and 2 (Wilmington, Del.: Scholarly Resources, Inc., 1978). *The Gallup Opinion Index, Gallup Report*, and *Public Opinion* were also consulted.

39. George Washington, "Farewell Address," *A Compilation of Messages and Papers of the Presidents, 1789-1897*, vol. 1, ed. James D. Richardson (Washington, D.C.: Government Printing Office, 1896), p. 222.

40. Frank Klingberg also suggests that mood phases grow over time, as he notes two distinct

stages of growth within each phase: "liberty" (characterized by individual, group, and local pressures) and "union" (tendency toward cooperation or centralization). See Klingberg, "Cyclical Trends, 1979," pp. 37-55, especially pp. 42-43. Steven A. Hildreth projects Klingberg dates to the year 2001 using the liberty and union divisions. Hildreth uses a curve that looks similar to the mood/ interest curve as presented in various papers since 1976, but the two curves are based on different assumptions. Steven A. Hildreth, "A Projection of American 'Moods' to the Year 2000," (a paper prepared at Georgetown University, Washington, D.C., at the Center for Strategic and International Studies, Fall 1981, for the Army 2000 Project). An analysis of Hildreth appears in William J. Taylor, Jr., *The Future of Conflict: U.S. Interests,* The Washington Papers, 10, no. 94 (New York: Praeger, 1983): 35.

41. For example, Bruce Russett notes that "the other evidence available on generational changes provides a theoretically plausible interpretation for the Klingberg data," ("The Americans' Retreat from World Power," *Political Science Quarterly* 40 [Spring 1975]:12). Zbigniew Brzezinski calls Klingberg's work "a remarkable study of America's posture in foreign affairs" and Klingberg's prediction that America would begin a retreat to isolationism in the 1960s a matter of "remarkable prescience," ("U.S. Foreign Policy: The Search for Focus," *Foreign Affairs* 51 [July 1973]:709). Even Bernard C. Cohen, usually a supporter of elitist concepts, seems to make some concessions to Klingberg. (*The Public's Impact on Foreign Policy* [Boston: Little, Brown, 1973], pp. 205-08).

42. Brzezinski and Russett are less concerned about the dangers of current introversion than is the mood/interest analysis. See Brezezinski, "Search for Focus," pp. 710-14; and Russett, "The Americans' Retreat," p. 17. Cohen waits until the end of his analysis to treat Klingberg and says, "perhaps if we understand what it is that is happening, we can learn how to mitigate the dangers inherent in it," (Cohen, *Public's Impact,* p. 208).

43. Michael Roskin has considered the work of a number of scholars and develops a theory of shifting elite generational paradigms on foreign policy deriving some of its direction from a framework posited by Thomas Kuhn. In his study, Roskin identifies these other analysts who have noted fluctuations in American thinking: Stanley Hoffmann, Hans Morgenthau, Dexter Perkins, and Frank L. Klingberg. Roskin notes that Klingberg is the most specific of the four. "From Pearl Harbor to Vietnam: Shifting Generational Paradigms and Foreign Policy," *Political Science Quarterly* 89 (Fall 1974):585-86. The quotation in the text is on p. 586. For Roskin's dates, see p. 581. For a work arguing that more than generational changes are involved in foreign policy belief systems, see Ole R. Holsti and James N. Rosenau, "Does Where You Stand Depend on When You Were Born? The Impact of Generation on Post Vietnam Foreign Policy Beliefs," *Public Opinion Quarterly* (Spring 1980), pp. 1-22.

44. Klingberg, "Historical Alternation," pp. 241, 249, 262, and 266.

45. Arthur Schlesinger, Sr., *Paths to the Present* (New York: Macmillan, 1949), especially pp. 77-92. Quotations from pp. 90 and 85. Arthur Schlesinger, Jr., speculates on the recent meaning of his father's phases in "Is Liberalism Dead?" in Bruce Stinebricker, ed. *Annual Editions: American Government 1982/83* (Guilford, Ct.: Duskin Publishing, 1982), pp. 22-27. According to this analysis, the 1950s represented a conservative phase, the 1960s represented a liberal phase, and the 1970s until the present has been a conservative phase. This would indicate that the length of phases has been lessened since 1948.

46. Quotation from abstract of Michael A. Maggiotto and Eugene R. Wittkopf, "American Public Attitudes Toward Foreign Policy," *International Studies Quarterly* 25 (December 1981):601.

47. Ole R. Holsti and James N. Rosenau, "Vietnam, Consensus, and the Belief System of American Leaders," *World Politics* 32 (October 1979):1-56. Note that Holsti and Rosenau deal with a select group of Americans; this group most definitely is an elite group rather than a random sampling of the American public. Later sections of this work, however, show how elite policy makers follow and thereby reflect public mood.

48. Ole R. Holsti, "The Three-Headed Eagle: The United States and System Change," an

abstract of a presidential address delivered to the International Studies Association, *International Studies Notes* 6 (Spring 1979):1. See also Ole R. Holsti and James N. Rosenau, *American Leadership in World Affairs* (Boston: Allen and Unwin, 1984).

49. Maggiotto and Wittkopf, "American Public Attitudes," 601-31.

50. Michael Mandelbaum and William Schneider, "The New Internationalisms: Public Opinion and American Foreign Policy," in *Eagle Entangled: U.S. Foreign Policy in a Complex World,* eds. Kenneth A. Oye, Donald Rothchild, and Robert J. Lieber (New York: Longman, 1979), pp. 34-88.

51. See Adler, *Isolationist Impulse,* and Jonas, *Isolationism.*

52. Jonas, *Isolationism,* pp. 32-69.

53. Washington's statement in his farewell address about existing commitments emphasizes extending economic ties with other nations while avoiding political connections.

54. Mandelbaum and Schneider, "New Internationalisms," pp. 41-42.

55. See George Modelski, "The Theory of Long Cycles and U.S. Strategic Policy," in *American Security Policy and Policy-Making: The Dilemmas of Using and Controlling Military Force,* eds. Robert Harkavy and Edward A. Kolodziej (Lexington, Mass.: D.C. Heath, 1980), pp. 3-19.

56. James L. Payne, *The American Threat: National Security and Foreign Policy* (College Station, Tx.: Lytton Publishing Company, 1981), p. 324.

57. See Huntington, *American Politics,* especially pp. 246-59.

58. Klingberg, "Historical Alternation," pp.251-60. Sources used for subsequent mood/ interest theory research include: Fred L. Israel, ed., *The State of the Union Messages of the Presidents 1790-1966,* vols. 1, 2, and 3 (New York: Chelsea House-Robert Hector, 1966); *Inaugural Addresses;* and Johnson and Porter's compilation of party platforms. For an analysis of party platforms from 1844 to 1964, see J. Namenwirth, "The Wheels of Time and the Interdependence of Value Change," *Journal of Interdisciplinary History* 3 (Spring 1973): 649-83. This study identifies parochial value phases, which usually occur within a few years of the last third of introvert phases, and cosmopolitan value phases, which usually occur within a few years of the last third of extrovert phases.

59. Klingberg, "Historical Alternation," pp. 257-58 and 260. For the mood/interest analysis, data on army as well as naval expenditures other than those in Klingberg's 1952 article were obtained from U.S. Bureau of the Census, *Historical Statistics of the United States—Colonial Times to 1970,* Bicentennial Edition, House Doc. 93-78, 93rd Cong., 1st sess. (Washington, D.C.: Government Printing Office, 1975), part 2:1114-15. Sprout and Sprout, *American Naval Power,* was useful in determining and locating meaningful naval votes. Its references to the *Congressional Globe,* the *Congressional Record,* and other primary sources were particularly helpful.

60. Huntington, *Soldier and the State,* and Hartz, *Liberal Tradition.*

61. Klingberg, "Historical Alternation," pp. 241-50.

62. Foreign Affairs Division, Legislative Reference Service, Library of Congress for the Subcommittee on National Security Policy and Scientifc Developments of the House Committee on Foreign Affairs, *Background Information on the Use of U.S. Armed Forces in Foreign Countries* (Washington, D.C.: Government Printing Office, 1970), Appendix I, "Major U.S. Armed Actions Overseas, with Relevant Congressional Action, 1789-1970," pp. 39-49, and Appendix II, "Instances of Use of U.S. Armed Forces Abroad, 1798-1970," pp. 50-57.

63. For a description of varying interpretations of the events of American diplomatic history, see Gerald K. Haines and J. Samuel Walker, eds., *American Foreign Relations: A Historiographical Review* (London: Frances Pinter, Ltd., 1981).

64. Klingberg, "Historical Alternation," p. 242.

65. Public mood was a crucial consideration in the early days of the United States. For a study of the effects of public opinion on the foreign policies of presidents Adams, Jefferson, Madison, and

Monroe, see Doris A. Graber, *Public Opinion, the President, and Foreign Policy: Four Case Studies from the Formative Years* (New York: Holt, Rinehart and Winston, 1968). Pages 65, 124, 197, and 243 state how public beliefs could have a decisive impact on each of the four presidents. For an analysis of the influence of the public on American foreign policy until the end of World War II, see Thomas A. Bailey, *The Man in the Street: The Impact of American Public Opinion on Foreign Policy* (Gloucester, Mass.: Peter Smith, 1964), especially pp. 1-13. Many observations of Bailey and especially Graber about the influence of opinion can be applied to the influence of mood, since in the early years of American history there is not the present mass of conflicting and manipulatable short-term data.

66. Huntington, *Soldier and the State*, p. 198.

67. Sprout and Sprout, *American Naval Power*, pp. 50-72.

68. Ibid., pp. 91-93.

69. Huntington, *Soldier and the State*, pp. 214-17.

70. For an interesting analysis arguing that domestic politics were a critical determinant of the policy enunciated in the Monroe Doctrine, see Ernest R. May, *The Making of the Monroe Doctrine* (Cambridge, Mass.: Harvard University Press, 1975). An extrovert public mood, as indicated by the mood/interest analysis, could explain the strong assertions in the doctrine.

71. Huntington, *Soldier and the State*, pp. 203-205 and 217.

72. U.S. Bureau of the Census, *Historical Statistics*, p. 1114.

73. Arthur Schlesinger, Jr., "Congress and the Making of American Foreign Policy," *Foreign Affairs* 51 (October 1972):89.

74. Sprout and Sprout, *American Naval Power*, p. 184.

75. Julius W. Pratt, *Expansionists of 1898: The Acquisition of Hawaii and the Spanish Islands* (Chicago: Quadrangle Books, 1936), p. 278.

76. The neo-Hamiltonians, their beliefs, and their activities are described in Huntington, *Soldier and the State*, pp. 270-88.

77. Regarding Wilson and the neo-Hamiltonians, see Huntington, *Soldier and the State*, p. 271.

78. Adler, *Isolationist Impulse*, pp. 55-59.

79. Ibid., pp. 129-218.

80. Huntington, *Soldier and the State*, pp. 355-61.

81. Thomas P. DeCair, "Labeling the Defense Policies of Presidents John F. Kennedy, Lyndon B. Johnson, and Richard M. Nixon," (a paper presented for National Security Seminar, Holland, Mich., Hope College, 1971), pp. 7-22.

82. Department of Defense statistics taken from Congressional Quarterly, *Congress and the Nation, vol. 3: 1969-72* (Washington, D.C.: Congressional Quarterly, Inc. 1973), p. 901.

83. Department of Defense statistics taken from Congressional Quarterly, *The Power of the Pentagon* (Washington, D.C.: Congressional Quarterly, Inc., 1972), p. 74.

84. Congressional Quarterly, *Global Defense: U.S. Military Commitments Abroad* (Washington, D.C.: Congressional Quarterly, Inc., 1969), pp. 76-77.

85. See Larry Elowitz and John W. Spanier, "Korea and Vietnam: Limited War and the American Political System," *Orbis* 18 (Summer 1974): 527-30; and Gallup data in *The New York Times* (4 September 1968), p. 30.

86. *Congressional Record*, 20 January 1977, p. S1132.

87. William J. Lanouette, "Who's Setting Foreign Policy—Carter or Congress?" *National Journal* (15 July 1978), pp. 1116-17.

88. For an interesting discussion of the problems of American foreign policy in the late 1970s, see Robert W. Tucker, "America in Decline: The Foreign Policy of 'Maturity,' " *Foreign Affairs* 58 (America and the World, 1979):449-84.

89. For a description of the United States mood in the late 1970s, see John E. Rielly, "The

American Mood: A Foreign Policy of Self-Interest," *Foreign Policy* no. 34 (Spring 1979), p. 74-86. Quote from p. 75.

90. The study by Hildreth, "A Projection of American 'Moods'," suggests that the United States is still definitely in an introvert mood. See also Klingberg, *Cyclical Trends, 1983*.

2. Alternate Methodologies and Foreign Policy Concepts

1. See David C. McClelland, "Love and Power: The Psychological Signals of War," *Psychology Today* 8 (January 1975):44-48; David G. Winter and Abigail J. Stewart, "Content Analysis as a Technique for Assessing Political Leaders," in *A Psychological Examination of Political Leaders,* ed. Margaret G. Hermann (New York: Free Press, 1977), pp. 27-61; the Committee on Foreign Affairs, Appendix II, pp. 50-57; James David Barber, *The Presidential Character: Predicting Performance in the White House* (Englewood Cliffs, N.J.: Prentice- Hall, 1977); Arthur Schlesinger, Sr., surveys cited in Thomas A. Bailey, *Presidential Greatness* (New York: Appleton-Century, 1966), pp. 24-25; and Robert K. Murray and Tim H. Blessing, "The Presidential Performance Study: A Progress Report," *The Journal of American History* 70 (December 1983):535-55. The mood/ interest theory, McClelland, the congressional study, and the presidential rankings each encompass almost the entire period of American history. Winter, however, content analyzed only twentieth-century inaugural addresses. In order to provide a more complete basis for comparison, the authors analyzed inaugural addresses of America's two most recent presidents and nineteenth- century American presidents from Polk through McKinley. Also, the Barber study deals only with twentieth-century presidents and did not originally include presidents Ford and Carter. The categorization of presidents back to Polk and after Nixon was accomplished in the following manner: the authors and two student assistants assessed each president from Polk to Roosevelt as well as Ford and Carter using Barber's categories. Where discrepancies existed, discussion and further research were used to achieve consensus.

2. The mood/interest theory divides introvert and extrovert phases into thirds, illustrating the fact that each phase has three parts: retreat from previous extreme, compatibility with short-term national interests, and then proceeding to the opposite extreme. However, Klingberg divides the phases into halves that he labels "liberty" and "union" as part of what he calls a political cycle. Liberty phases feature an emphasis on individual, group, and local pressure, while stages of union emphasize cooperation and centralization. See Klingberg, "Cyclical Trends, 1979," pp. 42-43.

3. Committee on Foreign Affairs, Appendix II, pp. 50-57. Actions included protective actions and actions where military clashes were intended or actually took place.

4. During the 1950s, McClelland and his students spent five years developing the techniques, codes, and protocols used to measure a single motive, the need for achievement. They applied their findings successfully in a study of economic history. Plays and stories were content analyzed for imagery of an achievement, power, or affiliative nature in an effort to establish an empirical connection between the achievement motivation level of children, students, and businessmen and levels of economic development. See in this regard David C. McClelland, ed., *Studies in Motivation* (New York: Appleton-Century-Crofts, 1955), and David C. McClelland, *The Achieving Society* (Princeton, N.J.: D. Van Nostrand, 1961).

5. McClelland, a long-time pacifist, was anxious to establish the relationship between the dominance of certain motives in literature and the frequency of war.

6. McClelland, "The Psychological Signals of War," pp. 44-48. Although McClelland posits a lengthy lead-time between signals in literature and war, we have worked most of our comparisons from the date on which McClelland's content analysis takes place. Therefore, we use McClelland's analysis of 1795 as an indicator of what will happen in the decade from 1795 to 1805. As McClelland's analysis suggests, the lead time between motivational signals in literature and wars has continued to shrink across time. Why this is the case is not speculated about in this chapter.

7. Richard Donley and David Winter, "Measuring the Motives of Public Officials at a Distance: An Exploratory Study of American Presidents," *Behavioral Science* 15 (1970):229. See also in this regard David G. Winter, *The Power Motive* (New York: Free Press, 1973); Winter and Stewart, "Content Analysis," pp. 27-61; and David Winter, "What Makes the Candidates Run," *Psychology Today* 10 (July 1976):46-49 and 92. Emmet Hughes's rebuttal of the Winter position can be found in *Psychology Today* 10 (July 1976):51-58 and 80.

8. The mood/interest theory and McClelland each provide data for much of the entire two centuries of American history. In order to make the Winter data comparable, the authors have content analyzed the inaugural addresses of presidents Polk through McKinley, and our two most recent presidents, Ronald Reagan and Jimmy Carter. Given the difficulties involved in rating scores as either high or low relative to a comparison with all other presidents' scores, the authors adopted an approach that avoids these problems by taking each president in his own right and searching for his dominant motive. Our method was developed in several stages. Robert E. Elder, "A Comparison of Winter's Motives and Barber's Character: Toward a Unified Theory of Presidential Personality" (a paper prepared for delivery at the Political Science Section, Michigan Academy, University of Michigan, Ann Arbor, Mich., March 21, 1981), p. 4 suggested that presidents from early periods not be ranked high or low in a motive on the basis of a comparison with modern presidents. Winter and Stewart had previously developed a method of rating inaugurals on a per-thousand-word basis in "Content Analysis," p. 52. Hope College student Eric Brummel suggested a method aimed at determining each individual president's highest motive and the relative distance between the highest motive and the two additional motives. Because this study dealt with only the relationship between power and affiliation, the authors developed the power divergence percentage score. The authors are grateful to Eric Brummel for the insight he provided in this regard.

9. The authors use the 1:10 ratio in the text because President Jimmy Carter, an introvert, second-stage only president who served after the 1970 study, used force in attempting a rescue of American hostages in Iran. He is not included in the table, but we are reluctant to claim greater significance than warranted. For a study with an independent methodology that supports a relationship between dominance scores and propensity to use force, see Lloyd S. Etheredge, "Personality Effects on American Foreign Policy, 1898-1968: A Test of Interpersonal Generalization Theory," *American Political Science Review* 72 (June 1978):434-51.

10. Barber, *Presidential Character:* pp. 7-14.

11. Elder, "A Comparison."

12. McClelland, *The Achieving Society,* pp. 211-16.

13. These five studies are: Clinton Rossiter, *The American Presidency* (New York: Harcourt, Brace, and World, 1960); T. Bailey, *Presidential Greatness;* Arthur Schlesinger, Sr., in T. Bailey, pp. 24-25. (Both Schlesinger's 1948 and 1962 studies are included.) The final study is a poll by Robert K. Murray and Tim H. Blessing, "Presidential Performance Study."

14. The three studies averaged were two by Arthur Schlesinger, Sr. (1948 and 1962), and Robert K. Murray and Tim H. Blessing of Pennsylvania State University (1983). The Schlesinger studies are included in Bailey, *Presidential Greatness,* pp. 24-25. The Murray and Blessing study is in Murray and Blessing, "Presidential Performance Study." These studies were chosen because they represent three different time periods and consist of average rankings from numerous historians. The final average rankings were derived through use of a percentile score. Each president's rank in the study was subtracted from the number of presidents ranked in that study. This number was then divided by the number of presidents in the study. The result was the percentile score. The three percentiles were averaged to obtain a final percentile. Then the percentiles were arranged in descending order from highest to lowest. This became the final rank ordering. It should be noted that Truman and Eisenhower appeared in two studies each and Kennedy, L. Johnson, Nixon, Ford, and Carter in one study. This was due to the dates of the studies. These three studies along with the Maranell and Doddler Accomplishment Poll of 1970, the 1977 U.S. Historical Society ten best, and

1982 *Chicago Tribune* ten best/ten worst survey are analyzed in Arthur B. Murphy, "Evaluating the Presidents of the United States," *Presidential Studies Quarterly* 14 (Winter 1984):117-26. Works by Clinton Rossiter and Thomas Bailey also gave information that could be utilized to obtain presidential rankings. The authors calculated rankings of presidents using both the averages of five studies and only the averages of the three surveys and found differences to be unsubstantial. Later tables will compare presidential posterity rankings to long-term trends. The ranking derived by using the three surveys is preferable because it represents an average of surveys in three different time periods (1948, 1962, and 1983). When the works by Rossiter and Bailey are included the averages unequally reflect views in the 1960s, as both Rossiter's and Bailey's studies are from that period. Therefore, the ranking using the average of the three surveys will be used in later tables.

15. Bailey, *Presidential Greatness*, pp. 25-26.

16. Klingberg, *Cyclical Trends, 1983*.

17. David C. McClelland, "The Psychological Signals of War," pp. 44-48.

18. Bailey, *Presidential Greatness*, p. 297.

19. Walter Lippmann, *The Public Philosophy* (Boston: Little, Brown, 1955), pp. 23-24.

20. The pragmatism noted here is the American common-sense tradition and not that of a specific philosopher.

21. The states considered to be sparsely populated states of the Great Plains and West in this study are: Alaska, Arizona, Colorado, Idaho, Kansas, Montana, Nebraska, Nevada, New Mexico, North Dakota, Oklahoma, Oregon, South Dakota, Utah, Washington, and Wyoming. These sixteen states have approximately one-third of the total possible votes in today's Senate. The most populous of these states, Washington, ranked twentieth among the states in 1980.

22. Direct election of senators did not come about until after the Seventeenth Amendment was ratified in 1913, and many of the senators who composed the "Battalion of Death" in opposition to the League of Nations after World War I had begun their careers before this amendment really took effect. The leaders of these irreconcilables at that time were: Borah (Idaho), Brandegee (Connecticut), France (Maryland), Johnson (California), Knox (Pennsylvania), Moses (New Hampshire), and Reed (Missouri) See Adler, *Isolationist Impulse*, pp. 98-100.

23. This statement is based on the necessarily arbitrary proposition that those senators listed in the index with three or more mentions in the context of Jonas' book are the major isolationist senators of that era.

24. These seven were from sparsely populated Western and Great Plains states: senators Homer B. Bone (Washington), William E. Borah (Idaho), Arthur Capper (Kansas), George W. Norris (Nebraska), Gerald P. Nye (North Dakota), Key Pittman (Nevada), and Burton K. Wheeler (Montana). Among the remaining five senators, Bennett C. Clark (Missouri), Hiram W. Johnson (California), Robert M. LaFollette (Wisconsin), Robert A. Taft (Ohio), and Arthur H. Vandenberg (Michigan), the states of New England, the Middle Atlantic, and the South are conspicuously unrepresented.

25. Ekirch, *Civilian and the Military*, p. 257.

26. These eight senators were: Guy Cordon (Oregon), Edwin Johnson (Colorado), William Langer (North Dakota), George Malone (Nevada), Glen Taylor (Idaho), Arthur Watkins (Utah), Kenneth Wherry (Nebraska), and Milton Young (North Dakota). Other senators voting against the treaty were: William Jenner (Indiana), Forrest Donnell (Missouri), James Kem (Missouri), Robert Taft (Ohio), and Ralph Flanders (Vermont). U.S. Congress, Senate, 81st Cong., 1st sess., 21 July 1949, *Congressional Record* 95, part 8:9916.

27. These five were: senators Carl Hayden (Arizona), Henry Jackson (Washington), Warren Magnuson (Washington), Mike Monroney (Oklahoma), and Wayne Morse (Oregon). For the entire vote, see U.S. Congress, Senate, 83rd Cong., 2nd sess., 26 February 1954, *Congressional Record* 100, part 2:2374-75.

28. These nine senators included: Gordon Allott (Colorado), Henry Bellmon (Oklahoma),

Wallace Bennett (Utah), Peter Dominick (Colorado), Paul Fannin (Arizona), Barry Goldwater (Arizona), Clifford Hansen (Wyoming), Henry Jackson, (Washington), and Gale McGee (Wyoming). Other senators voting against the resolution were: Thomas Dodd (Connecticut), Everett Dirksen (Illinois), Robert Griffin (Michigan), Edward Gurney (Florida), Margaret Chase Smith (Maine), Strom Thurmond (South Carolina), and John Tower (Texas). See U.S. Congress, Senate, 91st Cong., 1st sess., 25 June 1969. *Congressional Record* 115, part 13: 17245.

29. Vote count taken from "Reagan Victories Dominate Key Votes of 1981," *Congressional Quarterly Weekly Report* (26 December 1981), pp. 2572-86. Note that the resolution voted on was disapproving Reagan's proposed sale; thus, the resolution failed by a vote of 48-52, meaning the sale was approved.

30. The 68-32 votes on the two treaties were identical. The seventeen senators from small population states of the West and Great Plains who voted against both treaties were: Dewey Bartlett (Oklahoma), Quentin Burdick (North Dakota), Carl Curtis (Nebraska), Robert Dole (Kansas), Pete Domenici (New Mexico), Jake Garn (Utah), Barry Goldwater (Arizona), Clifford Hansen (Wyoming), Orrin Hatch (Utah), Paul Laxalt (Nevada), James McClure (Idaho), John Melcher (Montana), Harrison Schmitt (New Mexico), Ted Stevens (Alaska), Malcolm Wallop (Wyoming), Milton Young (North Dakota), and Edward Zorinsky (Nebraska). U.S. Congress, Senate, 95th Cong., 1st sess., 16 March 1978, *Congressional Record* 124, no. 38, p. S3857, and U.S. Congress, Senate, 95th Cong., 1st sess., 18 April 1978, *Congressional Record* 124, no. 54, p. S5796.

31. On August 7, 1964, the Senate passed the Gulf of Tonkin Resolution by a vote of 88 to 2. The two senators voting against it were: Ernest Gruening (Alaska) and Wayne Morse (Oregon). See U.S. Congress, Senate, 88th Cong., 2nd sess., 7 August 1964, *Congressional Record* 110, part 14:18470-71.

32. See, for example, Huntington, *American Politics,* especially pp. 240-45.

33. "Is There a Crisis of Spirit in the West? A Conversation with Dr. Henry Kissinger & Senator Daniel P. Moynihan," Ben J. Wattenberg, moderator, *Public Opinion* 1 (May/June 1978):8.

34. Marian C. McKenna, *Borah* (Ann Arbor: The University of Michigan Press, 1961), pp. 8-9, 11, and 87.

35. Quoted in *The New York Times,* 29 September 1970, p. 38.

36. See Joseph P. Kennedy, "Disentanglement [1951]," *Readings in American Foreign Policy,* 2nd ed., ed. Robert A. Goldwin and Harry M. Clor (New York: Oxford Univesity Press, 1971), pp. 162-69, in contrast with John F. Kennedy, "The Goal of an Atlantic Partnership [1962]," Goldwin and Clor, pp. 170-73.

37. Robert L. DeVries, "Beyond the Boundary: Morality and Global Economics" (a paper prepared for delivery at the 19th Annual International Studies Association Convention, Washington, D.C., February 1978), pp. 9- 21; Ronald Kirkemo, *Between the Eagle and the Dove: The Christian and American Foreign Policy* (Downers Grove, Ill.: InterVarsity Press, 1976), p. 29.

38. For an example of a "New Right" viewpoint, see Richard A. Viguerie, *The New Right: We're Ready to Lead* (Falls Church, Va.: Viguerie, 1981).

39. As Samuel Huntington has observed, "Magnificently varied and creative when limited to domestic issues, liberalism faltered when applied to foreign policy and defense." Huntington, *Soldier and the State,* p. 148.

40. See X [George F. Kennan], "The Sources of Soviet Conduct," *Foreign Affairs* 25 (July 1947):575.

41. For Kennan's view of the "X" article after a quarter century, see George F. Kennan, "X Plus 25: Interview with George F. Kennan," *Foreign Policy* no. 7 (Summer 1972), pp. 5-21, particularly pp. 14-15.

42. For a statement of Henry Kissinger's position at the time Richard Nixon acquired his services, see Henry A. Kissinger, "Central Issues of American Foreign Policy," *American Foreign Policy: Three Essays* (New York: W. W. Norton, 1969), pp. 52-97.

43. The above ideas are among those developed in Huntington, *Soldier and the State*, pp. 193-288.

44. This neo-Hamiltonian characteristic of the Kennedy administration was brought to the attention of the author in DeCair, "Labeling the Defense Policies."

45. Graham Allison, "Cool It: The Foreign Policy of Young America," *Foreign Policy* no. 1 (Winter 1970-1971), pp. 144-60.

46. Roskin, "Pearl Harbor to Vietnam," pp. 563-88.

47. AIPO data on support of the Korean and Vietnam wars by educational level can be found in John E. Mueller, *War, Presidents, and Public Opinion* (New York: John Wiley and Sons, 1973), pp. 272-73. For both wars, the data indicates a shift in the direction of opinions which had the most initial support among those with only a grade school education. Regarding the Vietnam war, it is argued in Thomas R. Dye, *Understanding Public Policy*, 3rd ed. (Englewood Cliffs, N.J.: Prentice-Hall, Inc., 1978), pp. 299-301, that the crucial consideration is that matters remained the same until the elites changed their minds. The fact remains that the mass did resist elite efforts to sell it the advisability of limited war and the elites did move in the direction of mass opinion. That the elite (college-educated) opinion changed from majority support for the war to majority opposition in the year before the 1968 presidential elections, when mass public input was strongest, is also significant.

48. Samuel Huntington recently concluded that "prevailing American opinion on the use of force appears to have reverted to the pre-World War II assumption of a sharp dichotomy between war and peace." Samuel P. Huntington, "The Soldier and the State in the 1970's," in Andrew J. Goodpaster and Samuel P. Huntington, *Civil-Military Relations* (Washington, D.C.: American Enterprise Institute for Public Policy Research, 1977), p. 21.

49. "Korea Under Atom Shield, Carter Says," *Rocky Mountain News*, 30 May 1977, p. 3.

50. John E. Rielly, ed., *American Public Opinion and U.S. Foreign Policy 1983* (Chicago: Chicago Council on Foreign Relations, 1983), p. 37.

51. Graber, *Public Opinion*, p. 65.

52. For a discussion of the mass, attentive, and opinion-maker (elite) publics, see James N. Rosenau, *Public Opinion and Foreign Policy* (New York: Random House, 1961), pp. 27-73.

53. Such a tendency is also noted by Jerel Rosati in "The Carter Administration's Image of the International System: Content, Stability, and Change" (a paper presented to the International Studies Association, Cincinnati, Ohio, 1982), see especially pp. 8 and 9.

54. Gabriel A. Almond, *The American People and Foreign Policy* (New York: Praeger, 1960), pp. 58-60, 98-99, 106, and 124. (The 1960 edition contains the examples on the same pages as the 1950 edition.)

55. Kennan, " 'X' Plus 25:" pp. 14-15.

56. Samuel P. Huntington, *No More Vietnams?: The War and the Future of American Foreign Policy*, ed. Richard M. Pfeffer (New York: Harper and Row, 1968), pp. 39-41.

57. Almond, *American People*, 57-58, 66-68, and 239.

58. Ibid., p. 71.

59. These definitions make it possible for a person to be a member of both the leadership and consistent publics for a certain period of time; but when the leadership public shifts its positions in accordance with public mood, the person would have to decide between following the shift and remaining in the consistent public.

60. Cohen, *Public's Impact*, p. 205, see also pp. 206-8.

61. Some analysts, basing their work upon varying methodologies, have developed concepts related to possible cycles of recurring international violence. For example, see Melvin Small and J. David Singer, *Resort to Arms: International and Civil Wars, 1816-1980* (Beverly Hills: Sage Publications, 1982). The work concludes "that, with *some* level of such violence almost always present, there may be certain periodic fluctuations in the amount of that violence." Small and Singer, p. 156. Small and Singer's data on nation-months of war under way "with dominant peaks

about 20 years apart" have both similarities and differences with the alternating introvert/extrovert moods of the American liberal. However, in a larger sense, Small and Singer conclude that "we can examine the long range century-and-a-half trend and find little pattern, examine the short range trend of the past few decades and predict a continuing general decline, or examine the crude periodicity and predict an upsurge in international and civil war as a current decline 'bottoms out.' " Melvin Small and J. David Singer, "Conflict in International System, 1816-1977: Historical Trends and Policy Futures," in Kegley and McGowan, *Challenges to America*, p. 107. For an hypothesis suggesting "that an upswing in violence occurs about once every generation to a generation and a half," with the latter figure being most accurate since 1680, see Frank H. Denton and Warren Phillips, "Some Patterns in the History of Violence," *Journal of Conflict Resolution* 12 (June 1968): 182-95, quotation from p. 190. Denton and Phillips suggest three conditions that "may be associated with such a periodic increase in violence:" (1) as participants in "the last great war" fade into the background, descriptions of the conflict "shift from 'horror'-dominant to 'glory'-dominant," (2) a new generation of decision-makers who have not had first-hand experience with violence comes into power, and (3) a "continuity of conflict and hatred" can occur as the generations brought up on stories of the enemy's wickedness moves into power and seeks revenge. Denton and Phillips, pp. 193-94. Although comparisons can be made between their dates of recurring violence and the dates of the mood/interest analysis, both introvert and extrovert moods last longer than Denton and Phillips's upswings in violence. Also, as Michael Roskin points out, America's violent experience with World War II did not deter it from using force in foreign affairs in the decades immediately following (Roskin, "Pearl Harbor to Vietnam," p. 586). Quincy Wright discovered in world politics a "general fifty-year periodicity in critical war situations during the last 400 years," mentioned in Frank L. Klingberg, "Historical Periods, Trends, and Cycles in International Relations," *Journal of Conflict Resolution* 14 (December 1970):510, citing Wright, *A Study of War*, 1965 abridged ed. (Chicago: University of Chicago Press, 1942), pp. 227-32. Rather than shifts in mood orientations as emphasized in the mood/interest theory, Wright discovered regularly recurring "periods of intensive international warfare," rarely exceeding four or five years. Klingberg, "Historical Periods," pp. 505-6, citing Wright, p. 226. The mood/interest analysis differs from each of these three analyses in that it pertains only to the United States rather than to the world and covers all politico-military fluctuations rather than just fluctuations in violence. Thus, the statement in the text that United States introvert/extrovert fluctuations are more regular than worldwide fluctuations. For an analysis on nine different international system-periods from 1740-1960, see Richard N. Rosecrance, *Action and Reaction in World Politics* (Boston: Little, Brown, 1963). Rosecrance's periods also are less regular than those of the mood/interest analysis.

62. J. David Singer and Melvin Small, *The Wages of War: 1816- 1965: A Statistical Handbook* (New York: John Wiley and Sons, Inc., 1972), p. 214. This data is not contained in Small and Singer, which updates much of the material in Singer and Small.

63. Small and Singer, pp. 176-77.

64. Ibid., pp. 143-57.

3. American Foreign Policy Interests

1. Karl W. Deutsch, *The Analysis of International Relations* (Englewood Cliffs, N.J.: Prentice-Hall, Inc., 1968), p. 87.

2. Gordon, *Toward Disengagement in Asia*, pp. 9-30.

3. Ibid., pp. 12-15; and Amos A. Jordan and William J. Taylor, Jr., *American National Security: Policy and Process* (Baltimore: The John Hopkins University Press, 1981), p. 358.

4. Gordon talks about the United States interest in Latin America as being "to preserve the dominance of the U.S." (p. 15).

5. For a description of this turn of the century change, see Norman A. Bailey, *Latin America in World Politics* (New York: Walker, 1967), p. 44.

6. This is not to say, however, that Latin American disputes are of no interest at all; the

Caribbean Basin in particular has been called our "third border," and the events of that region do affect the U.S. See, for example, U.S. Department of State, "U.S. Interests in the Caribbean Basin," *Gist* (brief State Department reference guide, dated May 1982).

7. Gordon, *Toward Disengagement in Asia,* pp. 12-15; and Jordan and Taylor, *National Security,* p. 358.

8. Samuel Huntington talks about the estimate of major national objectives by the United States military's Joint Board in September 1941, which he notes indicated that "the long run goals of the United States were not the defeat of Germany and Japan, but rather the establishment of a balance of power in Europe and Asia. Victory over the Axis was desirable only insofar as it contributed to this end." The statement also recognized the importance of maintaining the integrity of the Western Hemisphere. Huntington, *Soldier and the State,* p. 331. Hans J. Morgenthau has written about the United States interest in a worldwide balance of power and more specifically in Europe and Asia. Hans J. Morgenthau, *A New Foreign Policy for the United States* (New York: Praeger, 1969), p. 193. Morgenthau also acknowledges the United States interest in maintaining its hegemony in the Western Hemisphere against European threat. (*A New Foreign Policy,* p. 173). Ronald Steel basically acknowledges the reality of the spheres-of-influence analysis in great powers' interests. His assessment of balance of power considerations in Latin America and Europe agrees essentially with the analysis of this book (*Pax Americana* [New York: Viking, 1967], pp. 326-27). Fred Greene specifically points to the existence of a "balance of power" interest of the United States in Asia. He states "U.S. security is closely linked to Asia's ability to avoid domination by any one power or political system by means other than voluntary association" (*U.S. Policy and the Security of Asia* [New York: McGraw-Hill, 1968], pp. 35-36). Some analysts support a balance of power analysis, but argue that now "security can no longer be usefully defined primarily in terms of geography." Samuel P. Huntington, "After Containment: The Functions of the Military Establishment," *The Annals of the American Academy of Political and Social Science* 406 (March 1973):5-8, quotation from p. 5. Of particular interest and salience here is Walter Lippmann's observation, in justification of American intervention in the Dominican Republic in 1965, that spheres of influence are natural and that to assume they are inherently evil because we live in one world is a utopian fallacy; and "recognition of spheres of influence is a true alternative to globalism." Originally from Walter Lippmann, *New York Herald Tribune* European ed. (5 May 1965), here cited from Steel, *Pax Americana,* p. 328. The analysis in the above text sides with Lippmann and history, though it recognizes the importance of worldwide considerations.

9. Gordon acknowledges that his "three-tiered concept of national interest . . . is predicated on the assumption that the United States has only *minimum* conditions which it seeks to see satisfied in international relations." The mood/interest analysis would change "it seeks to see" to "must be." Gordon continues: "To be most specific, it should be emphasized that whereas the hallmark of a *Level One* interest is the willingness to risk general war in connection with dominance in the three named regions, *Level Two* and *Level Three* interests imply no such automatic willingness" (p. 16). Thus, other regions involve more flexible strategies and lower priorities.

10. Samuel P. Huntington, "The Defense Policy of the Reagan Administration, 1981-1982," in *The Reagan Presidency: An Early Assessment,* ed. Fred R. Greenstein (Baltimore: The John Hopkins University Press, 1983), p. 103. Richard Halloran, "Reagan as Military Commander," *New York Times Magazine* (15 January 1984), p. 60.

11. With regard to preventing exclusion in "those regions of the world lacking indigenous major powers—Southeast Asia, the Middle East, Africa, and Latin America—the United States would feel and would be insecure if any major external power—presumably the Soviet Union, or conceivably, China—achieved a monopoly of external influence or control in any one of these regions and consequently was in a position to shut off American political, economic, and cultural access to the region," Huntington, "After Containment," p. 7. The analysis of the mood/interest theory agrees with Huntington on many issues, but emphasizes geographic priorities and includes Latin America under the United States sphere of influence.

12. Gordon, *Toward Disengagement in Asia*, pp. 12-15.

13. Regarding this conflict see Walter Dean Burnham, "1980 as a Historical Moment: Reflections on the American Political Crisis," *The Washington Quarterly* (Special Supplement, 1980), pp. 4-24, especially p. 21.

14. See, for example, Earl C. Ravenal, *Never Again: Learning from America's Foreign Policy Failures* (Philadelphia: Temple University Press, 1978), especially pp. 131-38. Ravenal argues that the growing complexity of the world situation is an argument for America's withdrawal from extensive commitments in world poltics. The mood/interest theory, on the other hand, argues that this complexity is what draws the United States further into world politics.

15. The declaration was passed on June 17, 1812, by the Senate by a vote of 19 to 13. U.S. Congress, Senate, 12th Cong., 1st sess., 17 June 1812, *Annals of the Congress of the U.S.* 23 (Washington, D.C.: Gales and Seaton, 1853):297. It was passed earlier by the House by a vote of 79 to 49. U.S. Congress, House, 12th Cong., 1st sess., 4 June 1812 Supplemental Journal, *Annals of the Congress of the U.S.* 24 (Washington, D.C.: Gales and Seaton, 1853):1637.

16. Julius W. Pratt, *Expansionists of 1812* (Gloucester, Mass.: Peter Smith, 1957), pp. 48-49.

17. With regard to the Mexican War, Frederick Merk records that in the House, "the war bill was passed two hours after it was received—by a vote that was overwhelming, 174 to 14," and "the Senate's vote on the war bill was as lopsided as that of the House. It was 40 to 2." He also explained the large amount of public support for the war as "a momentary hysteria on the part of the public which Polk converted into a stampede." Frederick Merk, "Dissent in the Mexican War," in Frank Freidel, Frederick Merk, and Samuel Eliot Morison, *Dissent in Three American Wars* (Cambridge, Mass.: Harvard University Press, 1970), pp. 39 and 43-44.

18. For example, "[John C.] Calhoun said later that not 10 percent of Congress would have voted for the war bill if time had been given to examine the documents." Freidel, Merk, and Morison, *Dissent*, p. 40.

19. Ibid., pp. 58 and 62-63.

20. Samuel Flagg Bemis, *A Diplomatic History of the United States* (New York: Henry Holt, 1936), p. 449.

21. Pratt, *Expansionists of 1898*, pp. 234-57.

22. Ibid., pp. 266-78.

23. Richard W. Leopold, *The Growth of American Foreign Policy* (New York: Alfred A. Knopf, 1962), pp. 190-91.

24. Fred W. Wellborn, *Diplomatic History of the United States* (Totowa, N.J.: Littlefield, Adams, 1970), p. 289.

25. See Thomas I. Emerson, *The System of Freedom of Expression* (New York: Vintage Books, 1970), p. 56.

26. The Gulf of Tonkin Resolution (August 7, 1964) clearly indicates support by its passage of 88 to 2. Similarly, a vote for supplemental funds for the Defense Department, primarily for the support of United States operations in Southeast Asia, passed in the house by 389 to 3 on March 15, 1966. See Congressional Quarterly, *The Power of the Pentagon*, pp. 72 and 112-13.

27. For example, see Robert C. Johansen, *The National Interest and the Human Interest: An Analysis of U.S. Foreign Policy* (Princeton: Princeton University Press, 1980). Stanley Hoffmann also provides an argument for interdependence, though more moderately than Johansen, in Stanley Hoffmann, *Primacy or World Order: American Foreign Policy Since the Cold War* (New York: McGraw-Hill, 1978). On related topics, a statement of current world interdependence is presented in *The Global 2000 Report to the President of the U.S.: Entering the 21st Century*, vol. 1 (Summary Report), Gerald O. Barney, Study Director (Elmsford, N.Y.: Pergamon, 1980). Melvin Small also questions the necessity of past American wars in *Was War Necessary?* (Beverly Hills: Sage Publications, 1980).

28. For a strong argument in this direction, see Payne, *American Threat*. Richard Nixon

argues a similar position, though more moderately than Payne, in *The Real War* (New York: Warner Books, 1980).

29. See Modelski, "U.S. Strategic Policy," pp. 3-19; and George Modelski, "Long Cycles, Kondratieffs, and Alternating Innovations: Implications for U.S. Foreign Policy," in *The Political Economy of Foreign Policy Behavior,* eds. Charles W. Kegley, Jr., and Pat McGowan, *Sage International Yearbook of Foreign Policy Studies,* 6 (Beverly Hills: Sage Publications, 1981):63-83. It should be noted that in the 1980 article, Modelski implies that the beginning of long cycles follows the global war stage (see pp. 4 and 9), while in the 1981 article he puts global war as the first stage of a cycle (see p. 65). Thus, the numbering of subphases may not be clear, but the succession of subphases and the point made above are the same.

30. Some studies, on the contrary, argue from the position that national interests are not so defined, and point to the interrelationships between politico-military, economic, and humanitarian interests. See, for example, Donald E. Nuechterlein, *United States National Interests in a Changing World* (Lexington: University Press of Kentucky, 1973), especially pp. 6-29; and Donald E. Nuechterlein, *National Interests and Presidential Leadership: The Setting of Priorities* (Boulder, Col.: Westview, 1978), especially pp. 1-37. Nuechterlein establishes his position by first analyzing historical situations and then asking what interests have been pursued. This analysis argues that perhaps we should ask first what our interests are, and then compare our historical actions.

31. George Washington, "Farewell Address," p. 222.

32. Adler, *Isolationist Impulse,* pp. 31-32.

33. Charles Frankel, *Morality and U.S. Foreign Policy* (New York: Foreign Policy Association, 1975), p. 12.

34. For example, see William Schneider, "Internationalism and Ideology: Foreign Policy Attitudes of the American Public, 1975," (a paper prepared for the 19th Annual Meeting of the International Studies Association, Washington, D.C., February, 1978), especially pp. 15-20; Zbigniew Brzezinski, "America in a Hostile World," *Foreign Policy* no. 23 (Summer 1976), especially pp. 86-88; and Barry B. Hughes, *The Domestic Context of American Foreign Policy* (San Francisco: W. H. Freeman and Company, 1978), especially pp. 29-31.

35. The concept of the military-industrial complex, considered important by many observers, does have some relationship to the trade in arms, but large American business in general also wishes to develop trade opportunities. In the largest sense, the military-industrial complex exists to support interests, not determine them. The manner in which the author believes this works is best described in the context of the Public Rule Proposition.

36. Sidney Ratner, *The Tariff in American History* (New York: D. Van Nostrand Company, 1972), pp. 80-81, quotation from p. 81. For a description of individual tariff fluctuations, see pp. 9-79.

37. Klingberg used "Business Booms and Depressions," a chart published by the Century Press, Toledo, 1950, for his analysis. Klingberg, "Historical Alternation," pp. 263-64.

38. A description of recent business cycle fluctuations can be found in Richard G. Lipsey and Peter O. Steiner, *Economics,* 4th ed. (New York: Harper & Row, 1975), pp. 584-92.

39. N. D. Kondratieff, "The Long Waves in Economic Life," trans. W. F. Stolper, *The Review of Economic Statistics* 17 (November 1935):105-7.

40. Recent applicability of the Kondratieff analysis is questioned in Leonard Silk, "50-Year Cycle: Real or Myth?" *The New York Times,* (1 June 1978) Section D, p. 2. However, an analysis arguing for the continued applicability of the cycles is found in Robert J. Samuelson, "Kondratyev's [alt. sp.] Revenge," *National Journal* (7 October 1978), p. 1608.

41. Jay W. Forrester, "Changing Economic Patterns," *Technology Review* 80 (August-September 1978):3-9 (pages are those of a reprint).

42. W. W. Rostow, *The World Economy: History & Prospect* (Austin: University of Texas Press, 1978), especially pp. 298, 571, 578, 625-43, and 650.

43. See Modelski, "U.S. Foreign Policy," pp. 72-74.

44. Ibid. However, Kondratieff argued that, especially in the case of wars or revolutions, economic factors were of primary importance, "Long Waves," pp. 112-13.

45. Jacob J. van Duijn, "Fluctuations in Innovations Over Time," *Futures* (August 1981), pp. 264-74.

46. Robert E. Elder and Jack E. Holmes, "Economic Long Cycles and American Foreign Policy," in *Long and Short Term Economic Fluctuations and Their Political Consequences,* ed. Paul Johnson and William Thompson (New York: Praeger, forthcoming).

47. Of interest in this regard are some of the considerations that have been raised concerning the economic benefits as compared to the politico-military costs of imperialism. See Parker Thomas Moon, *Imperialism and World Politics* (New York: Macmillan, 1926), pp. 526-58.

48. Frederic S. Pearson and Robert Baumann, "Foreign Military Intervention and Changes in United States Business Activity," *Journal of Political and Military Sociology* 5 (Spring 1977): 86. Although acknowledging increases in exports and imports between the United States and "targets" during periods of intervention, the authors minimize the significance of these increases (p. 86).

49. Russett and Hanson, *Interest and Ideology,* pp. 81-82.

50. McKenna, *Borah* p. 192.

51. Herbert Feis, *The Diplomacy of the Dollar* (Baltimore: The Johns Hopkins Press, 1950), pp. 5-6.

52. Cited in Doenecke, *Literature of Isolationism,* p. 29.

53. Russett and Hanson, *Interest and Ideology.*

54. Gordon A. Craig, "The United States and the European Balance," in *Two Hundred Years of American Foreign Policy,* ed. William P. Bundy, (New York: New York University Press, 1977), p. 77.

55. Foster Rhea Dulles, *The American Red Cross* (New York: Harper & Brothers, Publishers, 1950), p. 17.

56. Feis, *Diplomacy,* pp. 5-6.

57. See Thomas Bailey, *A Diplomatic History of the American People,* 4th ed. (New York: Appleton-Century-Crofts, 1950), pp. 338 and 790; and Congressional Quarterly, *China and U.S. Foreign Policy* (Washington, D.C.: Congressional Quarterly, Inc., 1971), pp. 5-6.

58. "The Peace Corps: Making a Comeback," *U.S. News and World Report* (21 July 1975), p. 54.

59. For relevant charts, see John W. Sewall and Overseas Development Council Staff, *The United States and World Development: Agenda 1977* (New York: Praeger, 1977), pp. 230-34; Marian Irish and Elke Frank, *U.S. Foreign Policy: Context Conduct, Content* (New York: Harcourt Brace Jovanovich, 1975), pp. 430-31; and Roger D. Hansen and contributors for the Overseas Development Council, *U.S. Foreign Policy and the Third World: Agenda 1982* (New York: Praeger, 1982), p. 23. See also John P. Lewis, Valeriana Kallab, and contributors for the Overseas Development Council, *U.S. Foreign Policy and the Third World: Agenda 1983* (New York: Praeger, 1983).

60. For an explanation of the traditional development strategies for foreign aid and how such decisions are made, see Elliot R. Morss and Victoria A. Morss, *U.S. Foreign Aid: An Assessment of New and Traditional Development Strategies* (Boulder, Col.: Westview Press, Inc., 1982); see also Richard L. Hough, *Economic Assistance and Security: Rethinking U.S. Policy* (Washington, D.C.: National Defense University Press, 1982). Hough gives a good explanation of such foreign aid strategies, the ideas that they are based upon, and proposals for change.

61. For example, see James Chace, "How 'Moral' Can We Get?" *New York Times Magazine* (22 May 1977), p. 48.

62. Klingberg, "Cyclical Trends, 1979," pp. 37-55, especially pp. 40-42 and 50-51; and Klingberg, *Cyclical Trends, 1983,* especially pp. 9-10 and 173-74.

63. For two long-range analyses of humanitarian interests in American foreign policy, see

Arthur Schlesinger, Jr., "Human Rights and the American Tradition," *Foreign Affairs* 57 (America and the World, 1978):503-26; and William F. Buckley, Jr., "Human Rights and Foreign Policy," *Foreign Affairs* 58 (Spring, 1980):775-96.

64. Boundaries of these regions generally are self-explanatory and some exact boundaries do not need to be delineated for purposes of this book. Some definitional distinctions are of importance. Mexico is included in Latin America rather than North America. South Asia includes India, Pakistan, Bangladesh, and Sri Lanka. Southeast Asian countries are included under East Asia. When a particular United States policy problem might pertain to policy regarding two or more regions, the problem generally is discussed under the region of primary impact. For an excellent summary analysis of current foreign policy issues and priority by geographic region, see Wallace Irwin, Jr., *America in the World: A Guide to U.S. Foreign Policy* (New York: Praeger, 1983); also see Robert E. Gray and Stanley J. Michalak, Jr., *American Foreign Policy Since Detente* (New York: Harper and Row, 1984).

65. Events were charted from Wellborn, *Diplomatic History*.

66. Kim Spalsbury, "Mood/Interest Theory in Relation to American Foreign Policy Toward Developing Countries: Does the Literature Support It?" (a paper presented to National Security Seminar, Hope College, Holland, Mich., 1976), p. 64.

67. The British had been able to press Jay to the "utmost line of concession" in negotiating the treaty. For details concerning the treaty, see Bemis, *A Diplomatic History* pp. 101-104.

68. An article by Worth H. Bagley, who served as vice-chief of Naval Operations and commander-in-chief of U.S. Naval Forces Europe, compares current difficulties in developing optimum naval strategy to difficulties in the 1920s and 1930s. See Worth H. Bagley, "The Decline of U.S. Sea Power (Through Incoherence and Indecision)," *Orbis* 21 (Summer 1977):225-26.

69. "U.S. Interests in the Caribbean Basin," *Gist*.

70. Dexter Perkins, a noted authority on the Monroe Doctrine, observes with respect to the Monroe Doctrine, that "caution and something very like indifference characterize the years from 1823 to 1841; and then comes a period in which popular attention is once more drawn to the principles of 1823." Dexter Perkins, *A History of the Monroe Doctrine* (Boston: Little, Brown, 1963), p. 67.

71. The verbal United States reaction to the possibility of a French canal across Panama can be contrasted to the active United States encouragment of the 1903 revolution in Panama in order to obtain better terms for building a canal.

72. W. T. R. Fox states, "American isolationists and internationalists alike have perceived the power politics of Europe as unclean; it was, therefore, good to stay clear of it," "The Military and United States Foreign Policy," *International Journal* 38 (Winter 1982-83):39-58, quote from p. 43.

73. For a statement of actual Eisenhower administration policy as revealed in the Pentagon Papers, see NSC 162/2 (30 October 1953) in U.S. Department of Defense, *United States-Vietnam Relations 1945-67,* (commonly known as the government edition of the Pentagon Papers), 9 (Washington, D.C.: Government Printing Office, for the House Committee on Armed Services, 1971):171-200. Pages containing statements of special relevance to passages in the text include 174, 176, 181, 193, 195, 197, and 198.

74. For an analysis of the Reagan administration's defense policy and the issues involved, see *U.S. Defense Policy* (Washington: Congressional Quarterly, Inc., 1983); also Huntington, "Reagan Administration."

75. The Carter administration, facing a more introvert mood than the five previous administrations, paid less attention to the massive retaliation/flexible response dilemma, although tending toward flexible response. Such a flexible capability seemingly was emphasized in Western Europe, which was viewed as the major military concern outside of the United States. Asian capabilities were not emphasized, and a withdrawal of ground forces from Korea was contemplated. President Carter was reluctant to emphasize atomic capabilities or develop the neutron bomb.

76. For example, "the inability of NATO ground troops to fight in a nuclear atmosphere, the

vulnerability of current delivery systems, the likelihood that West Germany would be destroyed while being defended, and the lack of a limited nuclear war strategy combine to weaken the credibility of resorting to tactical nuclear weapons." Phillip A. Karber, "Nuclear Weapons and 'Flexible Response,' " *Orbis* 14 (Summer 1970):284-97, quote on p. 292.

77. See McGeorge Bundy, George F. Kennan, Robert S. McNamara, and Gerard Smith, "Nuclear Weapons and the Atlantic Alliance," *Foreign Affairs* 60 (Spring 1982):753-68.

78. Lieutenant General Daniel O. Graham, USA (Ret.) "The High Frontier Study: A Summary," in *Understanding U.S. Strategy: A Reader*, ed. Terry L. Heynes (Washington, D.C.: National Defense University Press, 1983), pp. 93-117.

79. Hoover, "Our National Policies," 3-10, especially p. 7.

80. Brandon, "Walter Lippmann," pp. 25-27 and 134-40, especially p. 27.

81. For an analysis of how America's new domestic priorities interfere with its foreign obligations, particularly its alliances with Western Europe, see David P. Calleo, "American Domestic Priorities and the Demands of Alliance," *Political Science Quarterly* 98 (Spring 1983):1-15.

82. For an analysis of the differences between the United States and its European allies, see William Schneider, "Elite and Public Opinion: The Alliance's New Fissure?" *Public Opinion* 6 (February/March 1983):5-8 and 51. For an analysis of the new generation of leaders in Western Europe, see Stephen F. Szabo, "The Successor Generation in Europe," *Public Opinion* 6 (February/March 1983):9-11.

83. For example, see Secretary of State Dean Acheson's 1949 letter transmitting the China White Paper to President Truman. Dean Acheson, transmitter, *The China White Paper: August 1949* (Stanford: Stanford University Press, 1967) 1:xvi.

84. "The U.S. decided to gamble with very limited resources because the potential gains seemed well worth a limited risk." Neil Sheehan, et al., eds. *The Pentagon Papers*, New York Times Edition (New York: Bantam, 1971), p. 15.

85. National Security Council documents contained in the government edition of the Pentagon Papers document these policies. References can be found in *United States-Vietnam Relations*, vol. 10. For containment, see NSC 5429/2, p. 736; and NSC 6012, pp. 1282-83. For peace, see NSC 5429/2, p. 737; NSC 5809, p. 1250; and NSC 6012, p. 1294. For minimum effort, see NSC 5429/2, p. 736; and NSC 6012, p. 1286. For indigenous support, see NSC 5429/2, p. 737; and NSC 6012, p. 1283.

86. These policies can be identified from the government edition of the Pentagon Papers. *United States-Vietnam Relations*, see vol. 8 as follows: containment, 144 and 288; resolving the colonialist-nationalist dispute, p. 144; avoiding direct responsibility, pp xix and 96; and aiding the people in a missionary/humanitarian sense, pp. 96 and 144.

87. Troop figures taken from Department of Defense statistics in Congressional Quarterly, *Congress and the Nation*, p. 901. Cost figures taken from Department of Defense statistics in Congressional Quarterly, *The Power of the Pentagon*, p. 74. The high figures referenced in this footnote occurred during fiscal year 1969. However, this is not believed to alter the meaning in the text since it takes time to adjust military effort to policy.

88. See Terry L. Deibel, "A Guide to International Divorce," *Foreign Policy* no. 30 (Spring 1978), pp. 32-33.

89. Richard M. Nixon, "Asia After Viet Nam," *Foreign Affairs* 46 (October 1967):112. For another analysis of Asian and U.S. security interests, see Joyce E. Larson, ed., *New Foundations for Asian and Pacific Security* (New York: National Strategy Information Center, 1980).

90. For a discussion of hyphenated American lobbies, see Adler, *Isolationist Impulse*, pp. 73-89, 288-90, and 355-56.

91. See Abdul Aziz Said, ed., *Ethnicity and U.S. Foreign Policy*, rev. ed. (New York: Praeger, 1981).

92. See Louis L. Gerson, "The Influence of Hyphenated Americans on U.S. Diplomacy," in

Said, pp. 19-31. On page 28, Gerson writes, "There is no hard documentary evidence that the main courses of U.S. diplomacy were directed or altered by the influence of a specific ethnic group."

93. For a discussion of interactions among interest levels, see Gordon, *Toward Disengagement in Asia,* pp. 9-30.

94. This reaction is noted in Congressional Quarterly, *Global Defense,* pp. 76-77.

95. For figures on public support of the UN and foreign aid, see Walter Slocombe, Lloyd A. Free, Donald R. Lesh, and William Watts, *The Pursuit of National Security: Defense and the Military Balance* (Washington, D.C.: Potomac Associates, 1976), pp. 34-35.; also see Rielly, ed., *U.S. Foreign Policy 1983,* p. 13.

96. Figures on net flow of official U.S. development assistance as a percentage of GNP can be found in Sewell, *U.S. and World Development,* p. 231; also see Hansen, *U.S. Foreign Policy,* p. 234.

4. Mood/Interest Pluralism

1. Roskin, "Pearl Harbor to Vietnam," p. 581.

2. Regarding the war with Tripoli and the Mexican War, see Committee on Foreign Affairs, Appendix I, pp. 39-40.

3. Regarding the Civil War and the Monroe Doctrine, see Schlesinger, Jr., "American Foreign Policy," pp. 85 and 88.

4. Regarding the Boxer Rebellion, Panama, and Mexico, see Committee on Foreign Affairs, Appendix I, pp. 40-42.

5. For a chronological listing of 160 U.S. military hostilities abroad without an American declaration of war (1798-1970), see Committee on Foreign Affairs, Appendix II, pp. 50-57.

6. See Committee on Foreign Affairs, Appendix I, pp. 39-49.

7. Helpful studies of the Senate and treaties include Denna Frank Fleming,*The Treaty Veto of the American Senate* (New York: G. P. Putnam's Sons, 1930); William Stull Holt, *Treaties Defeated by the Senate: A Study of the Struggle Between the President and the Senate over the Conduct of Foreign Relations*(Baltimore: The Johns Hopkins University Press, 1933); and Royden James Dangerfield, *In Defense of the Senate: A Study in Treaty Making* (Norman: University of Oklahoma Press, 1933).

8. Andrew Jackson quoted in Schlesinger, Jr., "American Foreign Policy," pp. 85-86.

9. "A Runaway Congress?" *Great Decisions '78* (New York: Foreign Policy Association, 1978), pp. 80-81ff.

10. Schlesinger, Jr., "American Foreign Policy,"p. 89.

11. McKenna, *Borah,* pp. 219-23, quotation on p. 223.

12. Adler, *Isolationist Impulse,* pp. 132, 151, 171, 185-94, and 232-33.

13. Jerel Rosati makes an excellent analysis of recent literature on this subject in "Congressional Assertion in Foreign Policy: Fact or Fantasy," (a paper presented to the International Studies Association, Philadelphia, Penn., 1981). For an explanation of the expanding role of Congress in relation to the president, see Thomas E. Cronin, "A Resurgent Congress and the Imperial Presidency," in *Perspectives on American Foreign Policy*, ed. Charles W. Kegley, Jr. and Eugene R. Wittkopf (New York: St. Martin's, 1983), pp. 320-43.

14. See Randall B. Ripley, *Congress: Process and Policy* (New York: W. W. Norton, 1975), especially pp. 23-26.

15. For some literature advocating a basically "executive dominance" position, see: Barber B. Conable, Jr., "Our Limits Are Real,"*Foreign Policy* no. 11 (Summer 1973), pp. 73-80; Lawrence C. Dodd, "Congress and the Quest for Power," in *Congress Reconsidered*, eds. Lawrence C. Dodd and Bruce I. Oppenheimer (New York: Praeger Publishers, 1977), pp. 269-307; Lawrence C. Dodd, "Congress and the Cycles of Power," in *The Presidency and the Congress: A Shifting Balance of Power?* ed. William S. Livingston, Lawrence C. Dodd, and Richard L. Schott (Austin, Tx: Lyndon B. Johnson School of Public Affairs, 1979), pp. 46-69; Harvey G. Zeidenstein, "The Reassertion of

Congressional Power: New Curbs on the President," *Political Science Quarterly* 43 (Fall 1978): 393-409; and Charles W. Kegley, Jr., and Eugene R. Wittkopf, *American Foreign Policy: Pattern and Process,* 2nd ed. (New York: St. Martin's, 1982), pp. 315-51 and 393-432.

16. See, for example, Daniel Yankelovich, "Farewell to 'President Knows Best,' " *Foreign Affairs* 57 (America and the World, 1978): 670-93; James Chace, "Is a Foreign Policy Consensus Possible?" *Foreign Affairs* 57 (Fall 1978): 1-16; Lee H. Hamilton and Michael H. Van Dusen, "Making the Separation of Powers Work," *Foreign Affairs* 57 (Fall 1978): 17-39; Cecil V. Crabb, Jr. and Pat M. Holt, *Invitation to Struggle: Congress, the President and Foreign Policy*, 2nd ed. (Washington, D. C.: Congressional Quarterly Press, 1984); and James A. Nathan and James K. Oliver, *Foreign Policy Making and the American Political System* (Boston: Little, Brown 1983), pp. 104-10.

17. Samuel Huntington, "The Democratic Distemper," in *The American Commonwealth—1976*, eds. Nathan Glazer and Irving Kristol (New York: Basic Books, 1976), pp. 9-38.

18. In "Congressional Assertion," Rosati combines these two models under "co-determination" (see p. 21). The term itself, as well as support of the position in foreign policy, is found in Thomas M. Franck and Edward Weisband, *Foreign Policy by Congress* (New York: Oxford University Press, 1979).

19. See Rosati, "Congressional Assertion;" Edward J. Laurance, "The Changing Role of Congress in Defense Policy-Making," *Journal of Conflict Resolution* 20 (June 1976): 213-53; and Joshua Muravchik, "The Senate and National Security: A New Mood," in *The Growing Powers of Congress*, eds. David M. Abshire and Ralph D. Nurnberger (Beverly Hills: Sage Publications, 1981), pp. 198-282.

20. Neil C. Livingstone and Manfred Von Nordheim, "The United States Congress and the Angola Crisis," *Strategic Review* 5 (Spring 1977): 34-44, quotation on p. 41.

21. On this point, also see Christopher Madison, "Percy Tests His Bipartisan Style at the Foreign Relations Committee," *National Journal,* 6 June 1981, pp. 1008-12. The article points out the Foreign Relations Committee's independence from the executive under the chairmanship of Percy.

22. For analyses of the War Powers Resolution, see Enid Sterling-Conner, "The War Powers Resolution: Does it Make a Difference?" in Abshire and Nurnberger, *Powers of Congress,* pp. 284-316; and Gerald R. Ford, "The War Powers Resolution: Striking a Balance Between the Executive and Legislative Branches," in Abshire and Nurnberger, pp. 318-26.

23. Lanouette, "Who's Setting Foreign Policy," pp. 116-23.

24. See William Bader, "Congress and the Making of U.S. Security Policies," in "America's Security in the 1980s: Part I," *Adelphi Papers* no. 173 (Spring 1982), pp. 14-21, especially pp. 14 and 20. For an additional recent source that argues that Congress' present assertiveness will remain, see David Leyton-Brown, "The Role of Congress in the Making of Foreign Policy," *International Journal* 38 (Winter 1982-83): 76.

25. John E. Rielly, "American Opinion: Continuity Not Reaganism," *Foreign Policy* no. 50 (Spring 1983), p. 100.

26. Warren Christopher, deputy secretary of state for the Carter administration, recently argued for a "compact" between the presidency and Congress which would reduce struggles for foreign policy authority. This compact would involve five principles, stressing that Congress and the president each perform their respective foreign policy roles. It could be argued that President Reagan is to some degree following these principles; still, the arrangement reflects the introvert mood by involving considerable congressional control. See Warren Christopher, "Ceasefire Between the Branches: A Compact in Foreign Affairs," *Foreign Affairs* 60 (Summer 1982): 989-1005, especially pp. 999-1005.

27. A recent study noted, "For the forseeable future, however, this struggle [over the distribution of foreign and defense powers] will be waged by branches more equal than at any time since the end of World War II." Richard Haass, "Congressional Power: Implications for American

Security Policy,"*Adelphi Papers* no. 153 (Summer 1979), p. 34. This situation is typical of introvert phases.

28. For these and other examples, see Christopher, "Ceasefire," pp. 989-1005, especially pp. 990-95.

29. See Justice Sutherland, "Curtiss-Wright Case," in *Readings in American Foreign Policy*, 2nd ed., eds. Robert A. Goldwin and Harry M. Clor (New York: Oxford University Press, 1971), pp. 28-35.

30. Elder Witt, "Legislative Veto Struck Down; Congress Moves to Review Dozens of Existing Statutes," *Congressional Quarterly Weekly Report*, 25 June 1983, pp. 1263-64 and 1266-68; also see John Felton, "Congress Loses Major Foreign Policy Tool," *Congressional Quarterly Weekly Report*, 25 June 1983, p. 1265.

31. Samuel P. Huntington, "The United States," in Michel Crozier, Samuel P. Huntington, and Joji Watanuki, *The Crisis of Democracy* (New York: New York University Press, 1975), p. 92.

32. A full analysis of substantive policy by administration would be a helpful supplement to full understanding of such concepts. See Seyom Brown, *The Faces of Power: Constancy and Change in United States Foreign Policy from Truman to Reagan* (New York: Columbia University Press, 1983).

33. "The National Mood," and "The Nation's 'Most Important Problem,' " in "Opinion Roundup," *Public Opinion* 1 (May/June 1978): 22 and 32.

34. See Bruce Russett and Donald R. Deluca, " ' Don't Tread on Me': Public Opinion and Foreign Policy in the Eighties," *Political Science Quarterly* 96 (Fall 1981): 381-99, especially p. 395; and "Environmental Update," in "Opinion Roundup,"*Public Opinion* 5 (February/March 1982): 33.

35. Richard E. Neustadt, *Presidential Power* (New York: New American Library, 1960), p. 150.

36. For example, see Sheehan, et al., "Harkins' Message to Taylor Voicing Doubts on Plot," (30 October 1963), p. 221.

37. See Sheehan, et al., p. 441 for this quotation from "McCone Memo to Top Officials on Effectiveness of Air War," (2 April 1965).

38. Sheehan, et al., "George Ball Memo for Johnson on 'A Compromise Solution,' " (1 July 1965), pp. 449-54.

39. Huntington, *Soldier and the State*, pp. 305-7.

40. See Sheehan, et al., p. 44, for this quotation from "1954 Study by the Joint Chiefs on Possible U.S. Intervention". The words quoted are italicized in Sheehan.

41. I. M. Destler, "National Security Advice to U.S. Presidents: Some Lessons from Thirty Years," *World Politics* 29 (January 1977): 161 and 163. The words quoted are italicized in this source.

42. Some members of Kennedy's inner circle, admittedly, had a neo-Hamiltonian combination of liberalism and conservatism; their limited war advice, however, was in accord with the increasingly extrovert public mood and therefore did not serve to balance it.

43. For a comparative analysis of presidents Truman through Carter, see R. Gordon Hoxie, *Command Decision and the Presidency: A Study of National Security Policy and Organization* (New York: Readers Digest, 1977).

44. Quoted from Lawrence J. Korb, "The Structure and Process of the National Security Council System in the First Year of the Carter Administration," (a paper prepared for the 19th Annual Meeting of the International Studies Association, Washington, D. C., February 1978), pp. 5-6. Further comment on Carter's relations with the National Security Council is provided by Dom Bonafede, "Brzezinski—Stepping Out of His Backstage Role," *National Journal*, 15 October 1977, pp. 1596- 1601.

45. See R. Gordon Hoxie, "The National Security Council," *Presidential Studies Quarterly* 12 (Winter 1983): 111.

46. See Ibid.

47. Dick Kirschten, "Inner Circle Speaks with Many Voices, But Maybe That's How Reagan Wants It," *National Journal,* 28 May 1983, pp. 1100-1103.

48. For a discussion of Reagan's belief system and political style compared to past presidents, see Fred Greenstein, "Reagan and the Lore of the Modern Presidency: What Have We Learned?" in Greenstein, *Reagan Presidency,* pp. 166-81.

49. For some analyses of these two foreign policy staff members, see Dick Kirschten, "Clark Emerges as a Tough Manager, Not a Rival to the Secretary of State," *National Journal,* 17 July 1982, pp. 1244-48; and Joseph Fromm, "Foreign Policy: One More Try," *U.S. News and World Report* 93 (26 July 1982): 22-26.

50. Dick Kirschten, "Insider Clark Decides Now is the Time to Go Public on NSC Policy Issues," *National Journal,* 11 June 1983, pp. 1217-20.

51. Christopher Madison, "Schultz a Mediator and Implementer More Than a Maker of Grand Designs," *National Journal,* 2 July 1983, pp. 1382-87.

52. For an excellent analysis of Reagan's organization of national security policy, a comparison of the Carter administration's policy to that of the Reagan administration, and for Reagan's organization of the NSC, see Robert E. Hunter, *Presidential Control of Foreign Policy: Management or Mishap?* The Washington Papers, vol. 10, no. 91 (New York: Praeger, 1982) especially Appendix C, pp. 109-15. For an analysis of the key members and policies of the Reagan administration after two years and an evaluation of the results of Reagan foreign policy, see I. M. Destler, "The Evolution of Reagan Foreign Policy," in Greenstein, *Reagan Presidency,* pp. 117-58; see also S. Brown, *Faces of Power,* pp. 567-628.

53. Alexander L. George, *Presidential Decision-Making in Foreign Policy: The Effective Use of Information and Advice* (Boulder, Col.: Westview, 1980).

54. On this subject, Amos Jordan and William Taylor, Jr., outline the theory of concentric circles of influence on national security policy. They write that, "At the center is the president surrounded by his closest advisers . . . who . . . are involved in the national security issues that require presidential decision." See Jordan and Taylor, *National Security,* especially pp. 201-3, quotation on p. 201; also see Roger Hilsman, *The Politics of Policy Making in Defense and Foreign Affairs* (New York: Harper & Row, 1971), pp. 118-22.

55. Amos Perlmutter notes: "Most of the bureaucratic-politics analysts, like the power elitists, fail to see that the political struggle over foreign policy in the United States is neither a function of bureaucratic politics nor a struggle between elected politicians and experts, but a central institutional-constitutional political struggle." He concludes that the focus of foreign policy is the presidential political center, and that the president is the real source of power. "The Presidential Political Center and Foreign Policy: A Critique of the Revisionist and Bureaucratic-Political Orientations," *World Politics* 27 (October 1974): 90.

56. For support of the importance of low level bureaucracy in daily foreign policy decisions see Hunter, *Presidential Control,* especially p. 25.

57. For a description of this build-up, see Nathan and Oliver, *Foreign Policy,* pp. 21-29. In addition, an overall study of current governmental organization for foreign affairs, especially the role of the State Department, is contained in the report, *Commission on the Organization of the Government for the Conduct of Foreign Policy, June 1975,* vols. 1-7 (Washington, D. C.: Government Printing Office, 1975).

58. For one study noting many such limitations on the State Department's role, see Leslie H. Gelb, "Why Not the State Department?" *The Washington Quarterly* (Special Supplement Issue, Autumn 1980), pp. 25-40.

59. For information indicating that business liberalism is underrepresented in the State Department, see John Ensor Harr, *The Professional Diplomat* (Princeton, N. J.: Princeton University Press, 1969), p. 183. Laurence Radway notes that "over 60 percent of Foreign Service executives have specialized in the Social Sciences and humanities," *Foreign Policy and National Defense*

(Glenview, Ill.: Scott, Foresman and Company, 1969), p. 67. Individuals with such specialties are more apt to be reform liberals than business liberals.

60. Bert Rockman, "America's Departments of State: Irregular and Regular Syndromes of Policy Making," *The American Political Science Review* 75 (December 1981): 911-27.

61. A recent study notes that "the outstanding feature of our military experience has been its paradox. We have been anti-militarist in thought and sentiment while remarkably combative in character and practice." This is further explained in terms of three principles: "Americans have shown their dislike of organized war by a desperate attachment to three principles: unpreparedness until the eleventh hour; the quickest feasible strategy for victory regardless of political aims; and instant demobilization, no matter how inadvisable, the moment hostilities are over." See Barbara Tuchman, "The American People and Military Power in an Historical Perspective," in "America's Security in the 1980s: Part I,"*Adelphi Papers,* no. 173 (Spring 1982), pp. 5-13, quotations on p. 5. It can be argued that the principles outlined reflect the liberal distrust of the conservative military juxtaposed with the liberal desire for decisive action.

62. The general concept of civil-military relations utilized in this analysis is taken from Huntington, *Soldier and the State.*

63. For example, a series of articles exploring questionable activities of the CIA was contained in *The New York Times,* 25-29 April 1966.

64. "Intelligence Superchief: Turner's New Challenge,"*U.S. News and World Report,* 15 August 1977, p. 22.

65. "Shaping Tomorrow's CIA," *Time,* 6 February 1978, pp. 10-18.

66. A good discussion of current United States intelligence issues is contained in *Washington Quarterly* 6 (Summer 1983). Specifically note Barry Goldwater, "Congress and Intelligence Oversight," pp. 16-21; Anne Karalekas, "Intelligence Oversight: Has Anything Changed?" pp. 22-30; Angelo Codevilla, "The Substance and the Rules," pp. 32-39; and Richard Brody, "The Limits of Warning," pp. 40-48.

67. For elaboration on many of these points, see Huntington, *Soldier and the State,* pp. 143-62 and 289-94.

68. For development of most of the themes in this paragraph, see Adler, *Isolationist Impulse,* pp. 234-42 and 305-307.

69. In recent years the attention paid to the dangers of a military-industrial complex have also served to minimize the effects of such collusion. Samuel Huntington states: "In American society, wherever the power of an organization or group is being exposed, it is also in the process of being reduced." Samuel P. Huntington, "The Soldier and the State in the 1970's."

70. For an illustration, see Charles Wolf, Jr., "Military-Industrial Simplicities, Complexities, and Realities," in *American Defense Policy,* 3rd ed., eds. Richard G. Head and Ervin J. Rokke (Baltimore: The Johns Hopkins University Press, 1973), p. 648.

71. See John H. Brown, "Theories of the Military-Industrial Complex," (a paper presented for National Security Seminar, Hope College, Holland, Mich., 1976).

72. For a comparison of the two parties from 1946-1960, see Samuel P. Huntington, *The Common Defense* (New York: Columbia University Press, 1961), pp. 252-59.

73. Russett and Hanson, *Interest and Ideology,* see especially pp. 244-70.

74. Paul A. C. Koistinen, *The Millitary-Industrial Complex: A Historical Perspective* (New York: Praeger, 1980), p. 14.

75. For example, Jacques Gansler notes that the relationships currently allow neither economic efficiency nor strategic responsiveness to national need. See Jacques S. Gansler,*The Defense Industry* (Cambridge, Mass.: Massachusetts Institute of Techology Press, 1980), especially pp. 1-8; for a follow-up, see his "Can the Defense Industry Respond to the Reagan Initiatives?" *International Security* 6 (Spring 1982): 102-21, especially pp. 120-21. Also, James Fallows notes, among other things is the problem sometimes known as "gold plating": procurement of a few expensive, sophisticated versions of weaponry, rather than more less expensive and simpler weapons. See

James Fallows, *National Defense* (New York: Random House, 1981), especially pp. 173-76. For a view contrary to Fallows, however, see William Perry, "Fallows' Fallacies: A Review Essay," *International Security* 6 (Spring 1982): 174-82.

76. The general definition of military professionalism used in making the statement is that developed in Huntington, *Soldier and the State*. For an analysis of the current U.S. defense planning mechanism, see John M. Collins, *U.S. Defense Planning: A Critique* (Boulder, Col.: Westview Press, 1982). Further analysis of the Department of Defense based on the Defense Organization Study of 1977-1980 is given by Archie D. Barrett, *Reappraising Defense Organization* (Washington, D. C.: National Defense University Press, 1983).

77. For mention of conflicts between the professional military and Eisenhower administration, see Huntington, *Soldier and the State*, pp. 391-99. Julius W. Pratt notes that the business community "had yielded reluctantly to the necessity of a war with Spain" in 1898, embracing the cause only when the possibility of new commercial bases in the Philippines and Puerto Rico was realized. Pratt, *Expansionists of 1898*, p. 278. Pratt's analysis indicates that business was following its own perceptions and was not a protagonist for military perceptions. President McKinley was cautious during events prior to the war, but avoided alienating a hawkish public.

78. Quoted in Michael J. Robinson, "American Political Legitimacy in an Era of Electronic Journalism: Reflections on the Evening News," in *Television as a Social Force: New Approzches to TV Criticism*, eds. Douglas Cater and Richard Adler (New York: Praeger Publishers, 1975), p. 123.

79. For example, see "U.S. Weighing Base in Israel," *Rocky Mountain News*, 7 July 1977, headline p. 1, and story p. 3.

80. William Schneider, "Conservatism, Not Interventionism: Trends in Foreign Policy Opinion, 1974-1982," in *Eagle Defiant: U.S. Foreign Policy in the 1980s*, ed. Kenneth A. Oye, Robert J. Lieber, and Donald Rothchild (Boston: Little, Brown, 1983) pp. 60-63.

81. In the largest sense, freedom of the press is a crucial protection against tyranny, and its value in this respect overshadows the problems noted in this section.

82. Gallup, *Public Opinion 1935-1971*, vol. 1, pp. 3, 35, 71, and 120.

83. U.S. Congress, House, 74th Cong., 2nd sess., 10 January 1938, *Congressional Record* 83, part 1: 282-83.

84. U.S. Congress, Senate, 83rd Cong., 2nd sess., 26 February 1954, *Congressional Record* 100, part 2: 2374-75.

85. U.S. Congress, Senate, 91st Cong., 1st sess., 25 June 1969, *Congressional Record* 115, part 13: 17245.

86. For an analysis which argues that the public has had a major impact on the president and foreign policy since the adoption of the Constitution, see T. Bailey, *The Man in the Street*, especially pp. 1-14 on "The Sovereign Citizen." Another study, though, argues that, "The United States has one president, but it has two presidencies; one presidency is for domestic affairs, and the other is concerned with defense and foreign policy." The study goes on to say that presidents have, since World War II, had more control over the latter. See Aaron Wildavsky, "The Two Presidencies," in *Classics of the American Presidency*, ed. Harry A. Bailey, Jr. (Oak Park, Ill.: Moore Publishing Company, 1980), pp. 162-73. For a follow-up article, see Harvey G. Zeidenstein, "The Two Presidencies Thesis is Alive and Well and Has Been Living in the U.S. Senate Since 1973,"*Presidential Studies Quarterly* 11 (Fall 1981): 511-25. It should be noted that Wildavsky's description does not eliminate the possibility of public mood influence in foreign policy, rather, it indicates that domestic policy is perhaps more consistently a public concern than foreign policy. The latter is still under the influences of American liberal moods.

87. See table 15 for a further examination of bridgepoint presidencies.

88. Ernest R. May, "An American Tradition in Foreign Policy: The Role of Public Opinion," in *Theory and Practice in American Politics*, ed. William H. Nelson (Chicago: University of Chicago Press, 1966), p. 117. Quoted in Ralph B. Levering, *The Public and American Foreign Policy, 1918-1978* (New York: William Morrow, 1978), p. 152.

89. In May 1977, 78 percent questioned favored U.S. ownership of the Panama Canal, 8 percent favored Panamanian ownership. Source: Opinion Research Corporation of Princeton, cited in *Public Opinion* 1 (March/April 1978): 33.

5. American Introversion

1. Some presidents serving in introvert phases have presided over the conclusion (Wilson) or deescalation (Nixon) of a war, which is believed to be consistent with the statement in the text.

2. George Washington, "Farewell Address," p. 222.

3. Events for this analysis were taken from Committee on Foreign Affairs, Appendix II, pp. 50-57. If the 1940-1967 extrovert phase is included in the analysis, the ratio narrows from 1.27 uses per year to .69 uses per year, still a significant difference. The last extrovert phase can reasonably be excluded from this particular comparison.

4. K. Jack Bauer, *The Mexican War, 1846-48* (New York: Macmillan, 1974), p. 5.

5. Typical of this view is a statement by Thomas Jefferson to John B. Colvin in 1810: "A strict observance of the written laws is doubtless *one* of the high duties of a good citizen, but it is not *the highest*. The laws of necessity, of self-preservation, of saving our country when in danger, are of higher obligation." Thomas Jefferson, *The Writings of Thomas Jefferson*, ed. Paul L. Ford, 11 (New York: G. P. Putnam's Sons, 1905): 146.

6. Adler, *Isolationist Impulse*, pp. 134, 205-206, and 228-30.

7. See "United Nations Evaluation," in "Opinion Roundup," *Public Opinion* 5 (June/July 1982): 36.

8. See Congressional Quarterly, *Global Defense*, pp. 76-77.

9. Taken from AIPO data in Mueller, *War, Presidents*, p. 271.

10. See Lincoln P. Bloomfield and Amelia C. Leiss, *Arms Control and Local Conflict*, vol. I, Summary (Cambridge, Mass.: Center for International Studies, Massachusetts Institute of Technology, February 1970), p. 5.

11. Samuel Lubell, *The Hidden Crisis in American Politics* (New York: W. W. Norton and Company, 1970), p. 250.

12. Bruce M. Russett, *No Clear and Present Danger: A Skeptical View of the United States Entry into World War II* (New York: Harper & Row, 1972).

13. Leslie H. Gelb, "Domestic Change and National Security Policy," in *The Next Phase in Foreign Policy,* ed. Henry Owen (Washington, D. C. : Brookings, 1973), p. 279.

14. Russett, "The Americans' Retreat," pp. 1-2 and 12-13.

15. Klingberg, *Cyclical Trends, 1983*, pp. 137-52.

16. Hildreth, "A Projection of American 'Moods'," p. 29.

17. For data regarding United States ODA, see Hansen, *U.S. Foreign Policy,* p. 244; for data regarding DOD outlays, see Farid Abolfathi, "Threats, Public Opinion, and Military Spending in the United States, 1930-1990," in *Threats, Weapons, and Foreign Policy,* Sage International Yearbook of Foreign Policy Studies, vol. 5, eds. Pat McGowan and Charles W. Kegley, Jr. (Beverly Hills: Sage Publications, 1980), p. 102.

18. Among these works are, John H. Sigler, "Descent from Olympus: The Search for a New Consensus,"*International Journal* 38 (Winter 1982-83): 18-38; and James N. Rosenau and Ole R. Holsti, "U.S. Leadership in a Shrinking World: The Breakdown of Consensus and the Emergence of Conflicting Belief Systems, "*World Politics* 35 (April 1983): 368-92. For earlier works making this same basic argument, see "Arguments Against the Return of Extreme Introversion."

19. George H. Quester, *American Foreign Policy: The Lost Consensus* (New York: Praeger Publishers, 1982), quote from p. 1.

20. Robert W. Tucker, William Watts, and Lloyd A. Free note that in 1976 "the composite score given the federal government in handling international relations dropped a startling 14 points," and conclude that "the foreign policy stewardship of Dr. Kissinger . . . has lost much of its

former luster," *The United States in the World: New Directions for the Post-Vietnam Era?* (Washington, D. C.: Potomac Associates, 1976), p. 20.

21. For a description of the crisis, see Stanley Hoffmann, "In Search of a Threat: The UN in the Congo Labyrinth," *International Organization* 16 (Spring 1962): 331-74.

22. Quoted in *The Detroit News*, 25 May 1978, pp. 1A and 5A.

23. The California poll (presumably in 1976) showed that 54 percent of the Californians polled wanted Congress to have the strongest voice in foreign policy as opposed to the president (28 percent). An identical pattern occurred in Iowa (also presumably 1976), where 60 percent believed that Congress should have the stronger voice in foreign policy, compared to 29 percent for the president. Cited from the California and Iowa polls by Daniel Yankelovich, "Cautious Internationalism: A Changing Mood Toward U. S. Foreign Policy," *Public Opinion* 1 (March/April 1978): 15.

24. See John E. Rielly, ed., *American Public Opinion and U.S. Foreign Policy 1979* (Chicago: Chicago Council on Foreign Relations, 1979), p. 28.

25. Rielly, ed.,*U.S. Foreign Policy 1983*, p. 34.

26. For elaboration on many of these issues, see Congressional Quarterly, *U.S. Defense Policy: Weapons, Strategy and Commitments* (Washington, D. C.: Congressional Quarterly, Inc., 1978).

27. On this point see, for example, James Reston, "The New Isolationists," *The New York Times*, 16 December 1981, p. A 31.

28. For a discussion of the specific restraints that Reagan feels as a result of public mood, see Schneider, "Conservatism, Not Interventionism," pp. 52-60.

29. See, for example, Andrew M. Greeley, "U.S. Isolationism: It's Alive and Well," *The Detroit Free Press*, 2 April 1982, p. 9a; and Karlyn H. Keene and Victoria A. Sackett, "An Editor's Report on El Salvador," *Public Opinion* 5 (April/May 1982): 16-17.

30. Tuchman, "The American People," p. 12.

31. See, for example, Hedrick Smith, "Reagan Puts His Stamp on U.S. Foreign Policy," *The New York Times*, 5 September 1982, p. E3.

32. Bruce Russett and Miroslav Nincic, "American Opinion on the Use of Military Force Abroad," *Political Science Quarterly* 91 (Fall 1976): 414.

33. Russett, "The Americans' Retreat," p. 3.

34. See William Schneider, "Public Opinion: The Beginning of Ideology?" *Foreign Policy* no. 17 (Winter 1974-75), p. 108. Schneider cites (p. 109) Bruce M. Russett, "The Revolt of the Masses: Public Opinion on Military Expenditures," chapter 3 in *New Civil-Military Relations*, eds. John P. Lovell and Philip M. Kronenberg (New Brunswick, N. J.: Transaction Books, 1974), pp. 57-88.

35. Russett and Nincic, "American Opinion," p. 414.

36. *The Gallup Opinion Index* (February 1980), p. 9.

37. Slocombe, et al., *Pursuit of National Security*, p. 38.

38. Source: Department of Defense, Annual Report Fiscal 1979, quoted in Congressional Quarterly, *U.S. Defense Policy*, p. 9.

39. "Foreign Affairs: As the Great Debate Approaches," in "Opinion Roundup," *Public Opinion* 2 (January/February 1979): 29.

40. See, for example, Philip Odeen, "Domestic Factors in U.S. Defense Policy," in "America's Security in the 1980's: Part I," *Adelphi Papers*, no 173 (Spring 1982), p. 28; see also Russett and Deluca, "'Don't Tread on Me'," pp. 383-84. Odeen puts the figure at 49 percent in 1980, while Russett and Deluca cite 55-76 percent in 1980 and 50 percent in 1981; see also Abolfathi, "Threats," pp. 98-99. Russett and Deluca show results similar to Louis Kriesberg and Ross Klein, "Changes in Public Support for U.S. Military Spending," *Journal of Conflict Resolution* 24 (March 1980): 81.

41. See Alvin Richman, "Public Attitudes on Military Power, 1981,"*Public Opinion* 4

(December/January 1982): 45. It should be noted that this pattern corresponds to a 1980 and 1981 decline in importance accorded foreign policy.

42. Rielly, ed., *U.S. Foreign Policy 1983*, p. 28.

43. "Opinion Roundup," *Public Opinion* 6 (April/May 1983): 28.

44. Abolfathi, "Threats," pp. 98-99.

45. "The Limits of Containment: A Time-Louis Harris Poll," *Time*, 2 May 1969, pp. 16-17.

46. For 1976 figures, see Tucker, Watts, and Free, *U.S. in the World*, p. 29; and for 1980 and 1981 figures, see Richman, "Public Attitudes," p. 45. For other studies showing similar trends, see Rielly, ed., *U.S. Foreign Policy 1979*, p. 26; and "Choose One From Column A and One From Column B," in "Opinion Roundup," *Public Opinion* 2 (January/February 1979): 34.

47. Rielly, ed., *U.S. Foreign Policy 1983*, p. 31.

48. Russett and Nincic, "American Opinion," p. 413. The reader wishing to pursue comparisons should refer to this source, which notes precise questions asked at each time.

49. In this regard, public opinion polls show that in 1976, "by a two to one margin (49 percent to 22 percent), the public opposes the signing of a formal treaty with Israel promising to come to her aid with arms and troops if she is attacked." Likewise, "while the public feels that the communists do constitute a threat to Africa (75 percent) and that more African countries going communist would be a serious loss to the United States (72 percent), the public opposes the United States giving military security guarantees to African countries theatened by a communist takeover." Quoted from Yankelovich, "Cautious Internationalism," p. 13.

50. These perceptions are taken from *Gallup Report* (December 1983), p. 5. In years when both a domestic and an international issue were listed as the most important problem, each received a half year. The energy crisis in 1974 is considered an international issue, while energy problems in 1978 and 1979 are classified as domestic issues.

51. Noted in Tucker, Watts, and Free, pp. 22-23.

52. "Environmental Update," p. 33.

53. "Performance: Short Term Blips," in "Opinion Roundup," *Public Opinion* 6 (April/May 1983): 25.

54. AIPO data taken from Rita James Simon, *Public Opinion in America: 1936-1970* (Chicago: Rand McNally, 1974), p. 125.

55. AIPO data adapted from Almond, *American People*, p. 73.

56. See Russett and Deluca, " 'Don't Tread on Me'," p. 395; and Daniel Yankelovich and Larry Kaagan, "Assertive America," *Foreign Affairs* 59 (America and the World 1980): 696-702 and 713. Yankelovich and Kaagan point out the significant changes in public mood in 1980, but conclude that the "national mood of 1980 does not yet reflect the kind of clear consensus that existed on both domestic and foreign policy from the late 1940's to the mid 1960's [the last extrovert phase]." Quote on p. 713.

57. Evan Thomas, "Highs for Mondale and Reagan," *Time*, 26 December 1983, p. 13.

58. Brzezinski, "Hostile World," pp. 86-88.

59. Lloyd A. Free, "The International Attitudes of Americans," in *A Nation Observed: Perspectives on America's World Role*, ed. Donald R. Lesh (Washington, D. C.: Potomac Associates, 1974), pp. 142-48.

60. See Tucker, Watts, and Free, *U.S. in the World*, pp. 28-34; or William Watts and Lloyd A. Free, "Nationalism, Not Isolationism," *Foreign Policy* no. 24 (Fall 1976), pp. 5-6 and 16-21.

61. See Lloyd Free and William Watts, "Internationalism Comes of Age. . . Again," *Public Opinion* 3 (April/May 1980): 48-49.

62. See Klingberg, "Historical Alternation," pp. 250-59.

63. Craig, "U.S. and the European Balance," p. 77.

64. Quoted in *The Detroit News*, 25 May 1978, p. 5A.

65. Sprout and Sprout, *American Naval Power*, pp. 184-88.

66. Dulles, *American Red Cross*, p. 17.

67. Selig Adler says that Hoover's "foreign policy statements reflected the dominant principles of the more restrained internationalists." Adler, *Isolationist Impulse*, p. 208.

68. Herbert Hoover, "Proposal Submitted to the General Disarmament Conference, June 22, 1932," in U.S. Department of State Press Release, 25 June 1932; quoted in full in Ruhl J. Bartlett, ed., *The Record of American Diplomacy*, 3rd ed. (New York: Alfred A. Knopf, 1954), pp. 497-99. Quotation in text from p. 497.

69. U.S. Congress, Senate, 95th Cong., 1st sess., 20 January 1977, *Congressional Record* 123, no. 11: S1132.

70. See, for example, Raymond Aron, "Ideology in Search of a Policy," *Foreign Affairs* 60 (America and the World, 1981): 507 and 511.

71. Midge Decter, "Has the Third World War Already Started?" *Imprimis* 11 (April 1982): 3-4.

72. See Richard Cattani, "Political Science Elites," *Public Opinion* 4 (October/November 1981): 51-53.

73. See Adler, *Isolationist Impulse*, especially pp. 55-218, for an account of introversion in the first half of the 1919-1940 phase. Fluctuations he describes on post-1919 public foreign policy attitudes are believed to be broadly comparable to fluctuations of post-1968 public foreign policy attitudes.

74. Adler wrote that "the time was ripe for the supreme triumph of the isolationist concept— the neutrality legislation of 1935-1937. Six years of depression and cumulative aggression had stimulated introversive thinking." Ibid., 234.

75. For a useful discussion of problems posed by nuclear proliferation, see Michael Brenner, "Decision Making in a Nuclear-Armed World," *The Annals of the American Academy of Political and Social Science* 430 (March 1977): 147-61.

76. Herbert J. Spiro, *A New Foreign Policy Consensus?* The Washington Papers, 7, no. 64 (Beverly Hills: Sage Publications, 1979): 63-68.

77. Jonas, *Isolationism*, pp. 32-69.

78. Maggiotto and Wittkopf, "American Public Attitudes," pp. 601-31. Holsti, "Three-Headed Eagle," p. 1. Mandelbaum and Schneider, "New Internationalism", pp. 34-88.

79. For elaboration on the 1935-1941 period, see Jonas, *Isolationism*.

80. The text of the farewell address can be found in Washington, "Farewell Address," pp. 213-24. See especially pp. 221-23.

81. Here cited from Doenecke, *Literature of Isolationism*, p. 13, who makes this observation in a summary of John Milton Cooper, Jr., *The Vanity of Power: American Isolationism and the First World War, 1914-1917* (Westport, Conn.: Greenwood, 1969).

82. See, for example, George Modelski, "The Long Cycle of Global Politics and the Nation-State," *Comparative Studies in Society and History: An International Quarterly* 20 (April 1978): 214-35; and Modelski, "U.S. Strategic Policy," pp. 3-19.

83. Of interest in this regard, a 1973 survey on American business leaders indicates that only 38 percent thought "a retrenchment of U.S. foreign policy commitments would have a negative effect on U.S. economic expansion abroad," and only 33 percent thought " a 25 percent reduction in defense spending would have an adverse effect on the American economy." Russett and Hanson, *Interest and Ideology*, p. 277. See pp. 61-65 of this source regarding its methodology and sample.

84. Alexander and Darby, "Technology," pp. 17-18.

85. For a scholarly treatment of the failure of Marxism in America, as considered in relation to the New Deal of the 1930s, see Hartz, *Liberal Tradition*, pp. 277-83.

86. Jonas, *Isolationism* pp. 34-35.

87. Almond, *American People*, pp. 224-25.

88. For more detail on these and other parts of Borah's life, see McKenna, *Borah*.

89. See Doenecke, *Literature of Isolationism,* pp. 30-31 for a description of literature regarding Senator Vandenberg. Material concerning a number of other introvert senators is noted on pp. 28-35.

90. See Rusling, "President McKinley," p. 137.

91. As an example, Bruce Russett states: "It is important . . . not to exaggerate the similarities between the 1970's and the years between the two great wars. A full return to the isolationism of that period is unimaginable. American economic and political involvement in the world is too great to permit it, popular attitudes have not gone that far, and responsible leaders surely would not allow it," "The Americans' Retreat," p. 17. In 1973, Zbigniew Brzezinski wrote, "Isolationism on the level of policy thus tends to be a partial view and not a coherent all-embracing doctrine. Even its adherents accept the proposition that at least in some respects the United States should remain actively engaged in the world, and in that sense they partake of a residual though vague consensus that the world is becoming an interdependent entity, from which there is no complete withdrawal. A broad and undefined nation of global interdependence seems to represent the general principle which most Americans share," "Search for Focus," p. 712.

6. Conclusion

1. Naturally, American motivations also differ from those of countries whose policies are rendered inconsistent by unpredictable or opportunistic authoritarian rulers and revolutionary changes in government.

2. See Klingberg, "Cyclical Trends 1979," pp. 37-55; and Klingberg, *Cyclical Trends 1983.*

Bibliographical Essay

The researcher wishing to investigate this topic or a particualr part of it in detail would be well advised to read all of the notes to relevant sections of the book. This essay is designed to help the reader who may wish to explore topics in general prior to making a research commitment. The reader should not view selection of sources for inclusion in this essay as a quality judgment as much as an induction of useful introductory materials.

An essential start for understanding U.S. foreign policy moods is Frank Klingberg's article, "The Historical Alternation of Moods in American Foreign Policy," *World Politics* 4 (January 1952): 239-73. This is, after all, the source that forecast the late 1960s start of the current introvert phase some fifteen years in advance. Klingberg's other works, including *Cyclical Trends in American Foreign Policy Moods: The Unfolding of America's World Role* (Lanham, Maryland: University Press of America, 1983), elaborate on his introvert/extrovert cycle as well as introduce other cycles.

The work done in Chapter 1 on moods manifested in liberalism owes a particular debt to Louis Hartz, *The Liberal Tradition in America* (New York: Harcourt, Brace, and World, 1955); and Samuel Huntington, *The Soldier and the State* (New York: Vantage Books, 1957). Doris Graber's book, *Public Opinion, the President, and Foreign Policy: Four Case Studies From the Formative Years* (New York: Holt, Rinehart and Winston, 1968), is helpful because it covers the early presidents. Works on public opinion and U.S. foreign policy that are excellent conventional analyses of this subject are by Gabriel Almond, *The American People and Foreign Policy* (New York: Frederick A. Praeger, 1960); James Rosenau, *Public Opinion and Foreign Policy* (New York: Random House, 1961); Bernard Cohen, *The Public's Impact on Foreign Policy* (Boston: Little, Brown and Company, 1973); Barry Hughes, *The Domestic Context of American Foreign Policy* (San Francisco: W. H. Freeman and Company, 1978); and Ralph Levering, *The Public and American Foreign Policy, 1918-1978* (New York: William Morrow and Company, 1978). Edward Weisband, *The Ideology of American Foreign Policy: A Paradigm of Lockean Liberalism* (Beverly Hills: Sage Publications, 1973); Bruce Russett and Elizabeth Hanson, *Interest and Ideology: The Foreign Policy Beliefs of American Businessmen* (San Francisco: W. H. Freeman and Co., 1975); Samuel Huntington, *American Politics: The Promise of Disharmony* (Cambridge, Mass.: Harvard University Press, 1981); and Jon Alexander and Tom Darby, "Technology, Ideology, and Marginality: A Perspective on the New World," (a paper prepared at Carleton University, Ottawa, Canada, 1983) have completed interesting studies which comment on the relation of liberalism to American foreign policy.

Studies of longer periods of time are particularly valuable in looking for macro-patterns. Among those not noted elsewhere in this essay and of use to this author are

Harold and Margaret Sprout, *The Rise of American Naval Power, 1776-1918* (Princeton, N. J.: Princeton University Press, 1946); Thomas Bailey, *The Man in the Street: The Impact of American Public Opinion on Foreign Policy* (Gloucester, Mass.: Peter Smith, 1964); and Fred Wellborn, *A Diplomatic History of the United States* (Totowa, N. J.: Littlefield, Adams and Company, 1970). Julius Pratt, *Expansionists of 1898: The Acquisition of Hawaii and the Spanish Islands* (Chicago: Quadrangle Books, 1936); and *Expansionists of 1812* (Gloucester, Mass.: Peter Smith, 1957) document thoroughly periods of expansionism. Also helpful are works by Arthur Ekirch, *The Civilian and the Military: A History of the American Anti-Militarist Tradition* (Colorado Springs: Ralph Myles, 1972); Sidney Ratner, *The Tariff in American History* (New York: D. Van Nostrand Co., 1972); Gerald Haines and Samuel Walker, eds., *American Foreign Relations: A Historiographical Review* (London: Frances Pinter, 1981); Gene Rainey, *Patterns of American Foreign Policy* (Boston: Allyn and Bacon, Inc., 1975); Melvin Small and J. David Singer, *Resort to Arms: International and Civil Wars, 1816-1980* (Beverly Hills: Sage Publications, 1982); and U.S. Bureau of the Census, *Historical Statistics of the United States: Colonial Times to 1970* (Washington, D. C.: G. P. O., 1975). For a useful guide to the study of the U.S. prior to 1965, see Library of Congress, *A Guide to the Study of the United States of America: Representative Books Reflecting the Development of American Life and Thought* (Washington, D. C.: G. P. O., 1960), and the 1956-1965 supplement (Washington, D. C.: G. P. O., 1976).

The application in Chapter 2 draws upon works by David McClelland, "Love and Power: The Psychological Signals of War," *Psychology Today* 8 (January 1975): 44-48; David Winter, *The Power Motive* (New York: The Free Press, 1975); and J. David Barber, *The Presidential Character: Predicting Performance in the White House* (Englewood Cliffs, N. J.: Prentice-Hall, 1977). Also important in Chapter 2 are the two surveys conducted by Arthur Schlesinger, Sr., and noted in Thomas Bailey, *Presidential Greatness* (New York: Appleton-Century, 1966); Robert Murray and Tim Blessing, "Presidential Performance Study: A Progress Report," *The Journal of American History* 70 (December 1983): 535-55; and Library of Congress data on uses of force abroad, Foreign Affairs Division, Legislative Reference Service, Library of Congress for the Subcommittee on National Security Policy and Scientific Developments of the House Committee on Foreign Affairs, *Background Information on the Use of U.S. Armed Forces in Foreign Countries* (Washington, D. C.: G. P. O., 1970). Suggestive analyses other than those in this work could be based on material in these sources. Those sources of the most use to this author in relating pragmatism, moralism, conservatism, elitism, fortunate circumstances, and world events to liberalism had first been used in preparing other chapters; thus they are noted under other chapters in this essay as well as in the footnotes for Chapter 2.

The interests chapter draws heavily from the work of Bernard Gordon, *Toward Disengagement in Asia: A Strategy for American Foreign Policy* (Englewood Cliffs, N.J.: Prentice-Hall, 1969), which contains a particularly useful typology of interests. A number of other sources were used in preparing this chapter, as noted in the footnotes. Hans Morgenthau, "The Mainsprings of American Foreign Policy: The National Interest vs. Moral Abstractions," *The American Political Science Review* 44 (December 1950): 833-54; and Henry Kissinger, *American Foreign Policy: Three Essays* (New York: W. W. Norton and Company, 1969), are helpful in thinking about geographic interests and the problems facing the United States at various times. John Mueller, *War, Presidents, and Public Opinion* (New York: John Wiley and Sons, 1973), demonstrates well the difficulty facing an American president who tries to lead the nation in a limited war. Frank Freidel, Frederick Merk, and Samuel Morison, *Dissent in Three American Wars* (Cambridge, Mass.: Harvard University Press, 1970), indicates that the difficulties that face presidents of different eras are often related. James Payne, *The American Threat: National Security and Foreign Policy* (College Station, Tx: Lytten Publishing Co., 1981), presents an effective argument on the utility of military force in addressing policy problems. Roger Hansen et al., *U.S. Foreign Policy and the Third World: Agenda 1982* (New York: Praeger Publications, 1982), and other Overseas Development Corporation publications provide useful information on foreign aid and U.S. policy toward the Third World. N. D. Kondratieff, "The Long Waves in Economic Life," *The Review of Economic Statistics* 17 (November 1935):105-15; and George Modelski, "The Long Cycle of Global Politics and the Nation-State," *Comparative Studies in Society and History: An International Quarterly* 20 (April 1978): 214-35, are suggestive to persons researching the relationships among cycle theories. The notes mention a number of authors who have expanded upon the cyclical patterns in useful ways.

Some editions have compiled particularly useful sets of readings in terms of looking at considerations raised in this book, including Robert Goldwin and Harry M. Clor, eds., *Readings in American Foreign Policy* (New York: Oxford University Press, 1971); Charles Kegley and Patrick McGowan, eds., *Challenges to America: United States Foreign Policy in the 1980's* (Beverly Hills: Sage Publications, 1979); McGowan and Kegley, eds., *Threats, Weapons, and Foreign Policy* (Beverly Hills: Sage Publications, 1980); and Kegley and McGowan, eds., *The Political Economy of Foreign Policy Behavior* (Beverly Hills: Sage Publications, 1981). All three editions of the *Pentagon Papers* have interesting material that provides useful insights into U.S. policies in the 1940-1968 extrovert phase. The shortest edition, the New York Times edition, is Neil Sheehan et al., *The Pentagon Papers* (New York: Bantam Books, 1971). An intermediate-sized edition, called the Gravel Edition, is entitled *The Pentagon Papers: The Defense Department History of United States Decision Making on Vietnam* (Boston: Beacon Press, 1971). A twelve volume edition, popularly called the government edition, is U.S. Department of Defense, *United States Vietnam Relations 1945-1967* (Washington, D. C.: G. P. O., 1971). The government edition has some particularly valuable information about policies from 1945-1961.

Useful sources for understanding the role of Congress in foreign policy include the work of Arthur Schlesinger, Jr., "Congress and the Making of American Foreign Policy," *Foreign Affairs* 51 (October 1972): 78-113; and Jerel Rosati, "Congressional Assertion in Foreign Policy: Fact or Fantasy," (a paper presented to the International Studies Association, Philadelphia, Pa., 1981). Richard Neustadt, *Presidential Power* (New York: New American Library, 1960); Amos Perlmutter, "The Presidential Political Center and Foreign Policy: A Critique of Revisionist and Bureaucratic Political Orientations," *World Politics* 27 (October 1974): 87-106; I. M. Destler, "National Security Advice to U.S. Presidents: Some Lessons from Thirty Years," *World Politics* 29 (January 1977): 143-76; and Gordon Hoxie, "The National Security Council," *Presidential Studies Quarterly* 12 (Winter 1982): 108-13, give a good introduction to the president's overall role in foreign policy. Fred Greenstein, ed., *The Reagan Presidency: An Early*

Assessment (Baltimore: Johns Hopkins University Press, 1983), is a useful volume on the Reagan administration.

Particularly important for the understanding of American introversion is the work of Selig Adler, *The Isolationist Impulse: Its Twentieth Century Reaction* (New York: Free Press, 1957); and Manfred Jonas, *Isolationism in America, 1935-1941* (Ithaca, New York: Cornell University Press, 1966). Useful material on introvert leaders includes work by Marion McKenna, *Borah* (Ann Arbor, Mi.: University of Michigan Press, 1966); and J. D. Doenecke, *The Literature of Isolationism* (Colorado Springs: Ralph Myles, Publishers, 1972). Particularly helpful studies of opinion trends and changes in the early part of the current introvert phase are by Michael Roskin, "From Pearl Harbor to Vietnam: Shifting Generational Paradigms and Foreign Policy," *Political Science Quarterly* 89 (Fall 1974): 563-88; Bruce Russett, "The Americans' Retreat From World Power," *Political Science Quarterly* 90 (Spring 1975): 1-21; and Robert Tucker, William Watts, and Lloyd Free, *The United States in the World: New Directions for the Post-Vietnam Era?* (Washington, D. C.: Potomac Associates, 1976). Analysts who have looked at recent trends in a particularly useful manner include Ole Holsti and James Rosenau, "Vietnam, Consensus, and the Belief System of American Leaders," *World Politics* 32 (October 1979): 1-56; Michael Mandelbaum and William Schneider, "The New Internationalisms: Public Opinion and American Foreign Policy," in Kenneth A. Oye et al., eds., *Eagle Entangled: U.S. Foreign Policy in a Complex World* (New York: Longman, 1979); Michael Maggiotto and Eugene Wittkopf, "American Public Attitudes Toward Foreign Policy," *International Studies Quarterly* 25 (December 1981): 601-31; George Quester, *American Foreign Policy: The Lost Consensus* (New York: Praeger Publishers, 1982); and John Rielly and his associates who have compiled detailed information on attitudes by the public and its leaders in *American Public Opinion and U.S. Foreign Policy, 1983* (Chicago: The Chicago Council on Foreign Relations, 1983). See also the 1975 and 1979 editions of this work. *Congressional Quarterly, Foreign Policy, National Journal,* and *Public Opinion* have been particularly useful in keeping current with rapid changes. Useful speculation on future trends has been provided by Steven Hildreth, "A Projection of American 'Moods' to the Year 2000," (a paper prepared for the Army 2000 Project); and Frank Klingberg's 1983 book.

A final note should be made about government sources. Some use of these sources can be indispensable to an understanding of what presidents and Congress were trying to accomplish, while too much use of them can obscure important dynamics. The sources that were most useful are identified throughout the text. Of particular help was some of the background material prepared as Congress considered the war powers legislation in the early 1970s.

Index